TURNED

In puncto reflexionis

Emma Bloor

© Emma Bloor 2024
The moral right of the author has been asserted.
This novel does not include artificial intelligence content.

All rights reserved in all media. No part of this publication may be reproduced, stored in any retrieval system, or transmitted in any form or by any means, electronic, mechanical, recording or otherwise, without prior and express permission of the copyright owner.

The names, characters and incidents portrayed are the work of the author's imagination and any resemblance to actual persons, living or dead, is entirely coincidental. The people and situations in the real-life places mentioned in this novel are fictional.

This novel is written in UK English.

ISBN: 978-1-7391411-2-7

www.emmabloor.co.uk

Contents

One	5
Two	11
Three	20
Four	32
Five	42
Six	54
Seven	64
Eight	74
Nine	83
Ten	99
Eleven	109
Twelve	121
Thirteen	141
Fourteen	153
Fifteen	168
Sixteen	180
Seventeen	196
Eighteen	212
Nineteen	229
Twenty	243
Twenty-One	256
Twenty-Two	265
Twenty-Three	275
Twenty-Four	286
Twenty-Five	296
Twenty-Six	311
Twenty-Seven	320
Twenty-Eight	329
Twenty-Nine	343

Thirty	350
Coming Soon…	362
About The Author	363
Author's note	363
Acknowledgements	364

One

22nd March 2023, 03:30

Rooks on the rooftops called order. In the blur of a misty night, the glowing streetlights extinguished in pairs, plunging the target suburban house into darkness. Equipped with night vision goggles, a masked team in black overalls scaled its perimeter, landing soundlessly in a manicured garden. Backs pressed against brick, they lingered as the tallest comrade drew a silver disc from his pocket and removed the protective strip with gloved hands.

He aimed.

The disc arched over the flowers and bushes like a Frisbee. It triggered the sensor light, illuminating the colourful garden with a stream of sunshine that glistened on the metal as it flew.

A spark flashed. The stream fizzled out, and the growl of a nearby motorbike drowned the chink of metal meeting cement.

The team crossed the lawn, careful not to leave boot prints in the flowerbed's loosened soil as they neared the back door. At the path, the tall man eased out the disc wedged in the pointing between a severed wire, replaced the protective covering and secured it in his pocket.

Gaining entry with a duplicate key, the six team members crept into the large kitchen and separated into pairs. One went through the double doors into the connecting dining room, circled an extravagant table and bagged the elaborate candelabras. They placed a silver can under the table and moved on to secure the rest of the ground floor.

Another duo ran down the kitchen steps into a chilly cellar and located the main utility points. Water off, electricity off, gas on. The female member stabbed the gas supply and retreated, closing the door on the consequent hissing, then entered the adjoining garage.

The third pair disabled the alarm in the hall and tiptoed up the polished wooden stairs. Quiet and skilful.

They invaded every room, raided them for profit, and left a canister in the centre of each floor. All but the occupied bedroom. Here, the team leader fed a copper pipe under the door and attached the other end to another steel canister. At his companion's nod, they descended the stairs and joined their comrades waiting at the back door. The cellar door was ajar now, seeping gas as the duplicate key turned for the last time.

Clicks echoed. Popping sparks decorated the atmosphere like dust motes caught in sunlight, or virgin stars bursting constellations for the first time. They danced in the air, sucking it into their flame. Seconds later, fire clouds ignited the furniture, and tongues raced across the carpets to meet other flame-engulfed rooms. Unlike ordinary fire, the smell was potent and toxic.

Thunderous liquid and aerosol explosions shook the walls, and intensified wherever they found water. The liquor bar blazed with demonic fury.

The female member, distracted by the inviting, hypnotic sway of the fire, wasn't as quick up the wall as her friends. At the top, she shielded her eyes and stole one last look. A trance-like smile spread across her face.

Then, the natural gas caught.

The perimeter wall vibrated, puffing dust into damp air. The woman fell, landing on her shoulder with a thump and a yell. A teammate dragged her up and pulled her away while the house burst open and burned like a Roman Candle.

~

The assassin's pulled-low beanie met dark eyebrows over piercing blue eyes. They stared like icy shards at the coffee shop floor. The phone inside his long black coat buzzed another three times, but it was for the sender's benefit that Laszlo Sándor didn't read or listen to the messages. If Spinzer called him Lassie one more time, he would likely blow, and his temper was never pretty. Especially when his deceased brother's voice echoed from within it. So far, he'd controlled himself, but his mood now resembled a bubbling lava pit. They should have exchanged payment this morning, but Spinzer had postponed the meeting twice. Now Laszlo was playing the client at his own game. The thrill of deliberately keeping the cocky upstart waiting dampened his irritation and helped douse the desire to rip off the Italian's head.

Laszlo left the coffee shop, pulled his collar tighter, and set off in the drizzle to Spinzer's nightclub, crossing the road several times to avoid being seen. He paused as he entered the car park, watching the smokers and vomiters while numbing himself to the bass thumping through his muscular body. The activity helped quieten the demons inside his head, at least until Spinzer paid him for his recent work.

A scout loitered at the fire exit and pushed the door open as he neared. "He's mad."

Unperturbed, the assassin shrugged and followed a pale-blue corridor to the secure back offices. The young club owner and full-time weapons dealer, Mario Spinzer, sat alone at his cluttered desk. He lifted a thin, easily snappable neck at the intrusion.

"You're late. I don't like doing this business when the nightclub is open. Though I'll give you this, Lassie. When you do a job, you do it well. I usually end up docking part of the fee."

The brooding Laszlo leaned on the doorframe, staring with flinty eyes. When Spinzer stopped speaking, he straightened up, his shoulders filling the doorway and the frame tickling his black hair. "You could try, but I wouldn't recommend it."

Spinzer grinned, showing stained teeth. The smile didn't meet his eyes. "I said, usually. Shut the door and sit while I enter the account details."

'Lassie' didn't sit. Instead, he checked the time. Not enough to fashion a decent forensic clean. He rolled his chin and closed the door, radiating an aura of aggravated malevolence, but remained standing.

Spinzer pretended not to notice as his finger hovered over the send payment tab. "It's up and running. Ready to send. But did we really agree so much? I mean, it was only a ten-minute job." He squealed a laugh. "I'm only yanking ya, c'mon, sit down, Lassie. There's a good boy."

The arrogant man stepped dangerously close to realising who he was affronting. Assassins had reputations for a reason. The pepper spray in Laszlo's trouser pocket would do more than burn Spinzer's dirty brown eyes.

His left hand teased the small can as he fought a smile at the idea of watching Mario scream while his eyeballs melted. "You should not *push it*. I might demand more for the extra body."

"Where did you think Mrs Corpse would be? Didn't you expect her to be lying next to her husband at that time of night? An experienced man like you..." The sarcastic amazement trickled like sand through an hourglass. The particles were running dry. "Besides, she ain't had an affair since hubby fired the tennis coach. A skilled problem-solver, which I thought you were, would've already known this. A better leader would've also returned my team unscathed. Should I deduct Lara's medical bills from your pay?"

Fists clenching as if they gripped his temper, Laszlo felt his patience clog with heavy sand. Spinzer noticed.

"Now, then, Lassie–"

"I've recommended you don't call me that," he spat through gritted teeth. The nickname reminded him of his childhood, and even the hint of it jangled his nerves. He'd been polite, with frequent warnings, for long enough.

"What? Lassie? Would you rather you were my bitch?"

That canine insult forced him forward, pulling a silenced Beretta from inside his coat. He aimed at the man's heart, impulse squeezing the trigger before the arrogant prick took in his shocked breath. Then, as he leaned across the desk and stared into Spinzer's dying brown eyes, the dog tags around his neck fell loose from his shirt and clinked on the metal surface.

"My name"—he tapped the payment tab with Spinzer's finger—"is Laszlo. And I will take the fee we agreed."

Blood heaved from Spinzer's mouth, pouring over his designer-trimmed beard and staining his blue shirt purple.

With the demons quiet, Laszlo calmed and saw how his hasty reaction had created a bind. Did he risk leaving the body and crime scene for the authorities to scrutinise? He normally planned his cleans with precision, leaving no forensics behind, and preferably without loose ends like the scout at the door and a heaving nightclub full of drinkers only just hotting up. This was not the perfect time to dispose of or cremate bodies. Nor would it be acceptable to gamble with a murder investigation if a trace of his DNA remained.

Laszlo buttoned his coat to leave. Spinzer's men would only incriminate themselves and call attention to their boss's deeds if they called the police shouting murder. Spinzer had many enemies. Even if his men had heard the gunshot and assumed he was the killer, what could they do? They were child's play to a man like him.

He checked the corridor before leaving, using the same fire exit and ignoring the same dozy scout standing guard. Some guard. The clueless man didn't even realise his boss was dead. It saved his life. Laszlo would have silenced him if he made a fuss. Again, child's play. If any of Spinzer's men came for him, they would need to get to him, and that wasn't likely. Not them.

There were others Laszlo had flagged as threatening enough. He studiously monitored each one from the media sidelines. Nothing passed him. He ensured he knew the location of each dangerous player, what they did, who they used, and how close they might be to discovering Laszlo's wonderful talents. Though having high-fliers touting for his business would be useful, they would have equally high-flying contacts to assassinate anyone they chose.

Watching them from the sidelines would suffice for now. Until they entered his orbit and became a threat to him, Laszlo didn't need to be too concerned.

Fearless, he walked the streets towards his hidden car.

Two

12th April 2023, 06:50

Barking dogs. Loads of them. A chorus of woofs and howls harmonised with Addison's rhythmic snores and penetrated her pleasant dream with high-pitched yaps and deep-rooted barks. When her sandy Labrador, Sting, sprang from the bed, his claws clicking on the laminate floor became a ghostly sound in her fantasy world. An eerie growl and the tickety-taps of long fingernails drumming on the windowpane froze her heart.

Sting jumped up at the window, snarling, and thirty-three-year-old Addison Rae woke with a start. Squinting, she pulled the sides of the pillow over her ears, covering her pixie-cut dark hair, and crossed her arms over her face, unwilling to let the morning sun squeezing through the closed curtains burn her sleepy eyes.

"Sting. Chill out," she groaned in a husky voice.

Fast pattering paws reached the bed. Sting's cold nose startled her as he nudged the inside of her arm while his paw scraped the covers off her chest. Another well-brewed round of barks joined the neighbouring dog chorus.

She gripped the pillow tighter around her head. "All right, all right. I'm getting up!"

Surely, Sting wasn't that desperate to go out. He ran back to the window and shoved his furry head through the curtains, dousing the room with an angelic glow.

Addison sat up. A prickly atmosphere closed in on her, amplifying every sound and sensation. Squashing down her unease, she climbed from the bed and opened the curtains, giving Sting's ears a gentle tickle to calm him. His growls continued.

The Lechlade cul-de-sac looked normal under a low sun and cloudless sky, and the lake bordering her estate glittered in greeting. Stunning. Nothing could match the haze filtering through the shades of spring tree blossom. The weeping willow blocking the view of the semi-detached house across the street swayed its gentle fingers in the breeze. Posh cars parked on driveways, but not a soul in sight. What had riled the dogs to bark so much? As Addison turned to leave, she noticed a neighbour had repainted their front door, changing it from soft blue to claret red. She shrugged, unable to remember when she last paid attention to it.

"C'mon, boy." With a gentle tug on Sting's collar, she returned all four paws to the floor. The incessant barking continued.

Ignoring her commands to stop, he jumped back to the windowsill and wet-nosed the glass.

"What is the matter with you?"

And them. The reverberating clamour outside grew louder, drowning out the owners' shouting. The biting uneasiness hadn't shifted. Was that why she felt so cold? She touched a warm radiator on her way to join Sting, still whining at the window.

The elderly Mrs Tonks was returning from a walk, battling with a snappy Jack Russell gnawing on his lead. Strange. Taffy was usually better behaved. Mrs Tonks glanced around, mystified, as the canine song turned into panicked cries. Addison opened the window and called out, watching Taffy tug at the lead and snatch it from his distracted owner. He ran towards Addison's front garden, pulling the bouncing plastic handle behind him. Then the poor thing fell and rolled onto Addison's lawn, letting out high-pitch yelps.

Seconds later, a tangible, freezing pressure pulsed through the window, forcing Addison back as it passed, dragging her every vibrating cell with it. She sank to the floor light-headed, scorching hot, and fighting to catch her breath. Her skin itched and stung as if lice with pinprick teeth riddled it. Pearls of sweat formed like piercing thorns across her body. She scratched the crawling sensation through her pyjamas, but to no avail. Squinting from the sharp stabbing in her head, she took slow breaths to control her rising nausea.

Sting's unfamiliar howl centred her. That was new. He'd never peed in her bedroom before either, something she would now have to clean up.

She drew her knees to her chest and tried to stand. The ground felt like sand on a constantly tilting surface. Forward and back. Side to side. She lay down with a blistering cheek pressed to the floor, spittle peppering her lips as she exhaled, too frightened to move in case she vomited.

What the heck?

Her skin burned, soaking her cotton pyjamas with sweat. Even scratching didn't lessen the pinprick itching. Her head pounded an unmatchable pain. It seeped from her skull with a shrill ringing in her ears as her heart thumped and blood dripped from her nose.

"What the hell is this?"

Using the bed as leverage, she struggled to her feet, but despite trying, couldn't quell the motion sickness. At the top of the stairs, she swerved into the bathroom and vomited. After a minute of dry heaving, she dampened a cloth and dabbed her face and runny nose, aiming to restore equilibrium.

Partly recovered, Addison descended the swaying stairs, clinging to the handrail and the hallway wall. The blurry front door catch tore from her fingers as she tried to yank it open. Frustrated, she tried again, turning it back and forth. The catch released when she turned it the wrong way, but the door didn't budge. Puzzled, she checked the door. How had two bolts appeared overnight?

Eyebrows knitting together in alarm, she unlocked them and wandered into the street. The cool air refreshed her sizzling face, and focusing on her steps helped to ease her panic. She joined a shaken, but unharmed, Mrs Tonks, who kneeled on the grass with her beloved in her arms.

"Scatty dog! Reckon he's broken his leg. I dunno what's got into him."

"Didn't you feel it?"

"Feel what?" Mrs Tonks replied, distracted by the task of getting off her tattered knees while cradling a dog.

"Whatever knocked him over."

"His daft behaviour did that." Mrs Tonks studied Addison's face, her brow creasing. "Can't say I felt anything."

Her heart thrummed. People didn't fall over without cause and the force had floored her. That…or something else had. She helped Mrs Tonks to her feet. "Something's going on. Sting's barking woke me up."

"Oversleep after a good night out, did we? I thought you looked rough. And your nose is bleeding."

"I'm not feeling the best this morning." Addison wiped the tickle at her nostril and checked for blood. It smeared across her knuckles. Was she sick?

Mrs Tonks glanced at her watch and muttered as if she hadn't heard her. "I need to find the vet's emergency number. It's only ten past seven."

"Urgh, is it?! I'm late. Will you be okay getting to the vet? I can call work?"

"I'll manage, Addie, love. Thanks all the same. You go sort yourself out." She trundled off, sprightly, for a woman in her late seventies.

Addison went indoors, hoping she had the same determined energy forty-odd years from now. A hit of it would be useful. She leaned on the banister, dizzy and exhausted, and called for Sting. He wasn't at his food bowl or in his bed. Soft whimpers floated from upstairs and she found him cowering under her bed.

"Come on, boy. It's all right," she said, reassuring herself as much as him.

Eventually, she encouraged him out. He licked her face but only sniffed at his favourite beef meat. The gentle wag of his sandy tail was hardly worth the effort. Subdued, she cleaned up the mess in the bedroom and showered for work.

~

Even sitting in her parked car, the ground rocked like the deck of a ship. Motionless and breathing steadily, Addison fought another wave of nausea and tried to remember the drive to work. What the hell was going on?

Swallowing her fear, she followed the path along the front of Palowa Enterprises where the red-brick window ledges sat just above her head. This usually amused her, because inside, they were at her hips. Today, she barely gave it a passing thought as she reached the semicircle of tall steps surrounding the main doors. She stopped and stared at the revolving cube in the centre bearing the company's eloquent logo.

Yellow? But yesterday the lettering was green. For eight years, it had been green. Hadn't it?

Strolling through reception, she doubted herself. The scratched paint and trodden carpets were obviously not new. An overhaul of the company's branding couldn't happen overnight, and the walls and accessories were shades of warm yellow, not pastel green. As were the lift lights lining the wall behind the oval desk. Six in all.

On the fourth floor, she greeted her colleagues as she stole towards her workstation. Marsha sidled up to her in a lemon-yellow dress, a beautiful contrast to her umber skin, and handed her a file.

"You're late. I've never known you to be late. You missed the Wednesday staff meeting. And you look awful!"

Addison grimaced. She'd forgotten about the meeting. "The topic had nothing to do with yellow, did it?"

Marsha drew her dark eyebrows together. "Uh…no. We're merging with a SID auxiliary company and we're to expect unusual transactions coming through accounts. It particularly annoyed Barnes that *you* weren't there, considering you reconcile the bank. He asked to see you soon as. Why are you late? Today, of all days?"

Because things have been weird ever since I woke up this morning and nobody has noticed. Instead, she replied, "I forgot. I'm having the strangest morning."

"You're in for an even stranger one if you don't get going. Barnes was livid."

"Why? It was only one meeting." She sighed. "I'll go now. Would you fetch me a coffee for when I get back?"

Marsha nodded. "You don't look well, Addie. Are you alright?"

"No. And what's worse is everyone acting as if nothing has happened." Her patience drained when a curious Marsha raised her eyebrows. "Didn't you notice anything odd today?"

"Only this, right here, and you arriving late, talking about yellow staff meetings."

Addison placed her bag on her desk. "It happened around seven this morning."

"What?"

Unsure, she shook her head, unaware of her listening colleagues. "It was like pressure coursing through me. Freezing cold. But it's left me feeling so hot. Whatever it was, it set the neighbourhood dogs off. Then Sting wouldn't come out from under the bed."

"Didn't feel anything. I ate my breakfast. Drank coffee. Took a shower. Nothing different from any other workday. Was it a wet dream?"

"Funny."

Laughter erupted.

Cheeks burning, Addison turned. Eight faces stared at her.

"Demonic possession?" Bertie suggested.

"Don't be ridiculous! As if." Addison gave a wary laugh. "But something happened. Like a weird shift. The force knocked me on my backside and took my neighbour's dog off his feet. He broke his leg!"

No one else had noticed anything. They jokingly blamed it on Addison's lack of a sex life. When they moved from spirit possession to invisible aliens, she interrupted.

"Well then, what about this place? Yesterday, the colour scheme was green."

Marsha snorted. "What? Addie, are you okay?"

"Have I woken up in a parallel universe or something? I'm not lying!"

"Did you bang your head last night? You need to pull yourself together, Addie, and don't tell the finance director that a dog with anxiety made you late. It won't cut it."

"It won't, no." The smooth-headed Barnes approached. "My office."

Crap.

Addison pressed her lips together and followed him into a plain, tidy room. When she closed the door, the metal blinds rattled like the ones in her dad's old pharmaceutical office.

Barnes, early-fifties and immensely intelligent, secured the glasses on his nose and sat at his neat desk. He gestured to an empty chair and said, "Miss Rae, do you need to take some time to evaluate your mental health?"

"What's that supposed to mean?"

"Exactly what I said. There was no weird shift this morning, and Palowa has always been yellow."

"The chair, carpet and walls were green."

"Yellow."

"Then, I guess I had a very vivid dream." *Lasting eight years.*

"There's no need to be facetious."

She flopped into the stained yellow chair and glanced out of the window. "I don't know how else to explain it."

"Then don't. We'll move on. Right? Or backwards for me, because I'm repeating what you missed this morning."

Her eyebrow rose at his sarcasm. He had some cheek! Granted, she'd grown accustomed to his stiff manner—ever since she declined his subtle advances—but today, it irked. She felt...disconnected. As if she'd risen from the dead without a brain. In its place pulsed an agonising headache. She tried to focus on his summary of the staff meeting before he took the lead to fire her.

Palowa's acquisition of Convolve Ltd, a subsidiary of Space Infrastructure Developments—SID, was the only interesting item, but Addison chose not to share what she thought she knew. Palowa acquired Convolve two years earlier. Not from the US SID but from a company based in Brazil.

Her head hurt and body roasted, yet despite the prickle at her throat, she corrected her frown, slowed her breath to calm her heart rate, and smiled, nodding in all the right places.

What the hell was happening?

Three

12th April 2023, 14:30

The headache worsened throughout the day. Painkillers, which didn't even touch it, only made her feel worse. No matter how much she drank, her thirst raged, and she was still hot and queasy. At mid-afternoon, Marsha packed up Addison's things and stole her car keys.

"I'm taking you home. End of. You look tragic. I called a taxi to pick me up from yours in half an hour."

Addison stared at the figures blurring into one. She felt rubbish and wasn't much use at work. Resigned, she followed without argument and prepared herself for Marsha's marinating questions about the cause of her sickness.

"I'm not hungover and didn't bash my head. I honestly can't describe it. There's nothing to compare it to, except, I guess, an aftershock. The kind you get after an explosion. It raced through me like a dose of morphine, getting into all the nooks in my system. It took me ages to get off the floor."

"Was it, like, a poltergeist?"

"Oh, you're as bad as Bertie and the rest!"

"She makes a good point."

"I don't believe in ghosts."

"She wasn't talking about ghosts." Marsha pulled up on Addison's drive and saw her to the door, wrinkling her nose when it opened. "Urgh. What is that?"

Addison followed the hallway and threw her bag on the white kitchen surface. A mammoth, coiled pile of faeces greeted her at the back door. The culprit lay in his bed with his ears folded, looking guilty. Marsha gagged and waited for her cab at the front door, sucking in the fresh air.

"Aw, buddy. What happened? Where's Mase?"

Sting twitched his ears, listening for him, then lowered his head with a heavy sigh.

She bagged the mess with the back door open and her breath held. Nothing had changed since this morning—the nausea was as prominent as ever—but she would manage it better without the worst pong imaginable intruding on her senses. She sprayed the floor with disinfectant before breathing again.

On her way to the bin, she waved the soiled bag in front of Marsha's face.

"Dirty cow. Get it away from me!" Marsha laughed and backed along the path just as the taxi arrived.

Addison waved her off and returned to the kitchen, concerned that her brother hadn't come back from his night shift. Mason always ate or collected his dinner, then walked Sting home with him before he went to sleep. The food she'd made yesterday sat uneaten in the fridge.

Sting ran around the garden, nose down and huffing into the dirt.

"Where's Mase?" Addison pulled her phone from her bag.

At his responding bark, she looked for Mason in her call history, sure she'd spoken to him yesterday. But no numbers came up on the list at all.

Odd.

Mason's number was missing from her contacts—another list strangely light of names—only Palowa colleagues and her mum seemed to exist in her life. Her brow furrowed as she tapped the digits she knew by heart into the keypad.

A gruff voice answered. "Yeah?"

"Hey, Mase. Where are you?"

"Who's Mase? This ain't no Mase. Get off my phone!" The stranger hung up.

Chin low, Addison stared at the screen until it blurred, double-checking her double-check. Mason's number glared back. It mocked her mind and shaved away any chance of forming logical answers. She pressed her pounding head to the worktop. The coolness refreshed her burning skin. She closed her eyes, too ill to hunt her brother down. Perhaps, after a nap, she might face walking Sting to Mason's flat in case he was sick, too. With shaking hands, she took useless painkillers and went to bed.

She dreamed.

The green and yellow logos swirled in her subconscious, taunting and disturbing her rest. Palowa became acronyms, birthing words through its capital letters: Parliament Atrocities Liven Over World Anonymity; People Are Logistically Opposing Welcome Amnesty; Palowa Aims Low On Woke Associations.

Despite the fearful illusion they conjured, there was a familiarity in the now-flaming headlines. They burned until the flames became a ferocious chemical fire, devouring a residential property. Though distressing to watch, the slumbering Addison cared little for the man it killed. The smarmy face of Robert Naise, the now-deceased Mayor of London, invaded her already unpleasant dreams.

She thrashed in her sleep, further scaring the upset Sting. He wasn't accustomed to this behaviour while she slept. He put his front paws on the edge of the bed and nudged her sweaty face until she woke.

Groggy and head still banging, Addison reached for her phone, confused at how dark it was. 7.20. Had she really been asleep for four hours? She noticed twelve missed calls and a bunch of messages from Marsha. The latest read, *Call me, ASAP!*

Sting bumped her hand with his cold, black nose.

"Sorry, boy," she croaked. "I bet you're starving and desperate for a walk."

Sting barked. Addison cringed and groaned as it bounced inside her head like a pinball.

Downstairs, and still combatting the shifting ground sensation, she let him outside and prepared his food, then warmed Mason's sausage dinner for herself. She couldn't face it, but hoped eating would give her the energy to visit her brother and find out why he didn't have his phone.

The thought gave her the incentive to sit at the kitchen table and force down unwanted mashed potatoes.

When her phone trilled, she snatched it up, hoping it would be Mason.

"Where have you been? Why didn't you call me?" Marsha, again.

"Please, don't shout. I was sleeping. Sorry. I haven't read your messages yet. What's up?"

"HR interviewed me. They wanted to know why you went home. They asked if I knew the cause of your headache."

"Likely trying to wriggle out of sick pay."

"Not for an afternoon. It ain't worth it. It was weird."

"This whole, nasty day is weird, Marsha."

"Somehow, they steered me to state, on record, why you were late."

Stunned, Addison fell quiet. What trouble had her candidness brought now?

"Have you thought about seeing a doctor?"

Addison swallowed a mouthful of water. "I might have to if this headache doesn't shift."

"About your memory, Addie. They can scan in minutes these days and at a fraction of the cost."

"Good job. The NHS is crippling."

"Yeah, headaches suck."

She rubbed her aching forehead. "No...the..." *Don't say National Health Service, in case it no longer exists.* The day was baffling enough.

"What?"

"Never mind. Anyway, I should walk Sting before his staring melts me."

"See you tomorrow?"

"Yeah."

"Will you call the doctor?"

"Yeah."

Addison slid her phone into her jeans pocket and fetched the dog lead, though he didn't need it. Sting would walk impeccably beside her until they reached Farmer Cotter's field, but as it was the law, she obliged.

He tugged on the lead before she could close the door. Her hand tore from the handle and it slammed shut as he pulled her down the road, coughing and choking from his collar.

"STING! HEEL!" she yelled, but Sting wouldn't stop. He didn't run, but he kept Addison at a fast pace across the field and on to the small country town high street, speeding past the cafe, boutique and antique shops.

As puffed out and focused on her steps as she was, she surprisingly noticed a cinema advert for the hottest new movie, The Visa Card.

Wait. What?

"STIIIIING!" She grabbed the lead with both hands and yanked him as hard as she could. "Heel."

Sting heeled. Addison's peculiar behaviour broke the spell of instinct and urgency. The unrelenting headache echoed her yells as she walked back to the poster in the bookshop window. Sweet teenage memories of dating the beautiful Orlando from the Forest of Dean surfaced, while she stared at a 'debut' French actor's face with a racing heart. The preview was showing this Saturday, but Addison had already seen it. With Orlando. Well, most of it. At the time, she'd preferred kissing her then-new boyfriend.

The movie would be no better than it had been twenty years ago.

As they moved on at a more reasonable pace, she wondered if she'd lost her mind. Was a brain disease or tumour devouring her reality?

They neared Mason's flat. Sting tugged the lead and Addison let him, as eager as he was to see her brother. They rounded the corner into an alleyway and approached the pistachio-green door to the flat above a charity shop. Sting sniffed the worn doorknob, letterbox, and wooden step. Was it new? It used to have tooth marks from Sting's chewing as a puppy.

Addison sighed and lifted a shaky finger to the doorbell, but a persistent Sting wrenched her away before she could press it. He stopped at the tall garden gate, sniffing and whining.

She pulled him back to the tatty front door. Mason liked things nice. He'd painted it last summer and complained about getting colour on the intercom she now pressed. There wasn't a speck of paint on it.

A soft, female voice crackled through the speaker. "Yeah."

"Uh..." Addison stuttered, surprised. Mason hadn't had a girlfriend since Chloe finished with him last year. "Hi. Is Mason there?"

"Nope. Just me. Wrong flat."

The flat was correct, the phone number, too. Only they both apparently belonged to other people. "May I ask how long you've lived here?"

"Five years."

The year Mason moved in.

She gasped as her mind drifted to Mason's cheeky smile and mischievous earth-brown eyes. He seemed more real in her memories than he appeared to be in the flesh.

Though grateful the woman couldn't see her pale face bleaching further into shock, she felt certain she'd hear the wobble in her reply. "Okay. Thanks. Sorry to bother you."

Addison scratched her forehead, dragging a still-sniffing Sting away. Riddled with confusion, and fingers trembling, she pulled out her phone and called her mother. At least that familiar number remained in her contacts.

"Mum, where's Mase?"

Silence replied. It wasn't a tricky question needing time to consider, was it?

Finally, her mum said, "Who's Mase?"

"Mason, your son."

"Ads, what are you on about?"

"My 24-year-old brother, mum. Stop being so stupid!"

A pained gasp breathed down the phone. "Miscarrying was a horrible time for me. Why would you bring it up?"

The line disconnected.

Addison's skin chilled despite the strange heat still raging inside her. She stared at the home screen, widgets blurring into abstract, and like a submarine on urgent call, her insides sank to her feet. Fingers like claws, she leaned on the wall and vomited again.

Another man had her brother's phone number, a different person lived in his flat, and their mother denied him being born.

Addison remembered. She recalled Mason's constant crying more than anything else. It was the reason she built the shed that he had later named the Jockey. How could she not have a brother? Folk had gone mad.

What the hell is happening?

~

Heading home was less intense, but Addison walked with a heavy heart. All around, she saw differences, subtle but alarming. The red traffic light looked darker and the green lighter; the little green man was fat and carried a stick. Road markings seemed thinner and the drain grills were round, not rectangular. A prawn cocktail crisp packet skidded across the path. Shouldn't it be pink, not pale orange? And since when had the streetlights sprouted antennae equipment atop their angelic glow?

Trivial little things.

Addison had to be mistaken. If her eyes were seeing things correctly, then her brain must be corrupting the data.

She reached the shop before Cotter's field. The LED lights streamed through the automatic door, making her head spin and burning her eyes. She scrunched them up in protest and stopped walking, but the damn headache still pounded and the heat from this morning's weirdness raged inside her. Wine was the last thing she should consider, but she wanted it. After tying Sting to the post outside, she braced herself for the shrill bell to announce her presence as she entered.

No bell chimed.

There was always one at night. Always.

Wary, Addison grabbed a milk carton and moved towards the alcohol. Odd that the rugged man behind the counter wasn't the owner. She gave him a polite smile and felt the weight of his ruminating gaze. What was he staring at? Was he expecting her to speak? She tried to focus on selecting wine, but his eyes clung to her.

The dark-eyed stranger grew more curious by the second. "Aren't you going to say hello?"

Compelled to make a quick choice, she curled her fingers around the neck of a chardonnay and walked to the counter.

"Hello."

She placed her shopping by the till and glanced at his leathery, frowning face. Mid-thirties, with laugh lines and a square jaw. He dragged insecure fingers through his tobacco-coloured hair as if he felt inferior to her.

"Bad day?"

Addison gave a sarcastic laugh. "Yeah." She waited to pay with her phone in her hand.

The man tilted his head, put the milk and wine in a bag, and handed it to her, muscles flexing under his shirt.

"This is on me."

"Why?"

"You've refused a date with me fifteen times. So, the wine is me buying you a drink, and the milk is for breakfast coffee." He winked.

Fifteen date requests? But Addison had never met the man! She swallowed, not confessing it aloud. Her day had been horrible enough. Instead, she played along, detecting a touching vulnerability beneath a fake bravado that matched hers.

"You flirt with all the women."

"True." He smiled and brought his face closer, wafting an intoxicating musky scent. "But you're the only one I ask out."

"Why do I say no?" she asked, genuinely curious.

He shrugged and nudged the bag. "Enjoy your wine."

"What's a man like you doing behind the counter of a country shop? You're like…Vinny Jones in Open All Hours."

He laughed. "Maybe, if you'll have dinner with me, I'll tell you."

"Perhaps another time." She picked up her shopping. "Thank you. Be sure you put it through the till or Arnold won't be happy."

"Addie, Arnold sold up three years ago. Remember?"

Addie? He surely didn't know her well enough to call her that. And Arnold hadn't sold up. He was here only yesterday. Fear prickled on her cheeks. Did she forget or had her reality become so bad that she'd created another to make life bearable?

When he came around the counter with a concerned frown, she ran for the door.

"Wait up!"

Addison untied Sting's lead and speed-walked, trying not to think about the tilting ground, missing Masons and Arnolds, or the other strange things.

"Addie! Wait! I have something for Sting!"

The persistent man caught up and ripped open a packet of bone marrow dog treats. He ruffled Sting's ears, just the way he liked, and offered his hand. "There you go. Good boy." Funny how he knew how to stroke him in exactly the right place.

A second treat arched through the air. Sting jumped, caught it no trouble, and then sniffed inside Addison's bag for the open packet.

"Thank you. He appreciates them."

"He's a nice dog."

Addison tickled Sting's chin. "He is."

"Well, I'll see you."

Warmth gathered in her stomach as she watched him go. Something she shouldn't feel for a man she'd barely met. Really, what the heck was happening? Yesterday,

Arnold owned the shop. Today, some random man better suited to the boxing ring had replaced him. Tears formed as she contemplated the possibilities—mental health, tumour, time travel, dimensions. There would be other theories if she were home to research them.

Confusion tangled her mind, heat tormented her body, and on top of the moving ground and incessant nausea, she was crying.

She sighed and wiped her eyes, then walked to Cotter's field to let Sting loose, trying to concentrate on the things she did know. He raced off, disappearing into the shadow of thick trees, heading to the den.

Mason called it Jockey because he reckoned den was too understated. He never called it a shed. Yet that was what it was. Addison had saved for it, begged her father to fetch it, and—with little help from him—assembled it. At only nine years old. The year Mason was born, and the crying started. All the time. She'd needed somewhere quiet to read and do her homework. Over the years, the Jockey became worn. Mason repaired it a few times, but it had weathered since they left home.

Sting's faint cries drifted from its direction. Addison's jog through the wild growth turned into a run. Tucked against a high boundary fence behind the trees, she found a battered shed and a confused Sting sniffing the base of its scarcely hanging door. The Jockey shouldn't be so run-down and unloved. It had looked nothing like this when she came last summer. Dusty green moss coated the wooden slats, their brown paint peeled. Roof timbers had broken away, and the damp prevention flapped in the wind. It hadn't been updated in years.

Sting whimpered and scratched at the rotting door as Addison lifted and straightened it. The bottom hinge squeaked, and the top rattled loose screws as she dragged it over the grass. Lucky the padlock was missing—she didn't have the key with her.

Sting sniffed around the shed, nestling his nose into the mouldy beanbag and the remnants of Addison's childhood, none of which should be here—old books on the shelves, hairbands, and a half-used lipstick. Whimpering, he ran out and snuffled the surrounding hedges and tree trunks.

There was no trace of Mason or his things.

She fell to her knees, looking for his name. He'd carved it under the shelf when he was seven and hid it for three years before confessing. By then, at nineteen, she didn't care, but if she'd have found it when she first gave him the place, she might have killed him. She prayed it would be there now.

It wasn't. Nor was the pellet hole in the top-right corner of the window. He'd promised to replace it, but never did. Well-needed target practice and being out with his mates had taken priority.

Nothing of him existed anywhere. It was as if Mason had never lived.

Four

24ᵗʰ March 2023, 22:45

Two days passed without a sniff of a comeback from Spinzer's people or a murder reported on the news. Everything was about Mayor Robert Naise and the eerie arson that devoured his house in mere seconds. It couldn't have happened to a nicer bloke.

This was day three. The last night before heading home in time for sunrise. Laszlo had many rules, all kept rigorously, and lying low after completing a job was one he never broke. Then again, killing Spinzer felt more like pleasure than work, especially since his men had disposed of the body, cleaned the mess, and hadn't come looking for him.

Laszlo didn't relish another night hiding in a dirty strip club and considered leaving early. But then he saw the 'on-his-watch-list' high-flyer, Anton Jarvis, sit at the mirrored bar and give his order to a scantily clad waitress while rubbing the lace hem of her white thong in his fingers.

Interesting. This wasn't his first visit. Labour MP Jarvis knew better than to touch her elsewhere.

Jarvis pointed to his chosen blonde, and the waitress laughed, saying, "Of course. You don't need to tell me." To which he replied, "I don't want the other one."

Laszlo sat too far away to hear their exchange, so he could only imagine the sound of his retort. Lip-reading was a gem skill—Laszlo didn't miss a thing if he watched a moving mouth—but tone added flavour and intent.

He abandoned his plans to leave London. The chance to record Jarvis was too tempting Sleazy high quality footage of him might one day become a critical bribery source. Jarvis got the job done, true, but he was underhand, nasty, and a person to watch. The coincidental opportunity felt too good to pass up. Laszlo decided recording him live through his dog tags was worth the risk. He wagged his finger when the Goan beauty of a waitress looked his way.

Red fingernails wrapped around her pad as she approached. "Change your mind?"

"Something like that. Another Vodka straight. I'll also have a blonde in booth three."

"Not three. It's reserved."

"I always have three."

"Mr Sandman, please. Don't make this difficult for me. It's reserved and prepared for a patron."

Laszlo 'Sandman' knew that. He'd watched her prepare the booth and then spray something inside as he reclined on an olive-green sofa. The VIP glugging his pint at the bar was the obvious punter.

Unlikely to be denied a second request, Laszlo rubbed his stubbled chin and sighed in resignation, faking his disappointment. "Then I guess I'll have booth two."

"How long?"

"For however long it takes. You have my credit card." As the waitress walked away, bum cheeks wriggling, he dropped his eyes and greased his mind for the task ahead.

The blonde he requested made no preparations for him. No fancy flowers, aromatherapy sprays, or champagne chilling in an ice bucket. Booth two had an aubergine-purple, low L-shaped sofa that widened at one end, a round side table beside it, and poles on the back wall. Stark white against black paint. They weren't for dancing. More for gripping.

Whatever suited, he thought, ignoring the excitement the picture gave him.

He closed the heavy front curtain and fingered the divider between him and Anton Jarvis in booth three. Solid. Not even a finger-space gap. Fat chance of hearing a conversation. Then again, Jarvis sought fun, not chitchat, and Laszlo hoped to record it, every ecstatic bit. Safeguarding. Insurance. At least one of the country's high-fliers would then be in his pocket and unable to threaten or use him against his will. That would be worth another night in the room upstairs.

He climbed on the seat, drew out his penknife, and tugged out the small screwdriver. The vent in the screen between the booths unscrewed quickly and swung loose, revealing a hole only wide enough for two fingers. Some air vent. After removing the lensed dog tag from his neck, he faced the camera forward and fed it through the slat to booth three. Once he'd angled it perfectly according to the screen on his watch, he roughly replaced the vent cover, sat, and swapped the knife for the comms connected to the tag camera. The curtain opened before he could slip it into his ear. He dropped it in his pocket as Debbie, the only other blonde stripper, entered carrying a neat vodka.

Approaching him, she plonked the drink on the table and kicked his legs open to stand between his knees. She didn't get the chance to step in. Laszlo grabbed her wrists and towered over her.

"Oh, hello!" she replied with a wink.

Transferring her wrists into one hand, he flopped onto the sofa.

He pulled her closer and stroked her stomach above the seam of her red silk knickers. As he trailed his fingers along the inside of her thigh, he said, "I don't go for that kind of thing, and you're not here for intimacy." When she cocked her frowning head, he added, "Take a seat. Let's talk."

"How much is it worth?"

"I've paid for your time."

"You pay me to thrill you. Which thrills me. Talking doesn't excite me."

Laszlo bit his lip, feeling at odds with his principles and upbringing. One thing he didn't do was use sex as a transaction. Usually. But...

"Stimulate me with your replies, and I'll stimulate you as a reward. How's that for a fair exchange?"

She smiled.

"Take hold of those poles over there. Knees up on the seat."

Debbie obeyed.

"Wider."

Laszlo sussed her out, fingers trailing while asking irrelevant questions. He noted the ticklish spots that made her twitch and the sensitive places where she caught her breath. With only a few strategic touches, he knew how to bring her to orgasm as climactically as possible...and how to control when or if she did. He would make her tell him everything before he let that happen. She would work for her pleasure.

With tweaks, kisses and bites, he made his way down her body, creating a wave of sexual excitement. Intensifying if her answers stimulated him. Most times, he rewarded the sheer effort she made by taking her to the edge, but never quite *there*. Should they disappoint, like her reluctance to share about the other blonde stripper, he would stop and cruelly starve her.

"Ah. You were almost there as well," he teased, dragging a fingernail over her breast.

Debbie answered his questions, seeking his touch. By the time he asked about Anton Jarvis, she was deliciously willing to give away anything to be satisfied.

"Why didn't he want you?"

Laszlo withdrew his hand when she took too long to reply.

She groaned and inched down the sofa, looking for him. "Don't stop. I don't know."

He bent her knees and ran his nails up the inside of her thighs, pausing close to the top. "Yeah, you do. What did you do?" He kissed her knee, trailing his tongue.

Anticipating his next move, she moaned and gripped the edge of the seat. "Nothing. It's because I have a brain and won't let him do what he wants."

Her sexual excitement crested into frustration, and after a forty-minute tease towards a crescendo, Debbie revealed something about the man leaving the booth next door.

"He wanted to share me for the weekend with Mayor Naise!" she panted. "I said no. Something didn't feel right. I got an inkling it wasn't only for the two of them."

Laszlo met her imploring eyes.

"Please, don't leave me hanging."

In seconds, she groaned in utter delight.

Still fully clothed, Laszlo reclined on the sofa. Most of him hadn't touched her, yet he wanted a shower. Instead, he gave Debbie a moment to recover, then sent her to order another vodka. He would at least wash his mouth out before settling the extortionate bill.

He removed the cover and reached into the vent hole, checking twice that his dog tag had gone. Heart racing, but keeping his cool, he swallowed the panic and slipped into a messy booth three. He checked the empty vent, the carpet, and between the seat cushions.

Nothing but an abandoned bra. Steps determined, he moved to the bar, hoping for signs of who had found it, preferring it to be the other blonde rather than Jarvis. Only Debbie waited, clutching a receipt.

He swallowed with a dry mouth as he approached. "Did he leave already?"

"Fled like he was being chased," she whispered. "Whatever did she do to him?"

Still cool, Laszlo washed the vodka around his mouth, checked out, and headed for his car. Despite his crimes, he wouldn't drive over the alcohol limit. He would rather sleep in the car tonight than stay at the strip club. Jarvis might come looking for the sleazy spy. It wasn't worth the risk. A risk that shouldn't even be in Laszlo's crosshairs. An unlucky consequence of a tiny lens being noticed in a faintly lit booth.

Huddled on the back seat with a tatty quilt and a snazzy laptop, he first disabled the transmission between the dog tag and his hidden IP, aware that a man of Jarvis' stature might have already made tracks into finding it if he knew how. If he had tech savvies on speed dial, forty minutes was ample time to trace the connection. It may not lead them to him, but it would show the device still recording. The astute and well-connected Jarvis would eventually uncover the owner from the partly revealed identification number. That would lead them to him. An oversight, he admitted, never expecting the beloved dog tags to leave his neck.

Stupid. It was stupid. Ego.

You took the opportunity, Laszlo, and screwed it up. Nice going. A radar is coming for you.

Before deciding if he should ditch his secure house, he watched the recording, eager to locate his tag and reveal who'd taken it. He hoped his next job wasn't cleaning up the body of a Member of Parliament.

~

Metal tapping the window startled him. He blinked awake. The sun was rising, and moving in front of it was a flaming copper.

This just gets better, he thought, sure his luck had deserted him.

The policeman tapped again and didn't stop until Laszlo opened it.

"Parking charges at hotel prices, are they?"

"Almost." His cheeky grin covered his horror at the circumstances. "Sorry, officer. I needed a rest before driving across the country. In fact, I should have left by now."

"There are beds for that."

"I didn't intend to sleep. Just rest. I'll be on my way." Laszlo moved to get out.

"Driving licence, please."

He handed his phone through the window and waited while the copper scanned and logged it. In forty-five years, his name had never appeared on a police file. His luck was now so in the red it had sucked out the fumes and spluttered to a halt. Seeing Jarvis with his face close to the dog tag lens last night, declaring war, had been bad enough. But this? This was exponentially bad.

"Bath is hardly across the country, Mr Sándor."

Despite the loose British law, Laszlo couldn't see an issue with sleeping in his car. A twinge of frustration slipped out as he sensed precious time slipping away. "Width-wise, it is. Besides, even if it were a few streets away, I'd have still needed the rest. I didn't feel well. Better than crashing, isn't it?"

The suspicious policeman returned his phone. "An incident took place nearby. Overnight. We're taking extra precautions. There's a café around the corner. Opens in ten minutes. I suggest some sustenance before you leave." He nodded and walked away, not even looking back as he rounded the corner.

Laszlo climbed into the front seat and sped off, stopping at a drive-thru for breakfast before joining the motorway.

Though not the worst scenario he'd planned for, it sounded a loud alarm. His safety procedures faced their first test. The software to burn his home data files remotely had synced and pinged, ready to activate, should the need arise. He could walk away from his life anytime. It wasn't necessary to return home. Though it would be painful to leave certain personal items behind. Izsak. Mabel.

Too painful. He had to fetch them. It would take Jarvis time to discover the dog tag belonged to Laszlo's deceased older brother, Izsak Sándor. It wouldn't take a genius to connect his surname to the police report that placed Laszlo near the strip club. He needed to be long gone by then.

The roar of his Audi engine did nothing to soothe the anxiety fringing his instincts. He pressed on the accelerator pedal none-the-less and headed into Bath. The slow-moving traffic cost him another twenty frustrating minutes he couldn't afford to lose. Sensing precious time slipping away, he ran an amber light, refusing to tap his fingers and wait while more time passed. Impatient, he threaded the maze of tight side streets and reached his house frazzled.

Fear drove him like a mad viper twisting around his heart. The police knew his name, and Anton Jarvis would follow up with a home visit. The need to pack and hunker down weighed on his mind. Heavier than the annoyance he felt with himself. He'd broken a few rules these last twenty-four hours. Now, he must face the consequences.

Efficient as always, he enabled the failsafe on his home devices, saved the files he wanted separately on an external hard drive, and deleted the rest. Then, he filled a case and brought it to the kitchen where he kneeled to access a safe.

His watch buzzed. A gentle zap of electricity stung his wrist, alerting Laszlo to imminent company. He glanced at the external cameras on his watch screen, spying movement outside the front door and along the side of the house.

A glint of red flashed across the silver safe handle as he jumped up and plucked his weapon from the back of his trousers. How had Anton Jarvis found him so fast?

Dink, dink, dink.

Laszlo looked down at a black stun grenade shaped like a sleek mini fire extinguisher rolling into the kitchen. It looked like a toy. Only, a fatal one at such proximity.

With mere milliseconds to act, he covered his ears and dived as it gave a piercing crack and burst with light like an erratic flash bulb. The stunning sound drilled through his hands and vaulted off his eardrums like pinballs in a machine. Bedazzled by the reflection bouncing off the safe, he yelled and rolled behind the centre island, disorientated and immobilised. He lay with blurry blobs in his eyes, and ears ringing in a vacuum of deafness. He didn't see the men rushing through the back door, or those surging from the lounge.

Seconds later, phantasmic and as if in slow-motion, six men in armour vests surrounded him, pointing laser-sighted rifles. The red dots of what, in this country, could only be government-grade weapons, peeked around the fluffy spots in his eyes as he felt the ground for his gun.

Dull, distant shouting entered the vacuum of deafness. A knee pressed into the small of his back and rough hands grappled to bind his hands before he realised it was happening.

Shit.

Wrists bound, and unsteady on his feet, he fought to overcome his lack of senses as they checked him for weapons. He couldn't see or hear much but felt the hard drive transfer from his pocket into intruder hands before they pushed him into the lounge where more men had gathered around his waiting suitcase.

"Going somewhere?" A voice echoed.

"Not anymore." Still dazed, Laszlo's voice sounded as if it were confined in a chamber.

The professional team swept through his compact house, taking his mail, suitcase, and computer.

A sudden demand to "make him comfortable for the journey" was worrying. *What were they planning?*

As he looked up, the butt of a rifle came towards him.

Five

13th April 2023, 20:07 – The New

After spending the night sobbing on the sofa, contemplating her imminent insanity, Addison emerged more positive. Decisive, she called work and took the day off. Still nursing a slight headache, she slept and later fired up her laptop. She compiled two lists titled The Real and The New, logging the changes that had sparked her despair.

Before last night, she hadn't been in the lounge since Tuesday, but as she looked around, she noted changes like a game of spot-the-subtle-difference between her eyes and memory. An elephant ornament she bought on a family holiday wasn't on her modest dresser. Likely because Mason had encouraged her into the bric-à-brac shop. As he didn't appear to exist anymore, she probably never went in.

A shiny silver frame encrusted with fake gems in the corners held a family picture. She'd seen it in a boutique shop and fallen in love with the ruby and diamond decorations. A cracked display frame had been the only one available and, disappointed, she chose the sapphire version instead. It was just as pretty. Two days ago, the frame had blue gems and four people in the photo. Now they were red, and Mason was absent.

The missing knick-knacks and replaced photos could be an oversight, but another major change was an intriguing mirror hanging long and wide on the wall. In The Real, the large plant pot near the television stood there. She didn't even own an antique bronze mirror. In yesterday's maddening despair, she'd tried to yank it off the wall. Instead, it opened at the side. Unable to make sense of her surroundings, she'd slammed it shut, but now felt ready to investigate.

She slid her fingers down the frame until she found a small clip. The mirror swung open. Behind was a tall, spacious wooden compartment containing two folded blankets. She leaned in, surprised to find the converted flue had vent strips at the top. Why have a cupboard with air holes? The blankets would get damp. Even more curious was the small battery-powered LED light stuck to the panel above the entrance.

After closing the mirror cupboard, she psyched herself up for the kitchen. Yesterday, it had tipped the balance of her sanity. She took and held a deep breath before opening the fridge. The milk label mocked her. She should have seen a sketch of a cow's fat, cheerful face with Brookhouse Dairies written around it. Instead, she saw the Coleman Farm franchise and the dreary outline of its farmhouse logo.

The British corporation was fast monopolising the fresh food market in The Real. In The New, it appeared they had already taken over. Their products filled her fridge, but Addison preferred farmers who cared about the land and livestock, not revenue, sales, and squeezing every penny for a profit. The superior food quality mattered, too.

She wandered around the house, finding it difficult to decide what to add to her list. In some ways, things just seemed different, like a plant missing from the garden or the feel of the stair-rail paintwork. Confirming them proved tough. Only items she used or saw often were certain in her mind. A mind that made associations, patterns, and connections. One that would notice something unusual or off, even if she couldn't fathom what it was.

Addison sat on the bed, soothing a mourning Sting and going over her list, checking she'd remembered everything. She had—even the chewed/unchewed doorstep.

The doorbell interrupted her latest recap. She peeked through the curtain, spying Vinny Jones from the shop waiting in the security light on the driveway.

She opened the window. "Hi…"

He frowned. "Jon."

"How do you know where I live?"

"I'm worried about you, Addie."

'Addie' again. Only friends and family shortened her name. Suspicious, yet troubled to learn he felt familiar enough to use it, she snapped, "Answer my question." Her eyebrows raised at his melodramatic sigh.

"You slipped and sprained your ankle outside the shop last winter," he replied. "I drove you home, expecting you to remember it. I'm really worried about you."

"So am I," she mumbled to herself. "I'm fine. As you can see."

"Open the door, Addie."

Addison closed the window and exhaled a shaky breath. She didn't know this guy, yet he cared for her. So why would 'she' refuse a date with him fifteen times? As kind as he seemed, and as dreamy as his soft-brown eyes were, she could hardly be honest. If he pressed her into a confession, how would he react?

Rather than invite him in, she took Sting's lead off the hook by the front door and whistled. The excitable Labrador's paws pounded the hall carpet. She opened the door, hesitant to talk to the shopkeeper in any capacity, but willing to put his mind at rest.

"This way." She pointed right and set off at a fast pace with the satisfied Sting trotting beside her. At the alley to Cotter's field, where she always released him from his lead, Jon grabbed her arm and pulled her to a stop.

"Why do you pretend not to remember me? Or my name? We've known each other for three years."

She grimaced. The last time she tried to explain, her colleagues laughed and suggested she see the doctor. Physically, she might be well, but her mental health still looked dire.

"It might be better if I show you." She followed Sting's lead deeper into Cotter's field, pretending not to notice Jon side-eyeing her.

"You look better today. Did you enjoy the wine?"

"It was an immense relief, thank you." She winced at how little time she gave before answering. "Though it didn't help me sleep, and I still have a slight headache."

"From the wine?"

"I wish it were that simple, but unfortunately not."

An awkward silence followed, chased by doubt clawing at her psyche. She should keep quiet until she knew what the heck was happening. Without something to back up her claims, he'd think she was crazy like her colleagues did.

Off the lead, Sting darted along the side of the second field, snuffling the hedge and grass, often stopping to sniff the air.

Jon chuckled under his breath. "He sure loves sniffing."

"He's looking for a scent."

"Got a fancy, has he?"

Jon's wink raised a smile, despite Addison's forlorn reply. "More of a yearning. We're mourning, I guess."

When his forehead puckered, she sighed, wanting to confess. To offload would be a release, but only on someone who would explore this with her and not make rash judgements. She couldn't be sure Jon was the right person. He might have known her for three years, but she only remembered knowing him for five minutes. Could she trust him? The sexy, ill-fitting shop owner, with eyes like a chocolate vortex, could certainly suck her into sweet fantasies. He smelled good, looked strong, and liked dogs. Yet the Addison he knew hadn't agreed to his advances. What did she know?

What did I know?

Doubt rooted with firm tendrils, and her confession suffocated beneath her fears. She steered away from the Jockey, whistling for Sting, but he ignored her. Decided on their course, he ran for the trees and disappeared. Her instinct sparked and overcame her doubts. She should start at the Jockey.

"Come on. It's easier to show you."

She caught herself smiling as affection for the place swelled her heart. It fell when the battered Jockey came into view. She looked at Jon. "Have I ever told you about this?"

Jon shook his head, his frown deepening.

"It's in the top ten of my most important things. Look at the state of it. I'd never let it get like this." She took him inside and pointed at the dusty shelving. "See that?"

Jon looked closer. "Nothing there."

"Exactly." She approached the window. "See anything here?"

With a tolerant sigh, he shook his head again and stuffed his hands into his pockets.

"There should be a hole in the corner made by a pellet gun. My brother's name used to be under the shelf."

"Used to be? I didn't know you had a brother."

"Apparently, I don't anymore."

"Addie, you're not making any sense."

She sighed, regretting what she'd started, and knelt beside the panel under the shelf. Her fingers rubbed over sanded wood. "It used to say Mason Rae. On Tuesday, I had a twenty-four-year-old brother. I made him sausage and mash. Wednesday, he had never been born. Gone. Overnight."

"Addie, I don't think that's possible."

"Tell me about it! I have a list of changes, but the scariest thing is not knowing what's real. I'm missing a navy and white spotted dress that one of my closest friends bought and made me wear to a party. It's hideous. Glad to see the back of it, to be honest. But not at this cost. I met Chloe years back when she dated Mason. We instantly became like sisters. I'm too chicken to see if we still know each other because we probably wouldn't have met without Mason. There's a seven-year age gap between us."

"You're saying you remember a brother who doesn't exist?"

"But he did. My mum said she miscarried, but in my…reality, is it—or in my head, she didn't. I built this place to escape his crying. I was nine and preferred reading in the quiet. When I was fifteen, I sometimes let him inside." The memory provoked a wistful smile. "He treated it like a palace for a year. Wiped his feet, swept his biscuit crumbs, and helped me paint it. When I finished secondary school, I gave it to him. Even had a plaque made to mark the occasion." Addison laughed again. "It obviously wasn't enough because not long after, he carved his name under there and hid it from me for three years!"

Jon peered at her, a dubious frown forming. "If you built it to escape the crying, why is it still here if there was none?" Addison hadn't thought of that. "Look. I…uh…wanted to check you were alright. As I said, you look better today, and I'm glad. I also still need to cash up. So, I'd better be going." He pointed his thumb over his shoulder.

Of all the brush-offs she'd heard, this was notably the weakest. Betrayal wrote an essay across her face, but Jon had spun around and walked away without noticing.

Anger brewed. She kicked the bottom of the Jockey door with a growl, and the wood snapped, echoing its crack into the silent night.

Jon strode on.

~

The next day, the accounts office reminded Addison of an exam room. As she passed the cluster of desks, her colleagues kept their heads down. The suspicious silence made her uneasy. Only Bertie offered a sheepish grin and a shallow greeting. Certain that something was afoot, she fired up her system, puzzled by Marsha's empty workstation.

"Is Marsha sick?"

Bertie responded when no one else did. "She's in with Barnes."

"Has something happened?"

"No. Just busy preparing for the Convolve purchase."

Addison frowned. Barnes only announced it two days ago. There wouldn't be anything for accounts to do yet. She imported yesterday's daily reports, surprised to see invoices already raised, received, and pending payments. The process was moving too fast. To 'expect unusual transactions coming through accounts' shouldn't mean the next day.

Or the day of.

The automated daily bank statement for Wednesday, the same day the strange pressure influx occurred, showed a £5.9 million credit entry. Strange. Why had SID paid Palowa? As senior bank reconciliator, Addison would have expected debits if they were acquiring Convolve from SID. She scanned her digital in-tray, emails, and messages for relevant purchase documents. Coming up empty, she looked at the reports for the invoice processor.

Marsha.

Addison opened the calendar and viewed Marsha's bi-weekly meetings booked with Barnes. Disappointment gave way to relief that she was not leading the purchase this time. Acquiring the Brazilian Convolve two years ago had been one of the most stressful times of her life. Rightfully, it should be hers, again. Now it would be Marsha's. At least it was a US firm this time. Marsha could speak her own language. Addison had navigated broken English and learning Brazilian phrases to get her through.

Had Barnes's trust in Addison's abilities collapsed so much since missing one little staff meeting? Surely, there was more to it than that?

Thirty minutes later, a flustered Marsha rubbed her forehead as she left Barnes's office. She didn't realise Addison could see her reflection in the stairwell door opposite his office. Neither did Barnes. Addison had often seen him loitering, listening to unsuspecting employee conversations...as he had on Wednesday.

Marsha inhaled before rounding the corner with a fake smile. "Hey, Addie. You look better. The day off did you good." She sat at her desk without another word and started working.

"Much better thanks, Marsha. I was going through yesterday's bank entries and saw a payment made first thing, but I don't have an invoice to allocate it to."

"Oh. Yes. Barnes needed a few things processed for a meeting yesterday. He asked me to prepare everything. You'll find all the Convolve items done."

"What was it for?"

Marsha looked blank. Didn't she know or couldn't she say?

"Uh, it's their employee pensions settlement."

"Okay. Then, why the face?"

"Wondering why you were asking." Marsha donned her headset. Her calendar status updated with a red DO NOT DISTURB icon next to her name.

Bertie had her back to them and shifted uncomfortably, while Addison battled another wave of anger, the roots of which were tangled in fear and paranoia. She was the senior, not Marsha, and she asked because it was her job to know. Was she still the senior or had Barnes demoted her? Had she ever been a team leader? Addison couldn't trust her memories. How many of them were false truths?

The edgy vibe rippling from her colleagues elevated her anxiety. By lunchtime, she couldn't take stock of it. The doubts controlled her as she took the stairs to the roof where she always ate her lunch.

Marsha sat on the stubby wall around the roof edge with her back against the railings. She had a distant look in her eyes as she fiddled with a sandwich bag on her lap.

Today, Addison wanted to avoid company and backed away.

Marsha looked up. "Hiya. Thought I'd join you if you don't mind. It's a good place to chat without being heard."

Secretive chats? Whatever she planned to say could wait. Addison had her own question to ask. "Did you hear from HR?"

Her forehead creased. "What? Oh. That. No, nothing."

"What did you say, exactly?"

"The truth about what you said. They kept mentioning your headache. They also asked if you were sick."

"Yeah. Vertigo, I guess. Everything kept moving."

More like my equilibrium needed to catch up.

Marsha fell silent.

"How did they know to ask if I was nauseous?" When Marsha didn't answer, she pushed for more. "Did they ask you anything else?"

"Not really."

"Hardly a grilling then."

"Perhaps I overreacted." Marsha smiled, but the flick of her eyes caught her lie. "I do have something to tell you."

"Save it. I guessed you were leading the Convolve purchase."

"Only because you were off. Barnes just came out with it yesterday morning. Completely unexpected." Marsha fell silent, turning her sandwich around in her hands.

"What's really going on?" Addison took a bite of her ham roll to give her time to reply.

Eventually, she mumbled, "I thought about what you said, you know, about the pressure thing. You were so sure of how it felt when it passed through you. Was it real?"

Addison cringed at the reminder. The force had either been so cold, she'd feel forever hot afterwards, or so hot that it initially seemed like it froze her insides.

"Felt real to me," she replied. "But I must've dreamt of a green Palowa. Right? Like Barnes thinks."

"I guess so. Have you called the doctor yet?"

She shook her head. "The headache has eased now. I don't see the point and I couldn't be arsed yesterday."

"You should. Rule out anything physical."

"Prove if I'm a nutcase, you mean?"

Marsha's eyes widened. "That wasn't what I meant at all."

"Yeah, it was."

"I'm just trying to be an understanding friend and to be there for you. Help you if I can. What if you have a tumour or mandala dementia?"

"What's that?"

"It follows Alzheimer's, but instead of confusing your present with the past, you remember a different past."

"Do you mean I'm not alone?" Addison's eyes lit at the thought.

"There might be support groups not too far away. We can look together—after you've seen the doctor. Company insurance covers specialists. Barnes suggested I book you an appointment, so…" Marsha handed her a yellow Post-it. "Two-thirty, this afternoon. She'll meet you in the first-aid room."

"That's a little invasive, isn't it?" Addison took the Post-it as if accepting punishment for a wrong she hadn't done.

"Have you noticed other changes?"

Addison shrugged. "Little things. Mostly subtle and trivial. I wrote a list but won't continue to feed the lie. Do you know anyone called Mason?"

"My son is called Mason. You know that because he's nine now."

Marsha's nine-year-old was a girl called Letitia, and her younger brother was Lester. In The Real. Addison kept it to herself.

"What about the word jockey? Mean anything to you?"

Marsha scrunched up her nose and looked sympathetic. "Does it to you?"

Addison swigged her drink rather than reply.

"Have you told anyone else about this?"

Unintentionally lying, Addison shook her head, subconsciously protecting Jon-Vinny-Jones before she knew it.

"For your sake, until we know what's going on, don't. All right? You come to me. Anytime. Call for whatever you need. Once we know, then we can re-evaluate."

"Do you think I have this dementia thing? I'm thirty-three."

"From what I read last night, twenty-six is the youngest patient. How's your sleep pattern been lately? Restlessness is a symptom."

"Barely slept since I woke on Wednesday night. Why?"

"Before that?"

"Fine." *Everything used to be absolutely fine.*

"Barnes roasted the team for poking fun at you. They won't mention it. Nobody else knows. So, that's good. But are you sure you're ready to work? We can't afford any mistakes. The buy-out will be challenging. An undertaking, even. We'll need to rely on each other if it's to go smoothly."

"I feel okay. But like you said, see what the doctor says. Barnes was right to give you the lead. Don't feel bad."

Marsha smiled as she packed away a lunch she'd only nibbled. "Can you access your list from your phone?" When Addison nodded, she added, "Take a copy with you, so you don't forget to mention anything to the doctor."

Though Addison agreed, she quietly questioned why a doctor simply checking her physical health would need it. Surely, only how the shift had made her feel was important. She'd only listed what had changed, but if it wasn't real, why would it matter?

Six

25th March 2023, 13:30

Distant voices and humming tickled the fringes of Laszlo's awareness, inching him from unknown realms. Waking to the smell of vinegar and stale cheese made him want to gag, but he kept the physical response from manifesting. He didn't want the voices to know he was conscious, and aware of lying on the ridged floor of a moving vehicle. Instead, he cracked open an eye, and right in front of his nose were two pitifully well-worn, black trainers on crossed feet, casual legs stretched.

Score one. His captors were relaxed. Considering his thick head, and the remnants of a stun-grenade hangover, he needed them to be.

Score two. No fuzzy blobs in his vision.

Beneath the putrid feet were grey ridges digging into Laszlo's ribs and hip. He slid into a groove when the vehicle pulled onto a bumpy road. Then, like hammer blows drilling through his body, vibrations shook him, bashing his head and body on the ridges. The impossible noise coming from under the floor vied for the top spot as they drove over what felt like a triple cattle grid.

His migraine protested with waves of pulsing agony.

A stinking trainer pushed against his fleshy cheek, lifting his face. Its owner assumed he was still unconscious and let it go with a quiet laugh.

"You sure made him comfortable for the journey. Smacked him hard, man. He's gone."

"Barely touched the pussy."

Laszlo's patience dwindled. To avoid making another unnecessary hasty move, he planned his spiel. How could he con Anton Jarvis into thinking this was one big, rather unfortunate mistake? Jarvis had to be behind the grab. No one else would storm his home and kidnap him. Laszlo didn't keep enemies around long enough to suffocate his future, even though the MP's henchman appeared to be doing a decent job with his feet. The team might stink, but they were proficient.

The van slowed, and while the distracted captors were looking through the windscreen, Laszlo wriggled his stiff fingers and pulled on the cable tie securing his wrists. It hardly stretched. It wasn't a cheapie.

Unlike the black trainer poking at Laszlo's sternum.

"Wakey, wakey. Rise and shine for the master."

When Laszlo's eyes blinked open, gruff hands pulled him up and the trainer wearer unlocked the back doors and jumped out. Three more heavies crowded behind him. Two shoved Laszlo from behind, and another pulled him towards a well-maintained barn in the middle of a field.

Laszlo watched his step. Then his Italian shoes were all he could see, and his irritation soared at the scuffs across the toes. The cretins had dragged, not carried, him to the van. He powered the anger into his arms and pulled on the cable tie. It stretched enough to feel the blood warming his fingers.

Inside the barn, a specialised chair summoned him. It had clamps and hinges to lie flat if they chose. Not a good sign. It also had an audience of armed men. Again, not a good sign. Piled high around them were hay bales, animal feed and miscellaneous farming products and equipment. Stuff a pristine barn wouldn't usually store.

Laszlo sat, legs astride, unclamped, guarded, and wrists still bound, waiting for 'the master.'

The balding, silver-haired Henry Coleman, often pictured at luxury country clubs playing golf with influential people, strode through the side door like he owned it. Which he likely did. The Coleman food franchise did exceedingly well, and the van could have travelled as far as Surrey.

Laszlo sighed with exaggerated relief. "Thank f…"

"You glad it's only me?" Coleman's baritone cockney voice grated across Laszlo's shoulder blades.

"Glad it's not the strip club owner."

"Do you fear him more than Anton Jarvis?"

"The MP? What's he got to do with anything?"

Coleman rubbed his short, peppered-grey beard. "Don't insult my intelligence, Mr Sándor. You recorded them."

"Uh, you mean the girl."

He laughed. "You expect me to believe that?"

Laszlo drew on the details that the stripper Debbie had heroically provided. "Melanie Taylor, twenty-three, is an art and fashion drop-out and an alleged thief. I filmed her to prove it."

"How convenient."

Laszlo shifted his shoulders. "It is what it is. I can't embellish the premise to fit your script. Why should I care what Anton Jarvis gets up to?"

"Who did Melanie steal from?"

"A punter."

"Then why worry about the club owner if he hired you?"

Laszlo laughed. "Would his clients approve of CCTV checking on the staff? Might damage the club's reputation a bit. Besides, Melanie agreed to a private soiree, and the theft occurred there. I naturally assumed the club owner had caught me snooping and grabbed me."

Colemans's frosty eyes cooled the temperature of the room. "But I'm only going to ask the same questions. Afraid now?"

Laszlo smiled a toothy grin. "I'm not scared of you or him. It would simply be unfortunate for him to discover I'm spying on his staff. Especially on behalf of a customer who isn't certain of Melanie's guilt. I didn't intend for the club to find out until I had the evidence to prove it, and only if instructed to proceed. So, there you have it. Not exactly exciting, is it?"

"Who hired you?"

"Some guy I met in the pub."

Coleman laughed. "Oh. How cliché."

"All right. A client I met in the pub."

"Okay."

"It was. We're friends. He knows the extent of my abilities. I've worked for him before."

"Who."

Laszlo wouldn't say. If he didn't have discretion, he had nothing.

An unexpected fist flew from behind and took him by surprise. Spit hurled from his mouth when it connected. Ignoring the heat coming from his ear, he curled his lip and dipped his head to look back with dangerous eyes. The hatred crept across the floor from his rolling chin.

"Who's the client?" Coleman asked again.

"The whos are confidential," he replied, aggravated. He'd rather navigate the situation without the throbbing head.

A man carrying papers while swinging van keys around his finger approached Coleman. "He's wiped the computer clean. And nothing on his phone."

Coleman nodded at the papers. "What are they?"

The van driver turned to Laszlo. "I'm afraid you've got some outstanding debt. Best get that sorted." He threw the examined dispute letters into his lap. Laszlo was being stubborn with the gas company.

Coleman walked towards him, rubbing his cupped hands together. "Club owner trouble isn't worth wiping your hard drive, Mr Sándor. Anton Jarvis trouble, however, is."

Laszlo glared back, unafraid despite the circumstances and Coleman's frustrated sigh.

"Who hired you?" he went on. "Melanie wasn't your gig. Admit it was Anton. Confess the client's name. Otherwise, our persuasion will get heavier." He pointed at the hay bales and food bags. "I reckon we lie you back with one bag of feed on your chest. Though, maybe two, eh, boys? He's a big lad. Then a hay bale, another bag, and then another bale, criss-crossing up until you suffocate. Can't get heavier than that."

Laszlo was prepared for the second fist. Before it connected, he shot off the seat, letters skidding across the floor as the goon went over the chair shoulder first.

Shoulda clamped me, he thought, hunkering his shoulders, ready to defend himself without his arms. He pulled on the cable tie again, but it wouldn't snap. Besides, free arms would be useless against the weapons cocking around him. Now, he only had his wits available.

"Enough." The early forties, bistre-haired Anton Jarvis, appeared from behind the hay bales, wearing a navy suit and an expression he would never show in public. Sharp, dark eyes looked him over. "Relax. Sit down, Mr Sándor. Let's talk."

Laszlo sat, legs astride, avoiding the clamps, and angled his head, waiting—unafraid on the outside, wary inside. Being at the mercy of a corrupt member of Parliament could have unpredictable results. He recalled the undiscovered laptop with the downloaded strip club footage and relaxed.

Jarvis bent forward. His pink paisley tie swung free. Was the pattern back in fashion? No amount of funking could ever make him like it.

"Is it so wrong to want to know who's watching me?" Jarvis asked.

"Not if someone is watching you. But I would have sped through the film not even noticing you. My focus would have been on Melanie's sleight of hand. If she has one."

"Who's the client?"

"I won't tell you that."

"Then why should I believe your story? Let me verify it. Who's the client?"

Silence.

"Why won't you tell me?"

Laszlo shifted in the chair. "Because when you come to hire me, you'll do it respecting my perseverance to not give you up. No matter what."

"A reputation does nothing for a dead man."

"It isn't about reputation. It's about discretion. And honour."

"Among thieves?" Jarvis laughed.

"Melanie is the alleged thief."

"Is there footage of the other days you spent watching a pickpocket?"

"She only had one client last night before you found the camera, so no. Not anymore."

"Nothing? Didn't she steal anything?"

"No. I deleted the files."

Jarvis held up the confiscated hard drive with the recording of his naked self all over it. "Is this all there is?"

Laszlo faked his disappointment and nodded, knowing he had all the files hidden on his laptop.

"Respect to you, Mr Jarvis. I didn't expect you to find me so fast."

"I have excellent friends. Why did you only keep this film?"

"I haven't watched it yet."

"You haven't?"

Was the lie too much of a stretch? He shook his head. "Too busy packing up to leave."

Jarvis glanced at the men standing around Laszlo's chair. Each nodded in confirmation.

"Excellent. For your records, then, Mr Sándor, I can assure you Melanie Taylor didn't steal from me. You have my word. Maybe your client would like to meet to confirm that, or perhaps you will just accept what I tell you and lie. That way, you'll still be paid."

"The situation is unfortunate, but I would still get paid."

"Good. Your tax returns are healthy. You keep to the law, mostly. Until this morning. I was watching activity in the area, and what should pass me but a report of a dosser sleeping in a parked car near the club. Accented Sándors aren't regular in Britain. So, I searched your name and saw you had a brother. An Armed Forces brother." He waggled his fingers and Coleman placed the dog tag in it. "His records match most of the ID numbers on this. Imagine my surprise to link you so easily as the culprit."

Surprised, Laszlo raised his eyebrows. A lucky circumstance had found him, not Jarvis's skills. The police report wouldn't exist if he had stayed away from his car. His respect for the MP and his 'excellent friends' for finding him so fast disappeared.

"Know much about prison, Mr Sándor?"

"Never been. But I hear it's restrictive."

Jarvis tossed the dog tag into Laszlo's lap. "Your brother's murder is still unsolved. But I gather the detective knew who killed him. Right? The suspect went missing not long later. Duncan Frost never returned.

Did you avenge Izsak by killing the man responsible? Because I reckon you did. Are the dog tags your tokens?" He pointed to the one in Laszlo's lap. Its brother tag still hung around Laszlo's neck.

"I was twenty."

"Everyone starts somewhere, and you have officer training. Duncan Frost was only the beginning of the road you walked. A tip-off to a detective who asks the right questions would soon find out, wouldn't it? Would they dig up evidence if they looked closely at you? Do you need the grief?"

"No."

"Then we can make a deal."

"What do you mean?"

"I keep your secret and you do me a very specific job."

"And your secret?"

Jarvis raised his eyebrows. "What? I entered a booth with a young woman. You haven't seen it. What could you describe? She danced for me, so what? I was on a stag night. All part of the fun."

"How specific a job?" Laszlo asked, letting Jarvis think he had the upper hand.

Coleman whistled and made a phone sign with his thumb and little finger as the men from the van left them alone to talk. Who did he want to call?

Jarvis captured his attention once more. "Find out who hired and killed Robert Naise. Then–"

"That's easy. Mario Spinzer. Funnily enough, another mysterious disappearance." Inside, Laszlo laughed. On the outside, he cocked an eyebrow.

"Find him."

"Take it from me, Mr Jarvis. He has paid for his crime."

"You need to undo it."

"Anton," Henry interjected, "we agreed."

"Undo what? Resurrect Mario?" Laszlo laughed.

Jarvis didn't. "Resurrect Robert."

"Who do you think I am? You need a church or a flaming miracle."

"Anton, please. We talked about this."

Laszlo continued with his sarcasm as if he didn't hear Coleman. "I'll just hop in the DeLorean, shall I? Meet with Doc Brown and get everything put right for you?"

Jarvis frowned, offence propping up his curling lip. "I don't care how you do it. That's your department. But you will undo it."

"How, genius? I'll take my chances with the detective, thanks."

Jarvis held out a business card. "Call this man. He'll point you in the right direction."

Henry pulled Jarvis and the card to one side. "Ross won't be happy. Anton, this has got to stop. It's too risky. We agreed."

"You agreed. I'll do whatever it takes. Robert deserves as much, and we need him alive." Jarvis held out the card again. "Do you accept, Mr Sándor?"

"I would take it, but…" When Laszlo showed his bound wrists, Jarvis went to the door and mumbled to the men outside, returning moments later with a set of cutters.

The long-awaited snap echoed, and the cable tie loosened. Laszlo rubbed his wrists, stubbornly ignoring the sore burn marks. He snatched the dog tag from his lap first, then collected his scattered letters and tucked them into his pocket.

Jarvis extended the card once more. "Do you accept?"

Laszlo kept his expression neutral. *The man is a fruitcake! I should just agree and slip off quietly.*

He had contingencies prepared. A solid identity in a small Scottish town—far, far away from a London MP.

Without a word, not wishing to reveal his thoughts, he took it and sat.

"Is that a yes?"

"No. It's impossible. You must know that. It also isn't a fair exchange. A copper's attention is way less challenging than your proposal."

"It won't be. I can assure you."

A twitchy vibe chilled the room. Its tangible aura descended into Laszlo's skin. Goosebumps swept his arms, and he swallowed as they pricked his throat and neck. Jarvis wasn't a man to mess with.

"First, speak to Ross. Then come to me with your solution."

The stinky Trainer-Guy tapped on the door. A taxi awaited. Booked and presumably paid for with Coleman's hand-sign for a phone.

On his way out, and wishing he had a fifty to throw at him, Laszlo said, "Do something about your cheesy feet, mate. They don't make nice smelling salts."

Seven

14th April 2023, 14:27 – The New

The door to the first aid room stood open, waiting for the patient to enter. Addison hesitated in the corridor, reluctant to discover which asylum would become her new home. *Mandala dementia*, Marsha had called it. Was that what she had? She took a long breath, squashed down her fears, and strolled inside.

The strawberry-blonde doctor looked up and smiled. Wrinkling laugh lines and the splash of gold freckles around her pale-blue eyes put Addison at ease. The woman seemed kind and mature enough to know her stuff. She signalled to a chair on the other side of the desk, saying, "carpet, showcase, vehicle."

Puzzled, Addison sat.

After the usual pleasantries, she performed an in-depth physical examination. Vitals and cognitive reactions were perfect. She knocked Addison's knee with a small rubber mallet and her foot swung without mental command.

Next, she took several vials of blood, transferred one into a compact machine, and closed the lid. It hummed, the whir increasing as it spun the sample at a remarkable speed.

"While we're waiting, let's go through a few questions and then you can talk about your experiences. Okay?"

Addison nodded.

"What's my name?"

"Doctor Collins."

"What were the three words I said when you first came in?"

Those weird words had spoiled the comfort of the doctor's smile. So strange, she had dismissed them as irrelevant. Sometimes, she repeated details to remember things.

"Sorry. Didn't know I was supposed to be paying attention."

Dr Collins smiled. "That's the point. Just give it a go."

Addison tried to think. "Um, vehicle," a pause, "carpet and, um...er...sh...shower?"

"Showcase."

"Two outta three ain't bad, right?" Addison sang, then coughed, embarrassed when Dr Collins didn't laugh. Instead, she asked Addison more questions.

What year is it? Who is the current monarch? Prime minister? Mayor of London?

"We haven't got one. Robert Naise is dead," she replied, proud to know this as absolute truth. Dr Collins nodded a "uh-huh" as she wrote notes and probed further into Naise's death. Addison provided the facts, even the gas used to assassinate him, happy to prove she could remember things correctly. After all, she'd had such a vivid dream about it only the other day. She straightened her shoulders. "See. My memory isn't so bad."

With a patronising smile, the doctor moved on, now enquiring about Addison's most and least favourite bands, songs, books and their genre, TV preferences, and school subjects. In school, the goody-two-shoes Addison preferred books to television—fantasy being her favourite. She loved being swept away into a fantasy world of dreams or nightmares.

Something not very different from this weirdness.

Dr Collins scribbled on a notepad, checking her boxes. Would she be comparing and diagnosing on the hop?

The questions stretched on. A personality quiz where Addison chose a colour that drew her the most took a tangent, digging into sleep patterns, anxiety, and depression. The probing into aspects of Addison's life, logical thinking, and social awkwardness felt intrusive.

Any confidence gained from remembering Mayor Naise soon diminished. It was an in-depth physical and psychological assessment. The way Dr Collins suggested her sleep pattern was poor rather than asking unnerved her. Had tiredness fuelled a false perception of reality?

Only three days ago, there had been nothing wrong with her.

Addison feared where the questions were leading and what Dr Collins might presume. So, the ping of the blood test results came as a welcome relief. It distracted the doctor long enough for Addison to gather her thoughts...and defences, should she need them.

"There are a few inconsistencies. Your iron is high. Ferritin levels are nearly 500. Though we expect to see that in cases like these. We'll do more tests, including a scan because you mentioned headaches."

"Is that bad?"

"It's treatable. Okay, now I have my data, you may start. Go from Wednesday morning. I'll cut in if I want to broaden something. All right?"

Addison started with the barking dogs and only summarised the weird pressure shift, but Dr Collins wanted every detail of its effects. Reliving it made the symptoms prominent again, though none had completely gone. She talked through the differences she'd noticed, and the doctor's ears pricked up when she mentioned Palowa's logo.

"What made you think it was green?"

"I just knew it was wrong, but when I got inside, I doubted myself. Overnight, everything green had turned yellow. Everything. At first, I thought we'd had an upgrade, but I couldn't recall a planned rebranding."

"And you're sure it used to be green."

"Yeah. At the time. Pastel green."

"And now?"

Addison shrugged. What could she say? She believed something false.

"Continue."

Sensing unease, she summarised the other differences, kicking herself when she mentioned her missing brother. Despite her reluctance, she explained.

"He looks after my dog when I'm at work. After his night shift, he drops by, eats or takes the dinner I made him, and walks my dog back to his flat. Usually, I pick him up on my way home, but Mason didn't come that day. It's ridiculous. Last week, I had a brother. Now my mum says she miscarried twenty-five years ago! How is that even possible?"

"Of course, it isn't. We'll fix it, Miss Rae. Trust me."

"Do you think I have this dementia?"

"I think it's likely, yes," Dr Collins replied as if it meant nothing.

Bad news didn't normally make Addison smile in relief, but at least she finally knew. "Thank you for being honest."

"If that's everything? It's half-five already."

Addison's eyes widened. Had three hours passed? When she stood to leave, her jacket pocket crinkled. Remembering, she reached inside.

"A colleague suggested I pass on a list of the changes I noticed. Would you like it? Personally, I don't see how they'll help."

"Anything can be a trigger, dear," she replied. "I'll be in touch when I've spoken to your GP."

Addison closed the door, bracing herself for Marsha's questions. Her phone showed three missed calls.

~

A half-eaten sandwich crusted on the table while she spent the evening researching on her laptop. She read articles and testimonies on the mandala dementia effects, and contemplated the likelihood of time travel and alternate dimensions. If it wasn't mental, it must be time, right? A quarter of a century ago. Twenty-five years. Months before Mason Rae was born. Changing time created new realities. Not just for Addison, but for everyone. One change could ripple and alter thousands of lives.

Today, time travel was only a concept. How cheesy that some future traveller had changed the past and affected her reality. It was too wild a theory when she might simply have this mandala dementia. Her symptoms fitted, and the doctor leaned in that direction. Funny how this only started on Wednesday, though. Was it a mini-stroke? It could explain the pressure she thought she felt and might have made her feel sick. Would evidence show up on a scan?

But…her brother. She definitely had a brother. Didn't she?

Head spinning, Addison shut her laptop, rousing Sting into action. He raced around the room and the hallway like he had when she came home from work. He'd growled, sniffed and yelped as if he tried to tell her something. It had taken ages to pull him from the patio doors and settle him.

She switched off the lamp and noticed lights drifting in from the street. She zig-zagged the furniture and went to close the curtains, but gazed at a momentary splash of stars peeking through the thick clouds instead.

One by one, the streetlights fizzled out, and the cloudy blanket that hid a starry night descended on her street. It didn't hide a transit van pulling up opposite with the headlights switched off.

Addison drew the curtains and peeked through the gap.

An armed man knocked on the van doors and held his thumb up to the rear window. A string of silhouetted figures jumped out, weapons hanging loose at their sides.

Her skin pricked. The news had said Naise's road lights blacked out right before he died. Without waiting to see the team's movements, she ran to the back door and whistled for Sting.

"Go. Find the Jockey. Go. Now!"

He gave a gentle yip and jumped the neighbour's fence. He'd make it. They always left their gate open. The armed men wouldn't notice Sting slipping away, but they would see her.

Addison opened the mirror and climbed in, grateful the blankets stopped her shoes from scuffing. She clicked the frame shut, heart thumping in an electro rhythm that matched the footsteps stomping past the mirror and up the stairs. Steadying her breath, she inhaled the cool air through the vent. Why have a vent inside a cupboard? Perhaps its purpose was to always have somewhere to hide.

It was tall enough to stand in without her hair brushing the wood. Had she needed a place to hide before? She reached up and pushed hard on the top. The ceiling lifted, swinging open on silent, hidden hinges.

Why would she need an escape?

"Clear," a distant voice called.

"Clear," called another.

"She's gone. Left her phone."

"Best guess?" an authoritative voice asked.

"Not long. The water in the kettle is tepid. A thirty-minute wash cycle finished as we walked in, and she sent messages to a Marsha Law twenty minutes ago. But her laptop battery is hot, and that lightbulb burnt my fingers, so not long. Minutes. Max."

Suspicious, Addison squinted. How had they accessed her phone without a fingerprint or passcode? Some fancy hacking tech, no doubt.

"Her colleague is called Marsha. What do the messages say?"

None of your business!

"They discuss a doctor's appointment and their concerns for the future. Addison is also anxious about the past and adamant about her brother. Her last one mentions a jockey. Do we know any jockeys? And shit, man. Will you get him to do something about his stinking feet?"

"Where's the dog?" the commanding voice asked, ignoring the request and drowning out the defender's retort.

Addison's heart raced as the voice headed into the kitchen. Whoever it belonged to was perceptive.

"A bed, bowl, and a lead hanging in the hall next to Miss Rae's coat, but no dog. She isn't walking it. They aren't in the car. So, where is it? Where are they hiding? Her phone and bag are here. She hasn't packed her clothes. Did you look everywhere?"

More stomping thumped up the stairs, and the back door clicked as they searched outside. Minutes later, they reconvened empty-handed in the lounge.

"Burn it."

Addison's eyes widened. Modern fires could incinerate quickly, especially when gases were involved. She'd seen the effects on the news and, more recently, in her dreams. The conversation with Dr Collins had freshened the memories. The combustible gas, chlorine trifluoride, poisoned the atmosphere with toxins and irritants, exploded on contact with liquid, and spontaneously ignited most materials. Swiftly. Only unsafe structure walls remained of Mayor Naise's house.

Would that terror be coming for her? She peered into the chimney shaft, resolved to climb it, and hoped the dim LED light would shine on her way out. Only thick black stared back. Hands shaking, she reached up, feeling around the coarse bricks until she found a cold, metal rung. She pulled herself up, feet pressing against the sides of the compartment, almost soundless until her shoe knocked the back of the mirror as she lifted her feet. Wincing, she lowered the hatch door and pressed her weight to close it.

Seconds later, the click of the mirror sounded. Abrasive fingers rasped against cheap wood like fine sandpaper, checking every part. When those hands reached the top, Addison hooked her shoulder under a rung and pressed down with all her might. She felt a push beneath her feet, followed by a thump that vibrated up her legs and startled her. The access cover didn't even rattle.

"A few blankets. Must have been the pipes."

"Burn it," came the command again. "Watch out for her sneaking around the neighbours' houses."

Addison climbed as fast as the tight space allowed, catching and scuffing her knuckles on the jagged cement. She reached for the last rung and sniffed. Was that smoke? Surely not this soon. Fighting the paranoia, she looked up, relieved to be more than halfway. The shaft narrowed, dashing her hopes. Could she squeeze through? It was her only way out.

Palms flat to the sootless sides, she climbed until her feet ran out of rungs and her shoulders filled the thin channel. The rest would have to be arm work and

Addison didn't know if she had it in her. She inhaled a determined breath and craned her neck to look at the twinkling night framed in chimney brick only a body length away.

Inching herself up, she felt for toeholds and finger spaces, surprised to find fitting spots. She paused. Who built the cupboard and added bolts to the front door? Had she or could there be another version of her that needed an escape route? A skinnier Addison. If she'd worn more than a shirt, or been fatter around her hips and backside, she would bake inside the chimney like a potato.

Or smoked. It swirled around her feet, creeping up her torso with a sudden rush of heat, snatching what little oxygen remained in the poky space. A cough forced its way out as she clambered up, holding her breath until she reached the top. She bent over the chimney stack and sucked in fresh, smokeless air.

For a moment.

Thick smoke chased her out, hiding the stars. She fell onto the tiles, enveloped in a grey cloud. Flames licked the walls above the bedroom windows and tickled the wooden fascia. She thought quickly, before the fire engulfed her. If the other Addison had built an escape, she would have planned an exit.

She scrambled low, looking for anything she might have left, but found only moss in the gutters. Until it caught alight. The roof tiles above her bedroom fell in. Flames leapt. Smoke whirled into the sky. With no way down, she clung to the chimney stack, trapped. Wood crackled. Tongues of fire flickered on every side. Heat raged from a cage of flames. They seemed to taunt her. Soon they would close in.

Thwop-thwop-thwop.

Rhythmic rotor blades sliced through the roaring fire, whipping the thick smoke into a dance. A helicopter hovered with a deafening racket and vibrations deep enough to set her teeth on edge. A dark-haired stranger kneeling in the hatch threw down a rolled-up ladder.

"Hop on."

Something niggled inside her. The man looked familiar, but she couldn't place him. Had she met him? He reached out and grabbed the fifth rung, ready to pull, but a set of dog tags came loose and swung at his neck. He released the ladder, secured them under his shirt, and looked back down.

"Get on, then. Or do you want to die here?"

Do or don't, Addison grasped a rung and her feet lifted.

Eight

28th March 2023, 19:16

Laszlo didn't stay home. He fetched his car, gave notice on his lease, and booked into a Swindon hotel under a false ID, planting himself a half-hour drive from the address on the company business card. He didn't call the number. Instead, he spent two days researching the name and its connection to Anton Jarvis, Henry Coleman, and Robert Naise. Henry and Anton were pretty pally in the barn, and both knew Robert Naise well. Ross was another one of them.

The close foursome met at university, according to the official report. As their ages spanned over a decade, it seemed suspicious and prompted a closer look. Unofficially, they were part of an invite-only, lucrative and private club. And there, Laszlo reckoned, was where their friendship had begun. Today, although they lived in different areas of southern England (Anton and Robert in London, Henry in Surrey, and Ross in Gloucestershire), all were within an hour's drive of Henley-On-Thames, the home of their Head Lodge.

As Laszlo sat in the bar, in a gold velvet armchair, scrolling the M4 motorway on his phone, he pondered which town on the way to London would be his next home. Bristol and Reading were already second-hand places because he had lived there in the last decade. He might be obsessive about his rules, but they kept him free.

Until he met Ross and got the measure of him, he'd stay in Swindon, and at some stage, he would have to make the call. Tomorrow. Tonight, the curvy brunette behind the bar had looked his way several times and often came to the table to see if she could fetch him anything. This time, she brought a complimentary bowl of nuts and wafted a sweet perfume.

She rubbed her neck, looking nervous. Deep tawny eyes stared at his knees as she placed the bowl on the stumpy-legged wooden table. "You don't look like an olive kinda guy. So, I hope I picked right."

"What does an olive guy look like?"

"Not you," she replied, smiling with perfect teeth. She tucked her hair behind her ear, fingers lingering at her earlobe. "I would have grabbed pork scratchings, but this place is too upmarket for those."

Surprising himself, Laszlo flashed a toothy grin. "And you made do?"

"More made the best of what I had."

Touched, Laszlo laughed and rubbed his stubbly chin. She responded by touching her lips to hide her smile, a mimicry that, along with the rest of her body language, more than confirmed her attraction to him. Trained to notice, the stunning, late-twenties woman's subtleties had captured his attention. That didn't happen very often.

"What, isn't there a steak in the kitchen?" he asked, drawn into her gaze as she searched his face. The spark in her eyes penetrated his emotional barriers with too much ease. He knew better than to allow that.

She checked over her shoulder for customers waiting, but the few punters inside were chatting amongst themselves. She moved closer, biting her bottom lip. "I'll see what I can do. Meantime, top-up?"

"In a minute. Night off last night, was it? I didn't see you here."

"I only work the three nights my mum can babysit my daughter."

Kids? Why didn't the mere mention put him off? Smokers, skinny women and mothers were usually his top turn-offs. Because of that, he hadn't had a girlfriend for some time, and he wasn't one for casual sex. What was the point of dating, anyway? Women hated him spending four days away at least twice a month. Most wouldn't accept it was 'just work'.

She held out her hand. "Lorrie."

"Laszlo."

Her warm hand lingered as she laughed, and when his quizzical head cocked, she let go to fold her arms. "You'll think I'm strange but...Lorrie and Laszlo." She laughed again. "It sounds like a car window sticker."

The corner of his lip rose in a smile. Audacious. He liked that in a woman. Honest, too. She also carried a cushion around her hips, and no matter how hard he tried, he couldn't stop thinking about holding them. Unlike with Debbie, he felt comfortable about this encounter.

Lorrie blushed under his perlustrate stare gliding up her body to meet her face. While her sensational tawny eyes darted everywhere but on him, he pushed his empty glass across the polished table.

"I'll have another, and a bottle of your best Bordeaux, delivered to my room. Two glasses." When she bent to pick it up, Laszlo stroked her wrist. "With or without steak, why don't you stop by when you knock off?"

~

Laszlo scanned the messy hotel room. Lorrie had accepted his invitation and brought the wine herself. He would have been content with only sharing a Bordeaux in her company, but things sizzled from the moment she arrived. The sheets were loose, pillows abandoned, clutter on the surfaces now strewn across the floor, and his thrown-off clothes led a track from the door to the bed. Hers had been with them until the early hours of this morning.

It was why he didn't date mothers. They always needed to go.

He left a healthy tip for housekeeping and went down for breakfast, feeling ravenous. His main course last night, when steak didn't arrive, was the Bordeaux Lorrie brought. He selected a full continental, stuffing himself with more than he needed while her heart-shaped face lingered behind his eyes.

As he left the hotel, he checked his pocket for the business card and recapped the route in his mind. He avoided technology tracking his movements, especially while working. Sat Nav was a classic tool to pinpoint where someone had been. He preferred a real map. No one could hack that.

Twenty-five minutes later, he pulled into Palowa Enterprises and circled the car park for a space. He parked near steep steps with a slow-spinning cube at the top and tapped Ross's number into his phone. He waited, watching the pastel green logo go round and around.

"Hello?"

"Have you been told to expect my call?" Laszlo asked.

"Depends on who it is."

"Surrey."

"Then, yes."

"Good."

"When can you meet?"

Laszlo released his seatbelt. "Well, I'm currently in your car park wondering what floor you're on."

"Now?"

"Why not? Are you busy?"

"Uh. Not really."

"Then let's get this over with."

"Fourth floor. Do us a favour, though, Laszlo. Grab two coffees from reception. We'll need them."

Getting the coffees wasn't a long detour. The only other person in the queue was a short-haired thirty-something woman, and Laszlo didn't mind playing waiter for a large cappuccino. Caffeine might sway him to accept impossible theories about resurrecting Robert Naise. Curious to find out what a finance worker at Palowa would know about such things, he took the drinks and walked towards the stairs. The woman from the coffee shop entered the lift and raised inquisitive green eyes, lips parting as if she wanted to say hello. Instead, she smiled again. Laszlo nodded and pushed the door to the stairs, used to people of all ages giving him the eye—the superficial, skin-deep attention he had learnt to ignore. Even though he was forty-five, he looked over ten years younger.

On the fourth floor, hovering in the corridor, he met a bald man wearing glasses and a charcoal-grey suit.

"Laszlo?"

"For my sins."

"Ross. This way." He gestured to his left.

Ross's closed blinds rattled when he shut the door to a basic office. The desk, cupboard and three empty shelves, which might once have held folders, were obsolete now that everything was digital.

Ross pointed to a pastel-green chair on a matching carpet. "In getting this 'over with,' we'll skip the pleasantries. There's only one way to achieve what Anton wants, and not all of us like it."

Laszlo sat and rested his foot on his knee. Underneath his flinty expression, he smiled. "The resurrection might get messy."

"Resurrection?" Ross shook his head, the strip-light reflection moving on his shiny scalp. "Anton is impossible. I'll just get to the point. We haven't discovered time travel, per se. We've discovered…how can I describe it? It's like a wormhole between realities, time, and worlds. Convolve studied it for decades and learnt how to anchor and manipulate it. We've relived a minute or two many times. Nobody noticed."

"What's this *we* business? You work for Palowa, not Convolve."

Ross smiled. "The problem we have is the further back we want to go, the fewer turning points, or travel points, there are. You can't program it for this date at this time. It's more like selecting the best turning point for the task. Imagine a tunnel with many holes. If I wanted to repeat this conversation, I would have thousands of holes, or turning points, in which to return and redo it. If I want to go back a week, I might only find one hole in this particular reality. And that's only if we find it among the innumerable points we are still researching. The next one on from that could be anywhere. Or time. Two years, two hundred years, or not even this world. It's impossible to see all the possibilities. We're still cataloguing."

Laszlo's face was a mask. Having trained as a captain in the British Army, he'd faced a few surprises, but none as outlandish as this.

Placating Ross, he replied, "Okay. You said, 'we're still cataloguing'. Who are '*we*'?"

"The people behind the dream of peace and prosperity. Bigger instruments than Palowa and Convolve. The point I'm trying to make is, the latest we can go back is twenty-five years."

"Don't you mean earliest?"

"The closest turning point in time, before Robert's death, is twenty-five years ago."

"That's the late nineties."

"It is. We don't know how successful travelling will be. We've only ever turned minutes at a time."

"I might die? This exchange is looking less attractive by the second."

Ross poked his tongue into his fleshy cheek. "Not just you, Laszlo. You won't be alone. We all go. The entire world. We draw the wormhole towards Earth, anchored to where we need to go. Fast. You feel it just going back a minute. Years?" Ross huffed, almost disgusted. "I imagine that would hit your stomach like a tree trunk, leaving you with a hangover for a week."

"That, I can handle. Repeating the last twenty-five years, however, is disturbing. More than. It's downright—"

"It's April. Before your brother died. Would that persuade you?"

Laszlo's stomach turned. It was two months before. Izsak would still be in Oman, strengthening British relations, and due home in six weeks. Could having his brother back be a genuine possibility? His heart tugged at the thought as he sipped his cappuccino.

"There is another, more challenging factor that Anton refuses to consider. But because the reality has Robert in it, he is happy to proceed. The turning point is close to ours, but not the same. Some might detect the differences. So, we've created responses and instances to blame if it crops up in the new future."

"What do you mean 'the reality?' We're going back in time."

"We're going back to *a* time. Turning points aren't necessarily this reality or this world, as I have explained. The turning point we explored is exceptionally close and the only one suitable for Anton's purposes. In other times or closer realities, Robert doesn't become mayor. I mean, travelling to one of those is pointless."

Laszlo shook his head, laughing. "I can't believe I'm even entertaining this!" He went to stand.

"A mayor and an MP are linked to this. Do you think it's so ridiculous? Palowa acquired Convolve with the specific intention of focusing on this. I'm here to hide the money funding research on time travel, universes, and all forms of realities—virtual, time, extra-terrestrial, and spiritual.

"I can't show you until we go and can't prove it with footage. Each time we go back, the camera hasn't recorded what hasn't yet happened. Obviously."

Ross spent a moment on his computer, then turned the screen. A man in a lab coat typed at his station and two women in similar coats stood nearby. One held out a distinctive blue and white porcelain vase, waiting for the nod before letting it go. It hit the tiled floor with a dink and shattered. Pieces scattered, coming to rest under fridges and cupboards, abandoned to gather dust in dark corners.

"Oh, no." The woman put her hands over her mouth and laughed, then held onto the counter. The other woman did the same. Bracing themselves.

For what?

Mysteriously, the man continued to tap his keyboard.

They moved like a gentle ripple. Only for a second. To be certain, Laszlo watched it twice, but it wasn't the screen playing tricks or a faulty recording. Their bodies rippled. Then, abandoned vase pieces left their dark corners and returned home, but before their journey ended, the picture fuzzed and vanished.

"This clip should have disappeared, like the rest. But we've learned, irrespective of its mysteries and boundaries, that iron can protect things moving between turning points. We saved this small part up to the moment we entered."

Or they had tampered with the clip to convey the desired impression. But at Coleman's Farm, Jarvis had shown such confidence in a resurrection that Laszlo's doubt faltered.

"How do I know it's true?"

"The vase is right there." Ross pointed to an exquisite Delfia ginger jar displayed on the sideboard.

"I watched them break it. Smashed to bits, as you saw. I took it with me as a reminder. Awed. Anything is possible."

Laszlo inspected the expensive jar. Not a chip, crack in the painted blue pattern, or line in the glaze spoiled its beauty. All the pieces were intact and home again. That's if it was even the same one.

"So, we'll remember everything?"

"We will," Ross replied. "The world won't. They'll be twenty-five years getting a second chance at their past. Guaranteed to make the same mistakes. Humans always do. There'll be exceptions. Some staff remember when they shouldn't. They usually have excess iron in their blood. Also, the neurodivergent. They recognise differences, patterns, and vibes. We've a record on most of them, but some go undiagnosed. They don't know that they are."

Silence descended as Laszlo tried to persuade himself it was true. To even process *how* it could be true.

"Are you in?"

Nine

14th April 2023, somewhere around 22:00

The man on the helicopter continued to grumble, impatient despite Addison gripping the blasted rope ladder as he'd asked. Now she spun in the air like a charm dangling from a necklace, twisting one way and then the other. As the thunderous blades drowned out his shouts to climb, he tried to stabilise the ladder. Flames licked the bottoms of her shoes. Her grip on the rung tightened, and she felt the burn in her wrists and knuckles. She didn't dare look down, so she looked up, dumbfounded to be hanging from a helicopter with the wind whipping at her legs.

"You'll be skimming the treetops if you don't hurry."

On cue, her shoes brushed the willow tree as they soared over her neighbour's house. She lifted her feet, aware they were heading towards Horseshoe Lake, where the trees were taller.

Although the man's grin looked friendly, his familiarity nagged in her gut. She was sure she recognised his unshaven square jaw, black hair, and muscular frame. Even his long, black coat raised a flag. Doubting her judgement, she glanced back at the orange glow of her burning house. Curious neighbours had scattered across the cul-de-sac, glancing between the raging fire and Addison's dangling feet. The arsonists had vanished…

Were they in the helicopter now?

Her sweaty palms tingled at the thought of climbing. Instinct raked anxious fingers down her spine, confirmed when the 'friendly' man released a frustrated sigh.

"Addison! Will you climb already, so we can get going? They'll be firing on us next."

She breathed, allowing time for rational thought. Who were they, who was he, and how did he know her name? How did he know she'd be in danger?

Fear froze her, knees bent as if she sat in a chair, while the burning in her arms tugged at the muscles in her shoulders and lower back.

The rope jerked and rose, one rung at a time. Panicked, Addison looked up, unsure of the trouble she might face, then looked down as the woolly fringe of trees ended and the smooth bottle-green glass of the V-shaped lake began. It would be cold in April.

The ladder kept rising. Was he a saviour or would she be stepping into the lion's den? If he pulled her to safety, she'd be grateful. The idea of slacking her grip to climb daunted her—she was bound to slip. But if he was the arsonist, she'd be better off letting go and taking her chances.

Only, the higher the ladder went as they flew north-west, the greater the distance from the water of the cool, green lake.

"WAIT!"

The obstinate man didn't wait. He lifted another rung, this time with a frustrated grunt and a flash of ice in his blue eyes. As he prepared to pull again, the dog tags almost swung off his neck. He growled and snatched them one-handed, steadying himself as the helicopter slowed and descended because she still wasn't on board.

Addison didn't have a choice. He might be a saviour, but he could also be part of the group so keen to root her out. If they caught her, they'd kill her. She knew it.

The calm water soothed her fear. Without riptides and waves to combat, she could manage it better than some of her holiday swims, and she'd swum underwater with turtles in Cyprus once.

Up the ladder might be fatal, as might letting it go, but at least it was her decision.

Instinct sparked adrenaline and Addison knew what to do. She gave in to her struggling muscles and loosened her fingers.

"No!" His yell faded in the bitter wind rushing past her ears and flapping the fabric of her baggy shirt. The helicopter dived, shining a searchlight towards her like she was the star of the show until she hit the lake.

She took several deep breaths. The last one she held when her toes broke the still, icy water. She crossed her arms and bent her knees as she slipped under the surface, liquid clogging her ears and nostrils.

Shocked by the cold, her limbs sprang out, defying cramp and swimming up, desperate for warmth and another breath. Her ascent scattered carp, and slimy unknowns webbed through her fingers. She swam faster, panicked when the searchlight glinted as she emerged.

Who was this guy and what did he want?

She gasped for more air as terror clutched her lungs. Moonlit water slid down her cheeks while the deep bass of the whirring blades neared—the beam homing in on the ripples she'd caused.

Spotting the nearest bank, Addison dipped her head and swam beneath the surface towards the main road, occasionally popping up to breathe. The persistent helicopter still circled, following the grassy edge until almost overhead. Dry land was so close.

The pale wood of a fishing pier dazzled under the searchlight as it turned towards her. Irritated, she sighed and sank under the water again, tired of treading. Her jeans pulled on her hips. Every aching muscle tensed from the cold. She shivered, freezing now that she'd stopped swimming to wait. The bank was just metres away, unsafe, while her pursuers hovered nearby.

The thump of rotor blades drilled through the undulating water, close enough to catch the skid if she swam to the top. She stayed low, lungs screaming, eyes itching, and heart breaking for an end to this nightmare week. With another gasp, she surfaced, swimming towards the fishing pier surrounded by bushes and trees with spring growth. Aching fingers and grazed knuckles grabbed the wooden frame. The rounded stones set into the platform broke her fingernails as she clawed to get out. Using the last of her pitiful strength, she pulled herself up, wood digging into her ribs and shoes slipping in the mud.

As she stood dripping on the beige stones, weighed down by sodden clothes that clung to her like a wetsuit, the searchlight swung back to the bank. She sank into the trees separating the lake from the road. They were sparse, but the dense bushes should hide her. Twigs and branches cracked, and the swish of bracken and leaves betrayed her. Shivering, she curled at the base of a mature birch tree, ignoring the nettle stings and roaring rotor blades. The noise overstimulated her edgy nerves.

"There!" his gravelly voice called. "Over there. It's wet."

Her throat pricked, senses alert. The water near the fishing pier rippled with a fringe of frothy white. A man jumped in, adding a splash to the puddle she'd left on the stones.

Addison sprang up and ran west along the path, keeping the trees between her and the lake. Burning lungs wheezed, blaring their complaints, and her side stabbed with a sharp stitch. The only sounds she made were her squelching footsteps as she neared the backs of the houses to her estate.

The foliage thinned. From all sides, Addison risked being seen. On her right, blue lights flashed between the houses. A fire engine spewed water on her smoking home while her neighbours murmured in the street. On her left, a dubious stranger, predatorily trying to save her. Friend or foe? Because although it looked like he wanted to help, he hunted her as if she were prey.

Her squishy running steps followed the track until she came close to the commotion at her house. Watching her step, she slid down the bank into water that felt like icy fingers. It clutched her chest and stole her breath. She followed the bank toward the V-base where the foliage thickened, passing the hum of the electricity substation.

Beyond were open fields. Behind her, and across the main road, were residential streets—all visible to a searching helicopter.

Though they weren't looking in this direction.

She chose not to risk a flight across the field. Instead, she explored her surroundings. The bare lakeside trees wouldn't hide her, but the bushes over the metal railings might. The boundary fence curved at the top to stop people from getting in. But not out. She took a run and jump, hooked her arms over the top and clambered over, landing on her shoulder in sharp thistles, thorns and nettles. She dug into the twiggy shelter, fighting a sob while wooden fingers combed her head and the sound of rotors skirted above the trees. Perhaps hiding wasn't the best idea, but neither was running. They would spot her for sure.

The helicopter lingered over a separate, fenced-off triangle at the V's tip. She guessed this mini lake was where they reared the baby carp. As she stayed low, wet and bleeding, she prayed the stranger wouldn't need a closer look, but a fearful breath escaped when the ladder descended over the carp pond and the dark-haired man shot down it like an SAS hero.

Who the hell was this guy?

As he hung there with the nose of the helicopter like a searching sunbeam, Addison froze, face pressed into leaves and branches, hoping the muddy-green residue coating her would pass as adequate camouflage. The minutes felt like years. Hardly breathing, she rode the cramp in her calves, chin chattering with sobs. She stayed until long after the sound of the rotating blades faded. Then, numb and shivering, she ran along the border between the fields and Cotter's Farm, afraid to cut across to the patch of trees where Sting should be waiting at the Jockey.

Tail wagging, he bounded towards her before she reached them. The warmth of seeing him again thawed a small piece of her. Wet or not, Addison couldn't help herself. She crouched to hug him, relief flooding in her tears. He licked her hand and face, tolerant of her cuddle when he would usually try to escape. He didn't leave her side as she jogged to the Jockey and pulled the broken door shut.

~

It was late. Addison knew that much, but she couldn't tell how long she'd sucked the body heat from poor Sting. Hours. It must be two in the morning, at least. Her hair had dried in clumps on the stinking, mouldy beanbag, and Sting's fur helped dry her shirt a little. Damp jeans clung to her legs, though. She glanced at her black pumps by the door, noticing a muddy-green tinge. Thank goodness she didn't lose them in the fishing lake. She dreaded putting her ice-block feet back into the wet canvas, but she needed to leave. She had Sting to consider before she embarked on an hour's walk to see Marsha in Highworth.

Cold and sodden, she slipped them on and tied the laces, focused. Sting first. Only one other person besides Mason appeared to know her dog well, and that man had walked away from her last night.

She exhaled to calm her racing heart. The shop was just ten minutes away. Just ten minutes.

"Ready?"

Sting leapt up and wagged his tail by the door.

"Stay close and heel."

They ran left through the trees and over the fields to a quiet road leading onto the high street. Cautious eyes scanned ahead. She pulled back as a car slowed to turn the corner, red lights glowing as it accelerated away.

Addison neared the main road. Sticking to the florist's wall, she looked over at the dark shop and lightless windows above. She hoped Jon-Vinny-Jones lived in the flat like Arnold and his wife did in her memories.

Before she could change her mind, she dashed across the road, Sting in tow, and banged on the door, eager to get off the street and away from security cameras.

Eventually, she heard footsteps. A bolt and catch sounded, and the door squeaked open. Jon's sleepy eyes bulged when he saw her, dirty, damp, and shivering.

"Something is wrong. Please believe me."

Sting darted through his legs and up the thin-carpeted stairs. Addison was too tired to grab his collar, too feeble to command him back, and too weak to stop her lip from trembling and tears from streaking her grimy cheeks.

Despite Jon's reaction in Cotter's field yesterday, his presence felt strangely comfortable. He seemed to calm her anxiety. But fear had held the shock at bay and now she froze, staring at his face, unable to find any words.

Jon grabbed her shirt and pulled her inside, ushering her up the creaky stairs and into the small kitchen. He fetched a thick, warm-looking robe, and flung it onto the table while she stared at the black floor tiles, dazed.

"I'll put the kettle on and set the washing machine. Both with my back to you. You undress and stick that on."

Respectful, Jon kept to his word, but Addison didn't even hear him. The image of the stranger on the helicopter rolled through her mind.

Where have I seen him before? Does he know me, like Jon, another person I've forgotten? Have I really seen him? Was it post-Tuesday, before this fearsome nightmare began and I was me, or after, when I appear to have stepped into shoes that belong to me, but pinch because they don't quite fit?

The stranger's face flashed into her mind again. Instead of the fiery backdrop of an inferno or a night sky, she saw the chrome picture frames and cream walls of the coffee shop inside Palowa reception. Another Vinny Jones-come-Vin Diesel character was unusual in a small town. She'd thought it at the time—as well as finding his tanned skin, black hair, and sensational blue eyes incredibly sexy. If the memory was true, the irony was hilarious. She'd ridden the lift with a girly smile, hoping she would see him again.

Did Palowa send him? Were they where it all began?

Suspecting Marsha might know, Addison's feet itched to move on to her intended next stop, but her muscles wouldn't work.

"Why did you come to me? Haven't you got friends?"

Jon's abrupt tone startled her into an awareness of her damp clothes and shoes. She noticed the robe on the table and a huge mug of steam-coiling hot chocolate by the kettle. The washing machine door was also wide open.

Her soft voice sounded distant. "I don't know anymore. And you're the only one living close enough to take him in."

"Who?"

With a lump in her throat, she pointed towards the lounge hoping to say Sting, but nothing came out. She froze, unprepared for the feelings leaving him invoked—

"Will you get out of those wet clothes? You'll make yourself sick. How long have you been in them?"

—just so she could figure out what the heck was happening and who had chased her.

"Addie?"

Sting's safety was paramount now. Then she'd find her answers.

Jon undid the buttons of her shirt, searching her eyes for signs of reproof. Detached and too dazed to react, she let him smooth it over her shoulders and down her arms, but couldn't hold his gaze when his fingers toyed with a stiff jeans button. Knuckles dug inside her waistband until it popped. Damp fabric curled as he pulled the zip, still staring at her face. She gaped at his taut throat, in shock from the evening's events and stunned by this intimacy. Why did she allow him? All thoughts of the men who had burnt down her house and hunted her frittered away.

Eyes up, Jon moved behind her and loosened her stained-brown bra. Delicate fingers brushed her arms, feeding the grubby straps over sweeping goosebumps. It fell to her feet as his hands tugged at the waistband of her jeans, pushing them down over freezing hips.

He draped soft, heavy fabric around her shoulders, and she noticed her jaw wobbling and tears falling.

"Put your arms in, Addie." He came round to face her, holding the front of the navy robe together in his fists. On autopilot, she slipped them in, yet couldn't catch her breath.

Jon knotted the rope, crouched, and lifted her foot. She leaned on his shoulder in reaction, gawping at his head as he removed her shoes and wet socks. He slid his hands inside the robe, tugged at the legs of her jeans, and pulled them over her pale feet. She didn't relax her grip on his warm shoulders, not even when his fingers touched her thighs and hooked into the sides of her knickers, thumbs pulling them down to her ankles to join the meagre pile. Unfamiliar tingles erupted in her stomach, confusing her further. Where did they spring from?

"Sit." Jon gathered her clothes and threw them into the machine. "Sit!" he repeated, lowering her into a chair. "I'll get you some socks."

Moments later, the boiler fired up, and her numb fingers warmed around a still-steaming mug of hot chocolate. She gulped it down, catching up with the present and processing how this relative stranger had been so considerate as he undressed her. It felt as if it had happened to someone else. Someone who'd wanted it. Those tingles she'd felt must belong to them as well.

Much of the drink was gone when Jon returned, holding a pair of tan thermal socks. He put them on her feet and sat in the chair opposite her.

"Finish that. I've run you a bath. Afterwards, you can tell me what's going on."

"I don't know what's going on!" she blurted, desperate to unburden herself. Perhaps it would make sense if she said it aloud, although she could hardly believe it. "At some point after ten o'clock, I escaped my burning house by dangling from a helicopter, jumped into the fishing lake and nearly froze, and got chased by a stranger. All because I woke up and things had changed!"

Perplexed, Jon raised an eyebrow, only for it to furrow as Addison told him about the thorough doctor's appointment and the raid on her home. Then she explained her research and the outlandish conclusions she'd made about time travel. The possibility was more attractive than admitting a health condition and finding out her brother had never existed.

Feeling a need to defend her position, she asked, "Do you have a printer and something to access the internet?"

Jon handed her his phone. "Bluetooth is on. It's connected to the printer."

As she accessed her Real and New list and printed it off, he went to fetch it.

"I'll look at this while you have a bath." Jon thumbed towards the hallway.

She paused. With her clothes in the machine, her trip to Highworth would have to wait, and a bath sounded inviting. She passed Sting on the way, fast asleep on Jon's grey sofa. Hopefully, the newly homeless golden hairs wouldn't be too difficult to vacuum.

~

After spending the time paranoid the men might find her soaking in the bath, a warmer Addison shuffled past the hot hallway radiator, wrapped in Jon's cosy gown and thermal socks. No one had followed her, and Jon hadn't called the police. For now, she was safe. Relaxed, she peered into the kitchen, searching for her clothes. The drying cycle was only halfway through. She turned to leave and spotted an empty plate on the floor with a water bowl beside it. Her heart warmed, despite her doubts. After all, she'd declined so many dates with him. But Sting was the quickest way to captivate her, and Jon seemed to always think about him. She switched off the light and moved to the lounge. The bottom of the door brushed the grey, long-pile carpet as she opened it.

Sprawled across the sofa, taking up most of the room, was Sting. Jon had squeezed on the end and slept with the dog's snoring head on his lap, his fingers still around his ear. For a moment, her heart stuttered, the sight like a picture perfect Christmas card, with three children under the tree waiting to be unwrapped. She yearned for a family of her own.

Beside her, a blanket lay on a half-open recliner. She climbed in with a sigh, wondering again why the other Addison had declined a date with him fifteen times and wishing she had her phone to look him up on social media. It usually served well if one wanted to learn a person's leanings. What did that Addison know about him?

Her eyes watered, desperate for sleep, while her heart mourned a brother she wasn't sure she'd ever had. She pined for her house and belongings—trinkets, photos, clothes, money, identity. Gone. How could she sleep? Besides, she knew she shouldn't. Once her clothes were dry, she'd need to leave if she wanted to be in Highworth before dawn. It was already three. The dryer still made a soothing hum.

Losing the fight to stay awake, she drifted off, to flames surrounding her and a rope ladder playfully dangling out of reach. As Addison jumped for it, it shied away. The man from the coffee shop chuckled, and in an evil childlike voice said, "Climb up, my pretty," while his dog tags swung in hypnotic sway.

She woke with a start after a few minutes. A pink tongue curled as Sting yawned and got up to stretch his legs, paws digging into the sofa cushions while he shook off his nap. He jumped down and dumped his head in her lap, nudging at her clenched fist for a stroke.

"Sorry." Jon sounded embarrassed. "I dozed off."

"I'm sorry we woke you. Twice."

"I have a delivery. I'd be getting up soon, anyway. Did you enjoy your bath? Can I get you anything?"

"Just my clothes." She stared at the carpet, feeling as uncomfortable as him. A faint recollection of his chocolate-vortex eyes studying her as his hands took off her damp shirt didn't help. Her heart raced as she shifted off the chair. "Thanks for seeing to that and letting me stay to collect myself. But I need to be somewhere before it gets light."

The machine beeped, and she moved into the kitchen, Sting at her heels and Jon at his. While she took out her warm clothes, Jon held up her shoes.

"These aren't dry yet."

"They'll do."

Addison placed a foot inside her knickers and looked up, her impolite expression asking him to leave. When he did, she dressed. Then she went looking for the shoes he had stolen. They were upside down on the lounge radiator.

Jon moved from the sofa to block them. "Don't leave. Go later when it's dark."

"It's dark now."

"Now. Not for long. Rest today. Wait until there's more time. What will you do when the sun comes up?"

Addison shrugged. "I'll know more by then, and perhaps I'll be able to answer your question."

"Where are you going so urgently that you can't take a dog with you?"

"I can't without a lead. I'm bound to be reported."

"Someone pragmatic like you can take care of that, right? Besides, I own a shop."

"Not all the way to Highworth," she answered over the top of him.

Jon's eyes widened. "That would take you an hour and a half."

"As do most dog walks."

"Wait until tonight, Addie, please. I'll drive you. What if the men you described are still looking for you? You should call the police."

"Right now, I can't even trust my employer. Nor should I trust you."

"Why? I'm the one helping you."

"So was he! And the too-keen man on the helicopter!"

Jon looked dubious.

"You don't believe me. Do you?" Addison swiped her shoes off the radiator.

"It's not that I don't. It's just, if it is what the doctor thinks, then are you in as much danger as you imagine? I saw the lights flashing over your street while you were in the bath. Fire, police, ambulance, or all three? I don't know. I only have you and strange stories." His fingers rubbed his brow as he paused for breath. "I want to believe you."

"But?"

He shrugged. "I don't know what to make of it."

Addison huffed, half-understanding him, and her eyes rested on his selection of films. A fantasy film jumped out that she hadn't seen in years and the sequel sat beside it, still wrapped in cellophane. She pulled it out, laughing.

"How long will it take you to watch this?" she asked, her smile and voice trailing.

"It only came out last year."

The cover shot pictured other characters to the ones she remembered. Almost as if it was a new film. She could swear she'd watched a sequel where the original actor played Alan Parrish. He and his estranged wife, Sarah, rescued their children from a magic board game. The poisonous pink flower had nearly devoured his daughter, and the bulbous helmet guy in a beige uniform was always on their tail. She recalled a wistful

Alan playing with his only toy, a metal soldier he'd left in his shelter when he escaped the first time. She even recalled his joyful expression to find it again, and seeing it fall as he relived his time there.

Another film wasn't as she remembered it.

"Is this the third movie?"

Jon shook his head. "Not that I know of," he replied, then looked it up on his phone. "No mention of another one."

Mouth trembling, Addison breathed, unable to prevent the wash of paranoia. Had someone tampered with her memories? Did she uncover a secret at work? Had they injected her with something to cover it up? Now, they were looking to finish the job.

"If I don't find out what is happening to me, I think I might go mad."

"And I think resting and untangling your shock is where you should start. Eat, sleep, and stop thinking. Wait. There'll be gossip in the shop. Someone might come in showing your photo. At least hold on until we…you… know something."

He selected a live local news app on the TV, but only found a mention of a devastating fire at an empty residential property. The police were trying to notify the owner.

A mini screen in the corner exalted Robert Naise for cutting the ribbon to a new school as if he'd paid for or built it himself. He'd only signed off on public funding, likely with a healthy backhander.

"They aren't still going on about him, are they? He's dead. Move on!"

Jon shook his head, ashamed of almost laughing. "No, he isn't. This is yesterday morning."

What. The. Heck. Is. Happening?

She tried to swallow, throat dry, and head thudding with the perfect assassination description she'd given Dr

Collins. She grabbed a pen and added Robert Naise to her printed list, along with the sequel, Jumanji 2.0. "Do you know what chlorine trifluoride is?"

"A toothpaste ingredient?"

"Pfft. You wouldn't want to brush your teeth with it." After she explained the gas and its behaviour, Jon agreed. "I didn't know it existed until last month. A skilled team used it to commit arson. The media were so shocked, they detailed it. You know what they're like. It killed Naise and his wife while they slept at home."

"I need a coffee. Actually, more than that, but extra-strong coffee will have to do."

When he didn't return, she went looking for him. The water for the coffee had boiled and Jon was at the kitchen table, writing a notice:

CLOSING TODAY
10:30-11:30
14:00-16:30

"You don't need to do that."

"I do. Zoe's off. Plus, I've already decided. We're going to work this out."

Ten

2nd April 1998, 07:06 – The New

Laszlo startled awake at his Hungarian mother's house. He didn't feel as if he'd turned into a new reality, twenty-five years behind the one he'd left. The ride was electrifying, and bright. It permeated every cell in his body with vibrating light and held them together as he travelled through the turning point. Now, back in his younger body, he felt invigorated. The fit muscles under his tanned skin didn't ache when he stretched.

The old bed frame creaked, making him wince. He'd forgotten the noise it made and decided he should move out faster than the first time. Telling his mother would be easier at forty-five. In Past One, he'd eventually grown a pair. When he eliminated Izsak's killer, Laszlo realised he excelled at executing the law and purging the evidence to avoid prison. Now, he didn't want her to notice his movements and find out her officer-class son murdered people for a living.

I shouldn't remember all this at twenty.

Nor should he remember the torture of wishing Izsak would call him Lassie one last time. Not when he'd hated it so much. Now Izsak could tease him all he liked and, this time, Laszlo wouldn't scowl. The desire to see his brother again had persuaded him to turn and resurrect Mayor Naise, but since then, ensuring the past couldn't repeat itself had cemented. He would save his brother, and unlike in Past One, he wouldn't need the extra Sandhurst training to harness the skills he already possessed.

Besides, government officials, global food suppliers and dodgy accountants, who were yet to reach their corrupt potential, employed him now.

Blinking sleep from his eyes, he looked around his old bedroom, spying the tatty posters of classic cars, and his idol, James Bond, stuck to the wall. In his unmanageable grief, he had torn them down after Izsak died. Fuelled by revenge, he used the baseball bat in the wardrobe to smash the rest of the contents, but it never dampened the rage he'd harboured. Only burying the culprit Duncan Frost had eased his torment. But then the voices started.

Laszlo climbed out of bed, reviewing the surveillance conclusions of his first cleaning job to drown out the memories. The dusty mental files were hard to find. He remembered leaving the crime scene so immaculate that forensics couldn't establish if a murder had taken place there. Assuming the accused had fled, the case stalled.

Would the same surveillance produce the same results? Because on Mondays, Frost had dinner with his mother. Laszlo would check that first. This was, after all, only a reality *'exceptionally close'* to the one he knew. He also intended to secure the same divorcee's cellar to bury Frost like before, and this time, perform the deed there rather than move the body from Frost's affluent home.

The accusing voices lingered. *"The brother killer hasn't committed the crime yet. Justice will be unearned."* But Laszlo didn't intend to risk his brother's name even reaching Frost's ears. Not this time.

At the kitchen table, his mother, Maria, ate breakfast and read the free local newspaper. She held out the community pages, pointing at an advert before he had time to pour himself a coffee. "Look at this. Poor woman. I doubt a builder will fill a hole for free."

Laszlo feigned confusion and hid his glee as he read the odd request.

> *Wanted! Due to a crime.*
> *Fill and smooth crevasse in cellar floor.*
> *Budget only covers materials.*

The divorcee's need had presented itself just as it had before.

~

Planning two jobs simultaneously was a first for Laszlo, but not beyond his remit. Frost would be easy now that he had re-familiarised himself with Frost's schedule and recalled his vicious fighting skills. The vengeful plot clicked into place within days, with no vital changes.

Abducting three-month-old babies, however, would be tricky. Practically and emotionally. The devoted and besotted mid-twenties mother tenderly fussed over him, as she had every time he watched them. How did a child with such a loving mother grow up to be a heinous weapons dealer running a sleazy nightclub?

Laszlo hardened his feelings. What did some stranger matter to him? If she only knew the things her son would do, she might agree to Laszlo taking him. Even taking him out if she should discover how many other sons and daughters it would save. Still, although Laszlo labelled himself as a despicable man, he didn't murder children.

He was proficient though, and he would stop Mario Spinzer from ever demanding Naise's assassination by preventing him from walking the same path. First, he would contact the divorcee in the advert and accept her request, then agree on a date to carry out the work.

~

After Duncan Frost ate his last meal and drove home from his mother's house, Laszlo lifted the elastic hood of his protective overalls, crept into the en-suite, and waited for him to stroll in. Blood cleaned up easier from bathroom floor tiles, and if Laszlo broke the man's skin again, he did not need it spattering the carpet.

A muffled cough in the bedroom alerted him to Frost's proximity. He lifted his baseball bat, undented since it hadn't yet smashed up a bedside table, but it swung as fast when Frost stepped inside the bathroom. The crack across his head sounded nowhere near as hard and satisfying as before, but then Laszlo had had twenty-five years to calm down. Last time, Frost had taken so long to come round that Laszlo thought he'd killed him, leaving Frost unable to endure the suffering he'd prepared.

He stared at the heap on the tiles, deciding on a different approach to getting Frost out of the house. Tossing him over the balcony when he wasn't dead was a no-go, so he pulled him onto his shoulder with a determined growl, ignoring his old drill sergeant's taunts as he huffed down the stairs to the car hidden at the side of the house.

"What's the matter, Sándor? Cotton wool for legs?"

If only Frost knew the labour that had challenged him this morning, and what still lay ahead. Laszlo didn't need to add more weightlifting.

After going through the cleaning process as impeccably as before, he drove to the divorcee's house with the cellar key already in his pocket. He switched off the headlights as he turned onto the side road at the back of her house and parked outside her gate. As expected, the neighbourhood was silent this early in the morning.

The gate bolt clunked as it opened, the latch tinkering, and stones crunched underfoot as he prepared the way, checking for threats all the while. He returned for Frost, pulled him onto his shoulder, and ran across her long garden to the steep steps leading to the cellar. It was empty except for a large concertina screen cordoning off the far end, the stairs to the house on the right, and two wooden slat-back chairs.

Duncan Frost now sat in one, with his hands secured to the slats, dribbling from his not-so raucous mouth. The tidy bump at his blond hairline would bruise—if it got the chance.

Laszlo opened a cellophane packet he'd left behind this afternoon, along with the rest of the equipment needed to prepare and finish the job—like the plastic sheeting he now stood on while pulling a crinkly fabric over his overalls and tugging on fresh latex gloves. He was shaking out the white apron when Frost stirred.

As he tied the rustling straps, he said, "On June 12th, 1998, you murdered my brother."

Frost's grey eyes squinted. Laszlo imagined the man's confused thoughts centred on the current month, and deciphering to which stereotypical box of lunacy his kidnapper belonged. Laszlo enjoyed the ambiguity.

"What?" Frost whispered. "You say that like I've already done it. That's messed up. It's only May 4th." His eyes darted around the cellar, checking for exits.

Laszlo clenched his fists and inhaled, long and drawn-out. "You stabbed him nine times because he intervened when you were beating up your girlfriend."

"I haven't touched her!" Frost tugged on the cable ties securing him to the chair.

"Yet."

Frost shook his head with a baffled smile—doubtless wondering how to explain something he hadn't done. "Seriously, mate. You've lost it."

"And you are making this so easy for me."

Sweat coated Frost's forehead as he pulled on his ties again. Laszlo circled him while his conscience scolded him over punishing a man for a crime he hadn't yet committed. He ignored it.

"You know how animals are killed, right? Hung upside down with blood draining from their throats. It's how I killed you last time. Over your bath. But, in fairness, I was angry then. Bloodthirsty. Today, it's a preventative measure. So, I will make it quick."

Frost's lungs swelled as Laszlo unsheathed his knife and studied it with pursed lips. "Nah." He placed it on the empty chair and unclipped his Glock with the same mock attention, deliberately drawing out his decision-making process before setting it beside the knife.

Frost cringed, likely unsure of how serious Laszlo was as he rounded the back of the chair and made his intentions known. He looped his arm around Frost's neck and tightened, pulling and stretching his torso. With his other gloved hand, he gripped Frost's raised chin.

"Ready?"

Socked feet slipped on plastic as Frost scrabbled for leverage on the concrete floor. He squealed and panicked when he realised Laszlo's neck brace held him up. The twist-and-snap was over in seconds. The crack echoed for a second more, followed by a snapping cable tie and Frost's surprised face dropping with a thud.

Rhythmic sounds of folding plastic and tearing duct tape soothed Laszlo's agitated mind, and the whispers of accusation and fault clawing at his concentration faded. He didn't have time to pander to the terror of making a mistake, nor did he desire a conscience. He relied on his years of training. They made him invisible and undermined the past's forensic ability. Today's would be like hide-and-seek at a little girl's tea party.

With Frost's body wrapped up, Laszlo gripped his booted feet and dragged him to his resting place, plastic scraping on the concrete. They thumped as he dropped them to move the partition screen aside.

The gracious, divorced homeowner yoo-hooed from the stairs and the chinking of crockery followed. Laszlo moved the screen around Frost and smiled. Why was she up at five in the morning?

"You're an early starter. I like that in a young man."

"It's okay, isn't it? I said I might come to do the work early if I couldn't sleep."

"You did. It's fine. It's another key to gain access to the house."

"Did I wake you? I was just getting started. Had a good poke around in there. Didn't find anything to worry about."

"Sleep is rare for me these days, Mr Brand. I only heard the scraping and your mellow-toned humming because I was making tea. I guessed you were a coffee man, partial to a custard cream?"

"Thank you. I don't mind either, but coffee's good this morning, and I'm always up for a bickie."

He took the tray and balanced it on the chair before she saw his weapons, relieved when it didn't topple.

"I'll let you get on, then." She stopped halfway up the stairs. "I'm glad you left the screen across. I don't like looking at it."

Nor would Laszlo if a member of his family had planted grenades in their cellar. Her husband hoped to bring the house down with her still inside it. Lucky three of them were duds. The other two only made an inconvenient hole.

Not so inconvenient for Laszlo. Keeping the area cordoned off, he ducked behind the screen. A bulbous yellow mixer beside piles of cement bags rested on the same cloudy plastic sheeting, standing ready. Bringing them down this morning had almost finished him, but he dreaded the next part of the job most. Filling it. Again. The task had been laborious the first time. He'd shifted most of the rubble yesterday, and once Frost was inside, he would refill, cement, and level it. For free, because the lady's advert said she could only afford the materials. Laszlo didn't mind. His labour charge would be Duncan Frost's eternal rent.

~

At 5 o'clock on Wednesday evening, Laszlo watched the Spinzer's dreary block of flats in Bristol. Mrs Spinzer worked late on Wednesdays, and her husband always drank while he babysat their son. Ignored him, more like.

People went about their business without noticing Laszlo in his black Renault. Would anyone spot him walking out with someone else's child in broad daylight? He would prefer the snatch to be later when folk were indoors and not bringing shopping home from work, but this job had a deadline, and he couldn't be late. The new parents were flying home from Portugal with an 'adopted' baby boy cover story, and it was imperative that Mario's arrival coincided with theirs. The urgency pushed him from the car and into the block of flats.

At twenty, Laszlo wouldn't have known how to pick a lock, but with his future-self topping up his talents, he accessed their flat in under five seconds. He pulled the chain across in case the father did a runner, but he needn't have worried. Deep snores came from the lounge. The man had passed out in his chair surrounded by empty cider bottles, his greasy black hair hanging towards his lap. Laszlo closed the lounge door and moved along the hallway, checking the rooms.

Baby Spinzer's room was at the end. Laszlo opened the door and gagged at the nauseating smell before he noticed Mario kicking his leg in a rickety old cot.

He considered sticking him in the car with the windows down and driving flat out. Instead, he looked around for supplies, accepting he'd need to clean the child before they left. He chuckled. Cleaning him this way wasn't quite what he expected the last time they met, and he was glad to be wearing his leather gloves as he wiped the remnants from Spinzer's arse cheeks. The moment put shooting the man in the heart into perspective.

Hello, future murder victim. Sorry about this. Just trying to avoid you making the same mistake.

Laszlo sighed, grateful it wasn't green like the first nappy he changed years ago, helping someone with a newborn. Though in today's reality, he hadn't met them yet.

Once he dressed Mario and swung the bag of baby supplies over his shoulder, Laszlo searched the kitchen. He dropped a bottle of refrigerated milk into his pocket, wrapped Spinzer in a blanket, and left.

In broad daylight.

Laszlo could hardly believe he was doing it, but he didn't look back. Neighbouring twitchy-curtain eyes would only see the rear of his head if he kept walking. The demons inside him yelled at once, both the nasty and the guiding ones. Adrenaline flowing, he reached the car, carefully dumped his armful on the passenger seat, and drove off, speechless at how he had got away with it. Now, he needed to avoid prison.

With his eyes fixed on the windscreen, Laszlo gripped the steering wheel, pretending there wasn't a baby beside him and this was just an ordinary day. Easy enough, once the hum of the engine sent Mario to sleep. The journey was straightforward, until, on the

A361 heading to Gloucestershire, Mario stirred. Laszlo didn't have time to pull over. Instead, he watched the road while searching around the seat, his fingers brushing over what some parents might call their favourite plastic item in the world. He shoved the dummy into the baby's mouth. Fierce suck noises responded. Then Mario spat it out and screamed again.

This happened four more times before Laszlo remembered the milk in his pocket. He loosened the seat belt and tugged the bottle out as he drove over an arched bridge into a small town, all the time shushing Mario's high-pitched screaming and navigating a sudden right turn at a set of pale-green traffic lights. Annoyed, he sped onto the high street, not expecting another sharp bend. He took it, frustrated, fiddling with the gears rather than popping off the bottle lid to shut Mario up and avoid having to stop. The sooner he got rid, the safer he'd feel.

He flicked the lid off one-handed and glanced down to find the baby's lips with the teat.

THUMP

A large woman in a beige coat careered over the bonnet and hit the tarmac rolling. Laszlo touched the brakes, watching her in the rear-view mirror, lying completely still. Then he tapped the accelerator and drove on, mouth dry, face pale, blanking the young girl at the side of the road with the terrified expression. He should have stopped. Instead, he listened to Mario's frustrated screams, and then his hungry suck noises, trying to ignore the taunting demons in his head.

Neither stopped until he arrived in Burford.

Eleven

15th April 2023, Saturday, 14:10 – The New

Sleep didn't come for Addison. Jon stopped by midmorning and forced her to eat a piece of toast, and returned later with a pasta ready-meal and a bulging black bin bag.

"This is only the first one. There's ten more. You're a popular gal."

Addison sucked in a breath. "What do you mean? Who else knows I'm here?"

"Only me. It's all right. I'm the drop-off point for people who want to help you get the house back together. These are clothes. Downstairs, we have kitchenware, bedding, toiletries, and a stack of food vouchers, courtesy of my shop. Then you can stock your fridge…when you get one. Someone even left you a TV. I had too many customers in to see who, sorry."

Addison smiled. "That's kind of people. Thanks. And thank them, too, would you? Did any strangers come looking?"

"I thought you'd ask, so I copied this from the security footage. Do they look familiar?"

She focused on the grainy image of two men, recognising the square jaw and dark hair of one of them.

"This looks like the guy from the helicopter. I think I saw him at Palowa. It's where I work."

"I know that."

"Sorry. It's weird because I haven't told you yet. Me. This Addison."

Jon squirmed, rubbing his hands together and avoiding her eyes. The fact Addison had only just met him was obviously an uncomfortable reminder. "I'd best see to dinner."

The door closed, leaving the topic to fester. Addison's heart sank. The emotional strength she'd struggled so hard to repossess wilted, and the confidence in her sanity drained away. Once again, fear and confusion ruled. Jon's dismissive reaction and the blunt reminder of her vulnerability (physical or mental) made her cheeks burn.

She paced back and forth, thinking of all the pointless preparation she had made not to fall apart, or let herself believe she had already fallen apart. Any courage she'd regained to leave and question Marsha melted away, along with her self-confidence and everything she planned to say. She stared at the door, flexing her fists while rage grew and urged her on to the kitchen.

Jon looked up from folding the charity clothes, and her anger simmered, though the adrenaline still trembled through her flesh.

"Say what's on your mind, Addie. Don't be shy."

"I am trying, really, really hard, to keep it together. I'm trying to convince myself that I'm not sick, not wrong, and there is something else going on here. And you…you just crashed me. In a second! I need somebody on my side who believes me and believes in me. I don't think it's you."

Addison dropped her eyes, noticing a thick, black coat with a fluffy-trimmed hood hanging on the back of the dining chair and wishing she'd seen it before she was rude.

"I am trying *really, really* hard, to understand and support you, but my only rationale is the medical one, not this…this other thing. What you're insinuating isn't possible, Addie."

"Which is why, with respect, you are not the right person for this. My friend will be. May I take the coat?"

"It's your coat." He turned away, then spun around when he heard her putting it on. "Not now? At least eat first. I detest wasted food."

Mission-focused, she continued zipping up the coat, muttering to herself about there being more important things as she left the kitchen.

"Addison, it's too early," Jon shouted after her.

At the top of the stairs, he snatched the hood to stop her from leaving. She grabbed his arm, spinning on her heels with a defensive temper returning to her eyes. His rugged face glaring back sparked something, and her breath raced for a different reason.

It disrupted her focus. She felt...divided. Conflicting emotions see-sawed. She didn't know this man, and if she had felt something for him, then later forgot, why did she refuse so many dates?

Tension hung as his soft-chocolate eyes studied the prism of green, brown and specs of yellow in hers.

"It's too early," he repeated in a gentler voice. "They're still looking for you. And hear that? The early dinner is ready."

Addison held her grip, navigating these new but unwanted feelings and drowning in confusion while the oven beeped. He unhooked his arm from her fingers and walked into the kitchen, taking the mercurial presence with him.

There won't be another fifteen date requests coming, then?

What did it matter? She didn't know or care about him.

Assured that Jon would care for Sting, she turned towards the stairs.

"Don't you even think about going," he called from the kitchen.

Addison grimaced and muttered, "Bossy much?"

She glanced at the fading, dusky light through the front door. The guy from the helicopter would be looking for her and traffic already sounded busy in the high street. Although she planned to use Monk's Path to escape town, her present doorstep was the bustling main road.

Yielding, she unzipped her coat and returned to the kitchen. She sat at the table before a healthy portion of pasta, thanked him, and picked up a fork.

"I will drive you to Highworth and sit in a car park to wait for you. Okay?"

"You shouldn't get involved."

"I'm already involved."

"You're looking after my dog, that's all. Since he can't be shut in all day while I'm at work."

Another memory tumbled, as real as the pasta she chewed. Mason demanded joint custody while he battled puppy-Sting's fast-moving, face-licking tongue. They agreed that day. While Addison worked, he would be with Mason. She couldn't leave Sting shut in when he was so used to freedom.

"Are you listening?" Jon asked.

"Okay. You drive me."

She had no intention of keeping her word. Once it was safe, she would leave and keep Jon out of it. Securely out of reach where danger wouldn't find him.

The moment came at eight that night. She switched off the light and gingerly peeked through the curtains. The black sky glittered like skin peppered with pimples behind a crescent moon. The trees were still. No rain. No wind. And the traffic had calmed. The occasional drifter ambled. Maybe they were tourists.

She scrunched Sting's ears, then layered up with a jumper and coat. While she loosely laced the size-too-small trainers, she said, "I'm gonna be gone a while. But Jon will look after you. And once I sort this and fix up the house, we'll be together again." She dropped to her knees and threw her arms around him, whispering into his fur. "I promise."

Tightening the furry hood, Addison stole down the stairs. The irritating micro-fibres tickled her cheeks, but the fur helped to hide more of her face. Cringing at every creak and squeak of the treacherous stairs, she prayed no one would discover her as she slipped through the door and speed-walked towards the church. The prickle of danger on her neck reaffirmed her decision not to use Halfpenny Bridge over the River Thames.

She sank into the darkness, jogging through the church garden, along the lane, and onto Monk's Path, following the river towards Buscot. The Trout pub glowed with pale yellow light, and Addison stopped to check an empty road before turning onto a long, arched bridge.

Panting and scuffing shoes stilled her heart. She kept her head down, avoiding eye contact with someone wearing muddy wellingtons and, as tempting as it was, resisted the urge to stroke their gorgeous cocker spaniel when she came sniffing.

"Evening."

"Hey there," she replied in her best fake American accent and scurried away before the polite man could reply.

At the bottom of the bridge, she took the steps down to St John's locks and ran across the fields towards a caravan park, and onto the road she would follow for the next hour and a half.

She shoved her hands deep into her pockets and sighed.

~

Dipping into the trees to hide wasn't always possible, and sometimes Addison had to walk on the road. Her muscles ached from dangling on a rope ladder and swimming in freezing waters, making climbing over or through the field boundaries painful. After an hour, her thighs were in excruciating pain and tender blisters had formed on her heels.

She stuck to the road now through tightly wound paranoia. Every snapping twig or bird in flight was something or someone sinister. Or worse, the guy from the helicopter chasing her again. Then an engine approached, and she sank into the hedgerow, ducking down as it passed. With sounds magnified, she heard everything, but the next car caught her unawares. She didn't hear the silent electric engine until it turned the corner, and the main beam glared.

The driver slowed. Misty brake lights glowed, conjuring a red smoky haze against the tarmac as the car pulled in. Her throat tightened, but she stayed calm and kept walking, deciding it was suspicious to dart into the fields without reason. The charity trainers she wore were a godsend should she need to flee. Though they pinched, they suited the hike better than her own shoes and would be broken in by the time she reached Marsha's house.

A heavy-set man, similar to the second person in Jon's photo, got out of the car.

"Can I give you a ride somewhere?"

"No, thanks," she replied in the same fake American drawl she'd used on the dog walker. She hurried past, relief rushing through her when she heard the door close and the car pull away. The accent and coat hood must have hidden her well enough.

Taillights fading into the distance, she moved off the road. The hedgerow clawed at her coat as she forced herself through it to climb over the wooden fence into the fields. She quickened her step, the constant nag of danger sweeping her neck with a sense of being followed, but only darkness lay ahead. Lambs bleated from afar. T-wit-t-woos from a pair of barn owls floated. She kept moving, convinced she was overthinking it.

She climbed the gate onto a closed farm track adjoining the main Lechlade road. The glow of a farmhouse pinpointed her location as twenty or thirty minutes from her destination. Opposite the track was a disused lay-by, blocked off, and concealed behind dense trees and bushes. With light feet, she ran across the A-road, over the mound of dirt at the entrance, and followed the trees, gritting her teeth at her rubbing blisters and the squelching moss underfoot.

A vixen's screech startled her. She paused, clinging on to calm and centring herself amid the array of nocturnal sounds. The eerie wheezing of barn owl chicks didn't help.

Sooner than expected, she approached another manmade mound, where the track met a lane leading to the main road. She halted, impulse drawing her backwards where the trees could hide her. When she caught sight of the small, silent hatchback that had stopped, now parked on the grass at the junction, she sank to her knees. Inside, a pale light glinted A phone? It vanished as the car door opened and the heavy-set guy stepped out.

"Where are you, you slippery bitch?" he mused aloud while scanning the main road with a pair of binoculars.

Thermal, she assumed, since it was nighttime. The trees and hedges wouldn't hide her body heat when he glanced her way. Heart thumping, Addison backed down the lay-by to another field and slid into the flood trenches. Soggy mud soaked her trainers. Tears threatened her resolve, but something urged her onwards. Fear? She pulled her feet out with a moist clop, clenched her fists, and smiled. Fake it 'til you make it, they said. Well, she'd try.

While her feet enjoyed their facemask, she headed west until she found a way onto the lane. She raced across, hoping the man didn't look behind him. Her pounding heart would be the reddest of reds through his binoculars. Thank goodness he couldn't hear it like she could.

How had they found her? She didn't have her phone. Her pockets were empty. Unless she'd swallowed something without knowing, they couldn't trace her with technology. Maybe they were watching the road in case she passed, but why, unless they knew she was walking?

Had Jon betrayed her?

The accusation fizzled and her vision blurred as a searing pain slashed across her head, pulsing above her ears. Legs collapsing, she coiled to the undulating ground with a treacherous yelp, recognising the nausea from before.

Eyes fixed, Addison blinked and then drifted away.

~

Hard earth dug into her stomach and stems of mature grass pricked her hands as Addison woke, chin chattering. A breeze blew, tickling her nose with the fluffy hood trim. She smoothed it, aggravated with the sensation. It signalled a lacking tolerance.

She rose to her knees, afraid the moving ground would make her vomit, but it was solid, and she no longer felt sick. Other than sore muscles, throbbing blisters, and itchy scratch marks, she felt normal. How long had she been unconscious? She looked around for the man, guessing he hadn't heard her, or he would have found her. Wincing at the pain in her body, she set off, determined. Marsha must know something. When

Barnes asked her to arrange a medical appointment with Palowa's own specialist, she had done it. They trusted her. Addison trusted her.

Her throat tightened. The men had been hunting her since she met Dr Collins. If Marsha wasn't on her side, going to her house would be foolish.

Despite her fears, Addison wanted the truth too much. She quickened her step and kept walking until she reached Marsha's unlit house glowing in the moonlight. With a hesitant fist, she knocked on the front door. Then louder and harder until...

"Shut up! It's two in the morning!"

A light came on and Addison stopped knocking. *Did she say two?* The door opened, the chain stretching as sleepy dark eyes peered through the gap.

"I'm sorry to turn up like this."

"Oh, my...Addie!" Marsha unlatched the chain and circled over-zealous arms around her neck. "Why are you here so late?"

"I wasn't supposed to be. I didn't know the time, and I left at eight. Should've been here at ten, latest, but...um, I passed out for a while, I guess. I'm tired, Marsha."

"Ten? Do you mean...?" Marsha's eyes squinted. "You walked from Lechlade?"

Addison nodded and took off her trainers. "Do you have anything for blisters?"

"Addie. What is wrong with you? That's miles. Sit down. Let me get dressed and I'll sort something while I make us a drink."

"Marsha," Addison said, her firm tone unmistakable. "Don't tell anyone."

"Who would I tell at this time of night?" Her footsteps creaked up the stairs. She returned a few minutes later carrying a box of plasters, a bottle of wine and two posh glasses. "I don't know about you, but I could do with this instead of coffee. Up for it?"

Though Addison would prefer coffee, she accepted with a polite smile. Perhaps alcohol would straighten her thoughts more than caffeine.

"I'm glad you're not burnt, Addie. Where were you? The police want to talk to you. Barnes reckons you're crisp."

"The report said the house was empty. So, me staying away isn't a crime."

"Well, no. But under the circumstances, the authorities are concerned for your well-being."

"What, I'm deluded now?"

"No, of course not. More, vulnerable."

Addison moved from the chair to sit beside her on the sofa. "Marsha, please. It's me. I don't lie, and I was perfectly fine on Tuesday."

"*I* know you're not lying, but I'm not sure you realise what the truth is," she said with a kind smile.

"But what if the truth you believe is a lie? What then?"

Marsha sipped her wine and didn't reply.

"You said your son Mason is nine. In my memories, you have a daughter that age and a son two years younger. Letitia and Lester. You married their father but divorced while Lester was still a baby, and you've struggled to keep this house running on your own."

"That might have been true if we'd married, and I'd inherited his debt, but we didn't. I don't struggle with my bills, and I don't have a daughter."

Addison gulped her wine, seeking the courage to reveal what she knew. "The Letitia in what I call The Real has a mole on her stomach. Right near her sternum. You described it as like 'soiling your daughter's body for a bikini' because you'd always hated yours. You have one in the same place."

Mouth agape, Marsha recoiled. "How do you know that?"

"Do your sons have one?"

Marsha shook her head.

"Good, because you said the gene only ran through the women. How else would I know unless Letitia had existed?"

After a moment, the stunned Marsha lifted her low jaw and whispered, "I've never told you and few people have seen it. I always keep it covered."

"Thing is, you did tell me. You cried about it and blamed yourself." Addison snatched her hand. "Look at me. How else could I know?"

Marsha stood, smoothing her trousers. She seemed nervous. "I don't know, Addie. I don't know what to think. Barnes asked me to counsel you, to dig into where your head was at. Make sure you were fit for work and had forgotten this shifting nonsense."

"Barnes?"

Marsha nodded. "He didn't want your 'mental health issues' messing with the Convolve purchase."

"When did he ask?"

"Friday, when you came back to work."

"Before or after the doctor saw me?"

Marsha's eyebrows furrowed. "Before. Why?"

"Because I'm deemed a higher risk since my appointment. People came for me and burned down my house."

"The police say the fire was accidental."

"It doesn't matter what they say or what they think is wrong with me. I know I had a brother, and you know you've shared things with me."

Marsha collected the empty glasses. "Reckon I need that coffee."

Alone, Addison let her eyes wander, resting now on a fashion magazine under the coffee table. She vacantly flicked through the pages until Marsha returned.

Addison pointed to a movie advert. "Have you seen this yet?"

"No." Marsha frowned. "Have you?"

"With a name like The Visa Card?" Addison blurted and laughed. "It sounds rubbish. You know I hate romances. That could never change, no matter which version of me I am."

Marsha's eyes squinted. "But…" Hands shaking, she placed the cups on shiny black coasters, her eyes darting around the room. A click from the kitchen interrupted whatever ran through her mind.

Addison sprang from the sofa and made for the door, bumping into a brawny frame in a black coat with a long chain around his neck. The man with the square jaw made a grab for her, but Addison twisted away, unsure how she knew the right moves. Fluke.

Marsha had called him after promising she wouldn't. 'Who would I tell at this time of night?' she'd asked. Well, the coffee-shop-helicopter guy was a good place to start. Why would she do this? Weren't they supposed to be friends?

Betrayed, and with every pore oozing injustice, she caught Marsha's eye. "What did you do?"

Twelve

13th April 2023 – Three days before – The New

Night after night, for a quarter of a century, Laszlo struggled to sleep. A mixture of images haunted his dreams. Frost often rose from his cement grave and chased him. Sometimes he caught him. Laszlo would dream-wake to find himself cemented alive in Frost's place. Then, he would wake for real, covered in sweat and vividly reliving the horror of digging his nails through the plastic sheeting and scraping concrete. Another draining nightmare involved a beige coat flying over the bonnet of his car. While its wearer rolled, a terrified girl looked on, and Mario's adult face attached to a baby's body, grinned from the passenger seat.

Laszlo yawned and rubbed his face, shaking the chilling decades-long pictures from his mind as he sat staring at an overgrown lawn from his Swindon house conservatory. He'd paid the deposit with the money he'd earned dealing with baby Mario, so it never felt like home. Unlike the one in Bath last time, in Past One. Now, in Past Two, he lived in Wiltshire, as requested, under the thumbs of Naise, Jarvis, Coleman, and Barnes as if he were their personal call-girl.

They called. He went.

Irritated, Laszlo slurped his coffee, then spat the tepid liquid back into his cup with a grimace. He went to the kitchen and poured another while answering his buzzing phone.

"Laszlo, it's Ross Barnes."

"It's been a while," Laszlo growled, more at him calling than the fact that he hadn't.

"It has. I need your assistance."

"Coleman's boys can handle it."

"It's a sensitive matter that requires delicacy. I recall helping you when someone saw your car close to an unsolved mis-per report and linked it to a cold hit-and-run case."

"You did that to help you."

"Needs must when you know politicians."

"I didn't need it or ask you. You inserted yourselves."

"You abducted a child and mowed down a pedestrian in your getaway car!"

The reminder morphed into another unwanted, vivid replay. He spread his fingers on the kitchen table, trying to stay calm, and refused to back down. "There was no proof."

"And our friends ensured it by clearing your name and further chaining your allegiances."

"Used it as an excuse to chain me, you mean. The authorities had nothing. For either crime."

"Replacing the wanted number plates with the originals, popping out the dent in the bonnet and scrapping it, didn't get you off the hook. The police questioned you about three crimes!"

"They only knew I drove a similar car!"

Barnes sighed. "We've been through all this."

"Then, listen up," Laszlo snapped. "I managed to look after myself long before I met you. You didn't think I could clean up, but I made the engine unsalvageable and had the car towed and crushed. It was a cube by the end of the week."

"We know. Coleman still has it somewhere."

Laszlo squirmed. He didn't know that. Swallowing the unease, he faked a smile that Barnes couldn't see. "I'm not worried. It's clean. Mario was for Naise's benefit, anyway."

"And Frost, yours. They all linger."

"The cops couldn't connect me to Duncan Frost. There was no motive."

"They were suspicious enough to watch and keep questioning you. You forget. This blew up because he didn't attack and put his girlfriend in the hospital. Consequently, she was never grateful to be free of him when he went missing. Instead, the abandoned and worried, love-struck glamour girl just wouldn't let it go. Would she? She hounded the police for news, which kept all three cases lingering because your reg kept coming up."

Laszlo shook his head. Didn't the man know him at all? "They wouldn't have matched the number plates to me."

Certainly not in 1998.

"And the politicians made sure. Now, I need you to help me."

Laszlo's melodramatic sigh showed his impatience. "With what?"

"You do realise what day it is?"

"Thursday."

"It's the first day of the future, Laszlo. The day after we turned."

"So, what? The future is grim and painful in either reality."

"I'm sorry the relationship with Izsak is sour."

"Sour?" Incredulous, Laszlo shook his head. "Your meddling in my affairs interested my brother. Curiosity led him to make those on-the-quiet enquiries, and thanks to you, it made him remember my old, fake number plates. He hates me."

"Come here. Today. One of my employees has arrived as her old self and she only turned yesterday."

Laszlo clenched his fist and growled, "Don't be stupid. We all went back."

"She didn't. She, um, hitchhiked. So far, she's the only one."

"So far?"

"Come to Palowa. And leave now."

When the line went dead, Laszlo threw his phone down and returned to the conservatory to finish his coffee. He'd go when he was ready.

~

The frantic, unanswered phone calls started ten minutes ago. Laszlo had only just clicked his seatbelt and would be another twenty minutes, despite the arrival time Barnes assumed. He would let the 'Jarvis puppy-handler' sweat. He was nobody's bitch, regardless of how they had conned him into submission. It didn't matter what they expected or thought. Jumping to anyone's command wasn't his style.

Succumbing to leadership for the rare call-girl appointments had been hard. He only tolerated them because he saw them as assignments he couldn't decline. Targets like those who had uncovered the turning point and threatened his freedom. Most of them meant nothing to him. Dispensable. Though one had been burdensome to execute. A pretty woman similar to Mrs Spinzer. He didn't know her crime. He hadn't asked, but the heart attack he'd caused was instant and the woman didn't suffer.

Laszlo pulled into the Palowa car park and stopped near the main doors as he had in Past One. He remembered the pastel-green logo spinning outside the entrance. Now it was yellow. He rushed past it, took the stairs to the fourth floor without stopping for coffee, and burst into Barnes's office unannounced.

As he sat in the garish yellow seat, he said, "Think I prefer the green. Easier on the eye."

"Hello, Laszlo," said Barnes, almost snapping the headset he held.

"Hello, Ross." Laszlo rested his foot on his knee. "So, the sensitive matter requiring delicacy?"

"Is a tricky one that we didn't foresee. But then we'd only turned minutes at a time, and never to another reality. It would have been impossible to know. Yesterday an employee described exactly what in puncto reflexionis feels like."

"In punk, what?"

"In puncto reflexionis. Latin for turning point or, more precisely, at the point of reflection. Remember, I told you it might be like having a hangover for a week?"

"Yeah, but I just woke up feeling normal."

"Me too. She didn't. I'm guessing it's down to an excess of iron in her blood that she didn't ride the turn like we did. She came yesterday, at the correct present time. I mean, she couldn't stay in a reality that no longer exists. So, she's forced here to become the Addison from here, but remembers everything from before."

Laszlo tried to get his head around that. He envisaged Addison skating the outside of the turning point instead of inside like the rest. Medicine had saved his memories, but he'd still had to live half of his life again.

Barnes swivelled the computer screen. "This is the HR statement made by a colleague yesterday."

The report read more like an inquisition, and Marsha Law's hesitant responses about her co-worker's sick day the day before were emotive. She explained how 'Addie' claimed her reality differed from the one she'd known, and in what ways it had physically affected her. He scrolled up to view the employee details. Name: Addison Rae.

Rae.

The name drilled through his gut like a rigger.

"It needs someone of your...talent to deal with it. Quietly."

Collecting himself, Laszlo glanced at her pretty but skinny, oval face and short, dark hair, struck by her fascinating green eyes that were sad yet scary. He didn't want his talent to 'deal with her', and her appearance had nothing to do with it—he preferred long hair and curves.

There had to be another way.

He recalled the safeguards drawn up for these exact occasions. It had been some time since they needed them. "Let's try the dementia story first."

"She's a bit close to home, Laszlo."

"Lay some groundwork and get her doubting. Any doctors in your circle? Have her attend an appointment with one of them and make the disease plausible."

"We could try that first. Easier to just..." He drew his finger across his throat.

"Know her well, do you?"

"Yeah. A bit."

"Like her?"

"She's a reliable worker."

Laszlo laughed. "That wasn't what I asked."

"Yes. I like her. She's all right, I suppose."

"And yet, you know...easier to just bump her off. Did she turn down a date with you?" He laughed again. "Thought as much."

"We'll need to explore the medical route tomorrow. Addison isn't in. She looked rough yesterday, so it's not surprising she's off sick. There is a sound basis for a medical condition causing her memory shifts. The dementia ruse might work."

It must—Laszlo had already taken a child from its mother. Taking its sister, who happened to be standing at the side of the road at the time of the accident, wasn't happening. It didn't matter if she was thirty-three now. Laszlo didn't want to. Nor did he want to keep thinking about the Raes on the Lechlade road, but the beige coat flying over his bonnet stuck with him all the way back to Swindon. Along with flashes of a girl in a shop doorway and baby Mario's perfectly timed drop-off at the Butler's mansion on the outskirts of Burford. If not for Antal Kovác, his father's old Hungarian colleague who used to work for the embassy in London, grumbling about the injustice of the adoption system and giving Laszlo ideas, he wouldn't have found the childless and desperate Mr and Mrs Butler.

Recalling their delighted faces eased him now.

Thinking of Mario, renamed Michael Butler, reminded him of the birth mother, Magdalene Spinzer. Laszlo had ruined another mother's life that day. Once home, he opened a browser on his TV and searched her out, surprised to find Mario's father prominent in the results, sober and running a charity investigating missing children. An article quoted, 'Finding his empty cot sobered me up instantly'.

Laszlo drew on that comfort. In Past One, Mario's father had died and his mother worked two jobs, with Mario giving her nothing from his spoils. Tragedy in Past Two had improved their lives and also those sharing in, and benefitting from, the positive charity work.

How had things fared for the son likely seeping acid into someone else's life? He scrolled through Michael Butler's familiar social media profiles, avoiding the info sections. He already knew he'd attended Burford School and now traded the stock exchange for a living. Butler was rich, inviting to the ladies, and volatile to his co-workers. He was more dangerous today than he had ever been.

That evening, Laszlo drove back to Lechlade-On-Thames and sat in the car outside Addison's house. Her front room window glowed, curtains open, and he watched as she catalogued her ornaments and items in drawers. She studied everything. Some at length. Others a brief glance. Certain things she logged into her laptop, others she put back and moved on. Curiosity brewed. Why would she catalogue her possessions?

Addison neared the inside wall of her lounge, moving out of his eye-line. He fumbled for the door handle while holding an unpleasant garage takeaway coffee and his phone in one hand. The hot liquid spilt over his thighs and halted his 'relaxed' stroll to get a better view. Swearing, he glanced at her shadow through the window. She must still be indexing. He fixed the leaking coffee lid, wiped his phone, and speed-walked, peering discreetly over his shoulder to see her disappear from the room. Laszlo spun around and gawked into her lounge as he passed. The only thing he could see near that wall was a large, full-length antique mirror.

What had she been doing for so long? Not posing. Her shadow streak had shifted too constantly for that. Maybe she'd cleaned it or was getting ready to go out. But so late?

Afraid to be seen in case she did go out, he returned to the car and let his eyes rest on the mirror he imagined behind the wall. Then they trailed up, past a light switching on upstairs, and to the chimney stack directly above it. His lips pursed, cheeks lifting in a smile. Maybe she wasn't doing anything *in front* of the mirror, but rather behind it? If his hunch that it led to the chimney was correct, she was a clever woman.

The engine purred. Laszlo was eager to leave, curious to learn all he could about this woman and how easily he could sway her to believe the dementia theory. How different would online data about the Addison of Past Two be to the one who had recently arrived from Past One? Would he garner anything useful to deceive her if the inner Addisons weren't the same? Every psychological approach fulfilled a need. Matching that need with the perfect method would be imperative. What was hers?

After an hour at home sifting through the meagre details of Addison Past Two, Laszlo found government censuses, education and medical histories, and a clean police file. No social media profiles and limited email usage, and accessing her phone through Wi-Fi was like breaking into City Bank with a feather. He would need to get his hands on it.

His search deepened, eyebrow rising at a lack of recorded long-term relationships. According to the electoral roll, she had never shared her house or had a partner's name connected to hers. Had she been single for a decade? Was that intentional, or did she yearn for love? Did the Addison of Past One?

Next, he accessed her financial information and credit score, which was excellent apart from the lack of debt. The woman had a healthy bank balance and had bought her house outright, courtesy of a family inheritance. No loan, credit card, purchase finance, or mortgage, although she had a few monthly subscriptions going through her account. Interesting that one was to a gaming corporation. His hopes rose—it proved she had a life in the digital world somewhere, and the genre of game she played would allow him to know her better and choose the most effective psychological approach.

If she went to work tomorrow, he would slip inside her house and find out.

~

Laszlo sat in a Lechlade café across from the grocery shop on the corner, watching the traffic and eavesdropping on the local idle gossip. Nothing about

Addison, but some woman's husband might want to know she'd discovered his ongoing affair. The change of scenery didn't alter the waiting game. His knee bounced as it had at home, adrenaline powering every thought. Barnes hadn't responded to his calls. He'd better have fallen out of this reality, or Laszlo would be furious about being ignored. It was now mid-morning, and he was keen to search Addison's house.

'Ross. Let me make this clear. A simple yes or no will suffice. Has Addison gone to work??'

The twinge of impatience in his text conjured the desired effect. Barnes replied, 'Fuck sake, yes'.

After leaving a healthy tip, Laszlo drove to Addison's street and parked near the junction. He followed the road on foot, drinking in the handsome sandstone houses he'd been too hyped up to notice yesterday. He hadn't realised the length of the street, either.

Eventually, he approached Addison's grey front door, lock pick in hand. Seconds later, he entered. As he closed the door behind him, he heard a thump from upstairs. Had Barnes lied? Was she at home? The unmistakable sound of a dog's yawn answered his question.

Annoyed he'd missed the detail, he shut the lounge door on the dog's barking and drew the cream curtains, giving himself time to search the room before someone saw him or the dog attacked. He enjoyed the smell of fruits and tracked it to a scented candle on a shelf as he glanced around for the TV controls.

The games console loaded with a noisy fan. While he accessed the games menu, the annoying mutt growled and scratched at the door. If only he could mute it as easily as the TV. Most of her stored games were popular violent crime or war simulations. Her penchant for fighting aliens, zombies, criminals and corrupt government officials surprised him, as did her username Soothsayer Shikari.

What a curious choice. A person able to foretell the future paired with the Indian word for a big game hunter. So now she hunted psychics?

Bemused, he scrolled the control settings and discovered she'd last played on Saturday night, three nights before the turning point. It didn't necessarily mean anything. Maybe she only played at weekends, but confirming would require a search warrant for her account data. Perhaps Addison was too preoccupied with illness and memory troubles. Still, it didn't help him understand his mark. Addison of Past One might not play video games.

Smirking at the dog snorts coming from the hallway, he shut the console down and pulled out his ringing phone. Barnes. Finally.

"Sorry. My silence was unavoidable. I haven't been alone until now. Why do you want to know so badly?"

"Research purposes. I'm getting inside her head before I get under her skin."

Snarls came from beneath the lounge door.

"What are you up to?"

"Looking at a mirror," Laszlo admitted. "French renaissance, I think. Though, I'm no expert."

His fingers brushed the ornate, hand-painted bronze frame. Solid, heavy, and worth hundreds of pounds.

"There's not much to report." Barnes's tinny voice was all but drowned out by the dog's frantic barking. "We set the medical appointment for this afternoon. She appears to be working as normal. The only odd thing is she never mentioned the original Convolve purchase to me or Marsha. It's been decades for me, only two years for her. I'll call later when I know more."

Laszlo didn't answer. Shocked that his hunch had been correct, he stared at the mirror swinging away from the wall to reveal a cupboard holding two thick blankets. The wood looked new, and the screws were shiny. It seemed like a recent build, but considering the chimney was its outer frame, it had to be more than a cupboard. He climbed in and pushed on the roof. It opened into a dark shaft.

Who was Addison Rae to have this in her home? Curious to discover more about both women, he planted a listening device, put everything back in its place, and slipped through the patio door.

~

A garlic and fish aroma steamed from a pot of risotto. Laszlo's complaining stomach took priority over his pinging phone. He loaded his plate and sat on the sofa, eating a mouthful as he tuned in to the football and scrunched his nose at the competing clubs in the FA Cup semi-final.

After stuffing another helping of rice into his mouth, he grabbed his phone and opened the attachment Barnes sent titled *The Real and The New*. The catalogue was the list he'd watched Addison make last night. He scanned her noted differences. New bolts on the front door, the hideous spotted dress present in The Real but not in The New. The mirror. Mostly he picked up the mentions of her missing brother who, in The Real, was the instigator of many knick-knack purchases. He also helped to look after Sting, who Laszlo assumed to be the dog.

The list was extensive. It even included town drainage. He vaguely recalled the rectangular grates. Being reminded made him homesick. Though he more-or-less lived the same life, deep down, he knew it wasn't home.

The trill of his phone startled him and thoughts of Past One floated away like dandelion seeds in the breeze.

"The medical went well. But the doctor said Addison won't cleave to the dementia story. She's too convinced of a brother working nights at a car production plant and intelligent enough to understand and describe Robert's assassination in impeccable detail. I'll send the recording. Then you'll be up to speed. Meantime, I've dispatched the boys. They'll arrive at nine-thirty."

"Dispatched them for what?"

"What do you think?" Ross snorted.

"Is that really necessary? I've another idea in mind."

"I thought you were a reputable cleaner? Who is she to you? The decision came from on high. Higher than you. We're picking her up for disposal tonight."

"Ross, you know this woman."

"Not really. She only works for me. But she won't be my downfall. I can promise you that."

Appalled, he sat back, staring at a now disconnected phone. He couldn't warn Addison and keep it secret. They'd track any contact he made. Technology in Past Two was far superior to Past One. Nothing slipped past the government if they wanted to know, and Robert Naise and Anton Jarvis would want to know.

First, he listened to the medical appointment and analysed the softly spoken Addison of Past One who was here today. Then, Dr Collins' phone call.

"The woman is intelligent, Ross. She'll piece it together because her brother's existence depends on it. I can already verify meeting a different Addison Rae to the one described on record. That troubled woman lived a sad childhood and was unruly at school. The facts don't match up. My initial diagnosis is a genetic condition that stores iron. She's also on the autistic spectrum. So instead of entering the turning point and returning to her younger self, she arrived at our old current time, also remembering her current memories."

Laszlo sighed. After hearing the doctor's stark conclusion, he could understand the ruffled feathers. Keeping Ross at bay would be difficult.

He glanced over Addison's Real list again, angling for a way into her trust. Frantic, he shaped a plan to intervene in her plight—purely by coincidence, of course. He snatched his phone and searched for his old friend Snowy, an army pilot from Arizona. It had been a few months since they'd spoken, and a few years since the call-girl appointment that gave Laszlo his only friend. The whistleblower's information led to the assassination of a US General and the Romanian sex-traffic circuit couldn't continue to be hidden by military officials.

But that was another story. Now he had his own favour to ask and Snowy's southern drawl comforted him.

"Hey, buddy. How's it going?"

"Touch and go, mate, and the reason for my call. Are you still posted at Fairford?"

"Yeah. Five more months. Why?"

"I need your 'copter services tonight. Desperately important. Can you swing it?"

"I can log a skills flight. What time?"

"I'll be there before half-nine, but I'll be listening at first, so I don't know."

Laszlo was calling in favours and going beyond duty for a woman he didn't know or care about, but he wanted to make amends for his careless deed. It would start with this. Then he would manipulate her into trusting him by being supportive of her mental illness and undermining her Real list as smoothly as possible. Control the situation rather than put it out.

Easy. Right?

The Addison of Past Two, who built an escape route from her house, would spot the manipulation signs with ease, he imagined. But she of Past One might not. He'd noted how she trusted the doctor in her psych eval, keen for someone to believe and help her. Laszlo would be that someone. If he got the chance.

~

At 9.20 that night, Laszlo pulled into Fairford RAF base and met Snowy at the security gates. He oozed positivity and American charm. He wore a knitted hat over his blond hair, and his khaki camouflage gear bore his name, squadron, and rank. The patch with a row of four black squares made him a fourth-level Chief Warrant Officer. A helicopter pilot, technical expert, and an excellent friend to have by his side.

Laszlo scrunched his nose at the musty aroma as they boarded the helicopter and picked at the peeled leather seats.

"What we doing and where we going?" Snowy asked, pressing switches and lighting up a colourful control panel.

Laszlo spread a cheeky smile. "Is this thing even airworthy?"

"I might be a CW4, Laszlo, but I couldn't log a skills flight. This is the banger, and every so often she needs a ride." Snowy raised his eyebrows, side-eying him. "I'm taking one for the team, you know."

Laszlo laughed. "It won't be much of a ride. It's Horseshoe Lake in Lechlade. But I'm hoping it'll be a successful rescue mission. Someone is on the cusp of receiving an unfair punishment."

"Which you aim to thwart."

"I'm many things, but I am not dishonourable."

Murder wasn't the only way to make people comply. Though, in hindsight, if he'd done that with Anton

Jarvis instead of humouring him, he wouldn't be in this present mess. He preferred his brother dead and loving him than alive and cursing every breath he took.

"Comms up. Where you at?" came the voice on group chat.

Laszlo glanced at Snowy. "They're ready. Any chance of hearing them through the headphones?"

"Yeah, but y'all hear me."

"Better not speak then." He added the receiver in the helicopter to the app on his phone. "It'll connect when you confirm your end."

"My mic's on mute, and that's okay while the rotor's quiet, but you won't hear me when we're up there."

Laszlo put his finger to his lips as the crew's voices filtered into one of his ears. His personal comms were underneath the other earphone, listening to Addison mooching inside her house.

"I'm online," he said, hushing their banter. "Is Ross with us?"

"We're all here now." An agitated Ross was a bad sign. "Plan A: fetch and dispose of her at the crematorium. Plan B: trap her inside her house and burn it. The crazy bitch was nuts after all and set the place on fire. There isn't a plan C. She must not survive or escape. Understood? She must not."

He couldn't understand why they were so desperate to be rid of her when other methods were available. His curiosity made him squirm in the seat as the van pulled up outside her house and Coleman's crew got out.

"Light beyond the hall. The rest is dark."

"Is she in?"

"Only one way to find out."

Yes, she's in. Laszlo scrunched his hands into fists, hoping for the chance to intervene before they took her to the crematorium and killed her. If they didn't kill her on sight.

The heart-stopping "clears" followed. Laszlo exhaled, satisfied that a click he heard was her accessing the mirror. Ross growled, muttering about her having a heads-up while the crew discussed her phone messages. Laszlo didn't believe that. No one else had a reason to protect her. No one had told her. She was just proficient enough to hide in time. That she could outwit them amused him.

"Where's the dog…"

The crew-captain's questions drowned under Ross's orders. "Laszlo. Suck up to Marsha Law. I need to know I can trust her because if she's overheard something and passed it on, she'll be next on my list. Probe her about what she knows and leave your details for her to call if Addison gets in touch."

"…so, where is it? Where are they hiding? Her phone and bag are here. She hasn't packed her clothes. Did you look everywhere?"

"She's gone and I've an idea who warned her. Make it glow anyway."

"Burn it," the leader translated to his crew.

"No! There are easier ways." Laszlo's compassion for Addison's mother clutched his heart. He wouldn't be responsible for her losing another child.

Snowy powered up the banger and lifted off while stinky feet Trainer-Guy discovered the cupboard behind the mirror. Was she cowering inside, afraid of the consequences, or would she be fierce and come out fighting?

"A few blankets."

Laszlo breathed again, relieved that she had made it to the roof even if she faced as much danger up there. He muted his mic and shouted to Snowy over the noise.

"How long?"

"Few minutes."

"Burn it" echoed in his comms again.

"Beds and clothes are cooking."

"Sofas, too."

Laszlo sighed. "She might not have that long."

Minutes later, the house came into view, flames lapping up the walls and the roof ablaze. Thick black smoke poured into the sky, but the downdraft of rotor blades dispersed it as they neared. It also dampened the fire, revealing a curious Addison clinging to the chimney and coughing. Gutters melted and smoked. Aggressive flames darted through the roof, wrangling with the air pressure and threatening the banger's stability. Heat equivalent to a Middle Eastern summer's day hit Laszlo like a hot plate and obstructed their rescue manoeuvres. The helicopter juddered as Snowy steadied the joystick, circling to get closer. Laszlo ignored the vibrations soaking into his knees as he searched the cubby for rope.

"Uh, buddy. We need to abort. The banger ain't built for this."

Laszlo paused at the open hatch, a strapped rope ladder in his hands. "No," he retorted, yanking at the Velcro fastenings.

"She's already too hot. Laszlo!"

He pulled his mic closer to his lips. "Do you see her? Look at her! No!" He secured the ladder clips and threw it down, urging Snowy to go lower by another metre.

"You're going to get yourself killed!" cried the loud voices only he could hear. *"You, him, and her to add to your many victims."*

"Hop on," Laszlo yelled with an itchy throat and eyes burning from the smoke. And thanks to the voices, his eyes burned with the victims' dead faces, too.

He tuned out Snowy cussing at holding the banger steady and reached down the ladder as far as his arm would go, expecting Addison to be eager to grab it. So why the hell did the stupid woman stand there while her house cooked? He inched lower, forgetting he'd loosened his shirt buttons in the heat. His dog tags swung free.

He let go of the ladder. Nothing was more important than Izsak's tags. They meant as much to him as they did to his brother. Laszlo had almost lost one of them once. Never again.

He buttoned his shirt and glanced down, frustrated. What was her problem? Surely she didn't prefer to stay there?

"Get on, then. Or do you want to die here?"

Snowy whinged about the heat, louder and firmer than before, and started counting down from fifteen. With the helicopter hot, stressed and juddering, they both breathed in relief when Addison took the rung and they finally moved away.

~

Laszlo smacked the steering wheel, growling, as he drove along the A361 to Swindon. No amount of shouting vented his fury. He'd dropped and lost his catch. Simple. Even his internal demons were too quiet to hear over his self-criticism.

Heaters at full pelt, and a crinkly dustsheet protecting his fancy seat, he shifted, trying to unstick cold, damp fabric from his skin. He thumped the steering wheel again, reliving the top of her head dropping until it slipped under the water. Now, after a pointless two-hour search, it was too late to approach Marsha Law to conduct an appeal for Miss Rae's safety. It would be wiser to wait until morning.

He swallowed at the thought of her name. Getting under her skin to manipulate and control her thoughts would be unpalatable enough without visions of her mother rolling over his bonnet. That would instantly take the edge off his seduction technique. Ross would have his way and cremate her, and likely while she was still breathing.

At least she was pretty. Her oval face and cupid's bow were pleasant to look at, and if he must use the ploy of love to get her onside and protect her, even the last resort of using sex as a transaction, then he would. She wasn't Lorrie, by any stretch, but…

Lorrie.

A whirlwind week of the most spectacular sex he had ever had. Gone. The barmaid from the hotel in Past One had lingered in his mind all these years. In Past Two, she was happily married to her daughter's father and had two more kids. Laszlo had tried to talk to her in the travel agents where she worked, but she wasn't the same Lorrie and it sparked no attraction. He missed her.

Forlorn, he entered his house and slammed the door shut.

Thirteen

15th April 2023 – One day before – The New

There had been no sightings overnight or early morning, and even though the high street burst with Saturday shoppers, Coleman's spying crew were confident Addison wasn't among them. Laszlo sat in his car outside Marsha's house, hoping to see someone up and about, hoping Addison's face might pop up at the kitchen window. No such luck. Instead, he saw Marsha filling the kettle.

He left his coffee and rapped on the door.

"Ms Law? Sorry to trouble you. My name is Laszlo Sándor and I'm from the Vulnerable Victims Unit connected to the local police and health service. May I come in?"

Marsha opened the door wider, glancing at the fake ID he held. He hadn't needed to use it for years, but always kept it updated. She stepped back into the hallway.

"I'm making coffee."

"Please. That would be great."

"You're here about Addison."

"Has she been in touch?"

She shook her head. "We spoke after work yesterday about an appointment, but nothing since."

"Did she seem afraid in any way?"

"A little," she replied, distracted. She over-poured the milk without asking if he took it. "Dementia this young would frighten anyone."

"Then she does understand the initial diagnosis. It's a start. Would you say she appeared…suicidal?"

Marsha's head snapped up. "Suicidal?"

"Miss Rae accidentally burnt her house down last night."

Her face fell, and she groaned as she stirred the milky coffee. When she handed him the cup, it was barely hot.

"Don't worry, Ms Law. No one was inside." Laszlo noted how her jaw unclenched and her eyebrows lowered. He swigged his drink and tried not to grimace when he swallowed. "Ross Barnes said you probably knew her best."

"Not really. We weren't social. Her moods were erratic. Some days she'd be chatty. Other days it was all work, you know. But she didn't look well on Wednesday. I drove her home myself. It's the only time I've been to her house."

"Would you say she's a tough person to get to know?"

"Addison is sarcastic, feisty at times, and keeps to herself outside work. She's always professional and considerate. As my senior, she took being side-lined at work better than I expected."

When he asked her to expand, she explained the Convolve purchase account that should rightfully have been Addison's. "She reckoned, under the circumstances, Barnes made the right choice."

"Do you know where she might go or who she'd turn to?"

"No. Her mother lives in a care home near here. There's no other family. No boyfriend that I know of. In fact, she's not mentioned having one in the ten years I've known her."

His heart sank. There must be a reason Addison had been single for so long. Would she even be interested in him?

"Do you know why? Is she gay?"

"No, I don't think so. Not found the right guy, I guess. More trouble than they're worth, anyway."

Laszlo returned her smile and handed her a contact card. "If she gets in touch, please call me. Try to get her to meet you, preferably here. Meantime, I'll be in Lechlade but will drop by to watch the street now and then. If you see me loitering, you'll know why. Thanks for the drink."

He put his empty cup in the sink and returned to the car. It became his home for the rest of the day, back and forth between Marsha's and Addison's houses and the shops, watching for her or her mutt. The locals rallied with a charity drive, bringing an assortment of household and personal goods, but Addison still didn't show.

He handed Trainer-Guy two fifty-pound notes. "There's a shop down the road with a TV in the window. Buy it and meet me at my car." By the time he returned, cable dangling and the plug whacking his knees, Laszlo had prepared a tracker just in case. Wherever Addison went, the charity items would follow. And who didn't take a TV? He removed the casing and added it. "Let's show our concerned support."

The heaving store bellowed with crying kids, gossiping women, and customers trying to get served before the shop closed at half-past-two. Strange it should close so early. A red flag pinned it in Laszlo's mind while he squeezed through the aisles, holding the TV so tight to his chest that he struggled to breathe. At the vast collection pile, he added his donation and waited, praying he didn't catch the coughing manager's germs when he asked if Addison had been in.

"She hasn't today, no. But I hope she's all right. Plenty of people are rooting for her." His strange, lifeless smile pricked the back of Laszlo's neck.

Where the hell was she? Not with her neighbours, her mother, or at the shops, and she hadn't contacted Marsha Law. She'd gone somewhere, though. The wet fishing pier and lake bank told him so. Her body wasn't floating in the water, either.

"Why do you keep closing?" someone cried. "I'm missing knit and natter to come early and get me bits."

He craned his head to see an elderly woman with a half-full basket.

The manager coughed again. "I'm not feeling too great and don't have a choice. Zoe's on holiday. I gave plenty of notice, Mrs Tonks, and would happily have delivered it if you'd rung, as well you know."

Mrs Tonks winked. "What, and miss all the drama? Beats knit and natter this week, hands down."

"Maybe give you something to natter about next week, eh?"

"Let's hope it's good. I'm worried about her. She had a nosebleed Wednesday morning. Did you hear the dogs barking?"

"No, Ma'am. You asked me that."

"Taffy isn't right. Not since. And it ain't his leg bothering him. It's something else. Dogs sense things. If you hear from her, you'll let me know, won't you, Jon?"

"Of course. Addison will be fine. She's made of sturdy stuff."

"Normally. But she wasn't her usual brusque self when I saw her last."

Laszlo stepped into view. "And when was that, exactly?"

"Yesterday, as I tended to my roses. She came home from work and asked after Taffy's leg. He broke it Wednesday morning."

"Did she seem all right?"

"Distant, but at least physically there. Now it's like she's disappeared in a puff of smoke."

"Rhetorically speaking. The house was empty when it burnt."

"Then where's she gone? She has nowhere else. Even the people in the helicopter didn't see her, and one of them hung on a ladder. I'm telling you. She disappeared in a puff of smoke."

"More like a lake of water," the voices teased. *"She's still down there, ankle caught in fishing line, mesmeric eyes wide open and short hair rippling like a crown around her head."*

With a loud sigh, Laszlo shook the murky picture away and turned to Trainer-Guy. "Take over the A stretch. I need to go."

"Now?"

"Something I said?" trailed from Mrs Tonks as he left.

It didn't take long to reach Swindon, and expecting a speeding ticket was painless compared to the rest of his troubles. He entered his kitchen, tossing his car keys into the shadow of the copper pans above the centre island.

"Alena," he shouted while he washed his hands. "Play Vivaldi Four Seasons. Spring and Winter. Loudly. Speaker seven."

From the lounge, Alena's voice repeated the command, and seconds later, beautiful instruments filled the quiet kitchen. Light spilled as he opened the fridge. When stressed, Laszlo liked to cook, and today was a fine day to tenderise meat, gouge out apple cores, and smack the hell out of biscuits for a cheesecake base.

He let the notes soothe him. In between dance steps and sipping a Bordeaux from a crystal glass, he chopped salad, crushed biscuits, and seasoned a T-bone, deciding that having this cut, and not a sirloin, wasn't too disappointing. He couldn't batter a T-bone, but the wheat digestives were extra fine.

At the beginning of Winter, he relaxed his grip on the rolling pin as prickles rode along his neck, chasing the adrenaline across his shoulders. Lifted, he thumped the copper pans in rhythm with the crescendo ending and breathed, tears streaming, calmer.

He selected something less emotive while he ate, channelling the anxious tension between Addison Part One now creating ripples on Part Two streets, and her, or any of Coleman's crew, suspecting he had any conflict at all. The only compromise he could allow himself was to control and not kill her.

If he could find her.

An opportunity presented itself later that night when a frantic Trainer-Guy called.

"Reckon I saw her. Spoke to her!"

"Where?"

"On the road to Highworth."

"What car?"

"Walking."

"Why would she be walking?" Laszlo asked. "Where is she now?"

"I wasn't sure it was her at the time. I'm still not. She refused a lift using an American accent, and it was dark, so I didn't see her face. I drove off, but it's niggled me ever since. What's some random woman doing walking alone, miles from anywhere? It's got to be her."

"Where are you?" Laszlo pulled up the satellite image of the A361 on his TV.

"Parked at the old lay-by facing a gated farm track, seeing if she walks past. Though night vision ain't picking up a thermal."

Laszlo found the area. The track looped along the A-road outlining a woodland lay-by. Looking carefully, he discovered there wasn't another farm track opposite the other junction.

"Take the car to the other side of the lay-by and wait in the lane. Because she'll see you parked if she looks before she crosses the track. Which side of the road is she walking on?"

"The wrong one."

Laszlo grabbed his keys, tempted to leave, but held off. Driving there on a whim would look suspicious. Coleman's goon might have stinky feet, but he could handle Addison Rae alone. He waited twenty minutes for an update report before calling and chasing it.

Trainer-Guy sighed. "No one's passed. Foxes and badgers, but no women."

"How long has it been?"

"Long enough. She wasn't dawdling."

"Maybe it isn't her then."

"I'm gonna get out. I'll ring you back."

The line cut and a vein in his neck twitched. When this was over, he should teach the man some manners, and lessons in hygiene. He'd already mentioned that his feet didn't make for good smelling salts, yet he never took the hint. Bathwater would be a fantastic first lesson, but Laszlo didn't like drownings. It reminded him of a primary school classmate who died in the river Kennet.

Visions of an asphyxiated Addison scattered when his phone rang.

"She ain't on the road anymore. Must have turned off. A few cars have passed me. She could have gone with one of them. But like you say, probably not even her."

"Sit at Marsha Law's place for a while. If it is her and she's heading that way, then my guess is she's going there. Even walking, she'd arrive by eleven. Keep your eyes peeled and call me if she turns up. No need to disturb Ross if it's late. Do not try to grab her. She won't be going anywhere, and we need to be clever if we're to catch her."

Eleven came and went. As did sleep. Laszlo dozed, woke startled, and checked his phone for missed messages.

Disappointed to see none, he flopped back on the settee and closed his eyes.

~

The phone on the glass table buzzed louder than Laszlo's alarm clock and he yawned away deep sleep before answering it.

Marsha's frantic whispers stammered down the line. "She's here! Downstairs. Right now. She's here!!"

He shot up, snatching his keys off the table. "Ms Law, first off, stay calm. Does she look well?"

"Yes. She's fine."

"Are you?"

"Yes. Surprised is all."

"Lock the front door, take out the key, and keep her talking. I'll be there in thirty minutes."

He disconnected before Marsha could complain. Arguing would only cost him time. Trainer-Guy must have been right about the woman on the A road being Addison. She had turned up in Highworth. But it bemused him why she was so late. A convenient delay? Lucky, whatever the reason. If she had reached Marsha's house with the goon outside, she'd be in Henry Coleman's hands now, and his agenda differed from Laszlo's. Addison would be dead.

A frantic message pinged when he entered Marsha's street. She was crumbling, but after a rant, she said the back door was open. Careful not to make a sound, he unlatched the side gate, followed the path, and peeked through the kitchen window as Marsha carried cups into the front room.

Laszlo breathed and focused on the job, manifesting the persona of a Vulnerable Victims Unit support worker and perfecting his compassionate smile. He crept in the back door, cringed at the unavoidable click of locking it, and moved towards the lounge, colliding with Addison. An almond scent wafted, raising a long-dead Past One memory of his mother's Christmas cake. She always added a splash of brandy to the marzipan.

Winded, Addison backed off, confused, eyes widening when she saw him in the doorway. Her shock morphed into betrayal and blazing cheeks lit the room as she scanned for another exit.

The discreet Laszlo frisked her with his eyes, foremost thinking of the plan and looking for something appealing to focus on. Though not his type, she was pretty enough to make the con work. Sex wouldn't be a transaction if he could spark an attraction.

"What did you do?"

He raised his hands. "Don't be afraid. I'm not who you think I am." He held out his fake ID, but she didn't look at it.

With a scornful laugh, Addison pushed up her sleeves, a determined expression on her face as she prepared to fight her way out. She wouldn't last a minute, but he hoped to avoid physically harming her.

"My name is Laszlo Sándor from the Vulnerable Victims Unit."

"Here to carry me off to the asylum? Thanks a bunch, Marsha!"

Marsha looked at the floor.

"Why would I do that?" Laszlo asked. "You're having difficulty with your reality, Addison, but you're not insane."

Relief softened her face, and a blush hit her cheeks as she exhaled. Though she tried to hide it, Laszlo watched the trepidation unshackle from her body.

"My current reality is people trying to kill me!"

"Who?"

"Those who burnt down my house." She played with her fingers.

Marsha looked up, and Laszlo knew what she was thinking. Having already cemented the lie, she believed Addison had set the fire herself.

Addison eyed him with suspicion. "And you–"

"What about me? I haven't met you before."

"You work for Palowa!"

"No."

"I saw you there at the coffee shop once. Before all this."

"That isn't possible."

"You were also on the helicopter. I recognise your face."

Of all her confused memories, she had to remember those so perfectly.

"Perhaps someone similar to me. I imagine it has been a scary time for you. I wasn't there and I certainly haven't had the excitement of a helicopter trip. It's understandable for you to be confused and imagine things."

"Like the brother I know I have." Her lip trembled. She bit the flesh to hide it, but Laszlo was too astute to miss it. Lately, he had been over-sensitive about her brother, Mason Rae, too.

Hiding his sinking heart, Laszlo smiled. "We have been looking for you to make sure you're alright. I understand more than you think. I've experienced similar situations before and it's why I'm here to tell you that you are not alone. To help you distinguish between what is true and what you think is true, so you are enlightened and confident about the things you remember. It's okay. It's my job and you have nothing to worry about."

Shoulders relaxing, a silent Addison stared at Marsha's navy carpet, while the fridge hummed from the kitchen and warm water flushed through creaky radiator pipes.

"Can we sit?" He stepped towards the armchair nearest the door.

"Shall I leave you to it?" Marsha asked.

Laszlo leaned forward. "It might be beneficial for Addison to have a friend—"

"She can go to hell for what she's done."

Marsha tore off the sofa and rushed past the recoiling Addison. She picked up a magazine and thrust it under Addison's nose. "Remember this?"

Addison snatched it and looked closely at the advert for The Visa Card. "Yes, Marsha. It was only a minute ago."

"According to you, you saw it on a date as a teenager."

Addison frowned. "How can I if it's only just being released?"

"But it is on your list." Laszlo took out a piece of folded paper from his pocket. "Check it."

With trembling fingers, Addison read the list and frowned. The mandala dementia deception was already budding.

Tears filled her eyes, and she choked. "I didn't go on a date with Orlando. I couldn't get home from the cinema and had to say no."

"Why couldn't you get home?" Laszlo asked.

"I don't remember. I guess my dad couldn't pick me up."

"Addison, will you sit? Please. Allow me to summarise the current medical trials for mandala dementia. They are underway and proving successful in every patient. We don't know what causes one's perception of reality to change, but uncovering trauma roots through hypnotherapy has been a phenomenal discovery this past decade. Also, rediscovering history through learning has helped. I've steered many to freedom, and now, by using our memory authenticity app, they are secure in mind."

The purpose-built, successful medical trials made the patients forget everything but what they should know.

He watched her eyes tighten as she thought about it. She couldn't prove her memories. Not now her Real and New list had let her down. Looking defeated, she flopped into the chair beside the window.

Laszlo smiled inside. Phase one complete. Phase two: encourage her to leave with him.

Fourteen

16th April 2023, 02:50 – The New

Thoughts muddled, instinct failing, and insecurity at its highest, Addison read the Real and New list over and over, veering into mental despair. She wanted to argue that the other memories were genuine and fresh in her mind, that the movie was a mistake, but she couldn't lie to herself. She remembered typing it, convinced she had kissed the luscious Orlando for an hour while watching it. Instead, her memories were hopes and dreams of a crushed fourteen-year-old girl who had lost out on love.

Shame filled her, embarrassment that the dementia had manifested in front of the kind VVU therapist Laszlo Sándor.

Marsha's hand squeezed Addison's shoulder, and she shook it off.

"Get away from me. I trusted you."

"Addie, I would never mean you any harm. I called him, not the police, Dr Collins, or Barnes. I believe he'll look after you."

"Barnes? Why would you call him?"

"He thinks you're dead!"

"You're reporting to him about me, aren't you?"

"Not exactly."

"Was the doctor a set-up? My life's been a mess since I saw her. Did you share things and help fuel this horrible nightmare?"

Marsha sighed and looked away. "Barnes asked me to keep an eye on you, but I told you that."

"And offer your *any time, night or day* support so I'd feel comfortable about coming to you. Right?"

Addison stood up, fingers splaying when Marsha yelled, "That isn't fair," right into her face.

"Save it, Marsha. I'm leaving."

"Don't," she cried, grabbing her arm.

Addison snatched it away, beleaguered, and a mortified Marsha raised her hands.

"Please don't. I'm only trying to help. Betrayal was never my motive. I'll leave. I need the bathroom anyway."

Addison didn't notice Laszlo covering the door until he moved aside and opened it. When Marsha left, he shifted to the sofa and took her shaking hand. With a gentle pull, she sat back down.

"Let me help you. Trust me."

"Trust you when I can't even trust the people I know?"

"If you come with me, I'll tell you the things I can't now, here…with her…" Laszlo jerked his head towards the door as he rubbed the back of her hands with his thumbs.

Drawn into the trance of his captivating eyes, Addison calmed. His tender gaze wrapped around her like a safety blanket. Doubts crumbled into dust as his rhythmic thumbs circled. Hypnotic. A tightness manifested at the pit of her abdomen, and she inhaled, slipping back to reality with a steamy bump.

"And go where?" she croaked. "There's only social care left since someone set my house alight and I won't surrender to the government." They frowned at each other. Bemused, she added, "I don't know why I said that."

"Is there anyone you can stay with?"

She shook her head, tears forming. "I don't know who I know."

Laszlo handed her a box of tissues from the fireplace. "I want to help you through this, if you'll let me. No hospital, doctor, or police station, I promise. A hotel would be too draining on the charity, but perhaps I could swing it." He pursed his lips. "I'll even take you to my house if it makes you feel safer. It's unconventional, I admit, but acceptable under the circumstances. Plus, I'm willing to risk it if it helps you recover."

His risk? Surely putting herself so fully into a stranger's hands was more her risk. Then again, Laszlo was the only one who seemed to understand and sympathise with her plight. In her vulnerable state, she ached for someone to lead her out…someone who knew how. Laszlo looked to be that person, considering the people she knew, or supposedly knew, were untrustworthy.

Her so-called friends hadn't made a good impression. Perhaps a stranger would. Laszlo had certainly made one so far. In her current frame of mind, someone stepping in, holding her up and taking control of what was slipping from her hands was tempting. Laszlo could help her explore the problem, and unlike Jon, he seemed willing. Why distrust a therapist just because she couldn't trust her own thoughts?

However, a professional team had come looking for her and burnt down her house. That really happened. But it wasn't this man. Why would he waste time talking to her about dementia instead of dealing with her while the traitor used the upstairs bathroom?

Addison had to stop suspecting everyone, especially a sturdy man with a face of dreams. An adonis of perfection. Despite what she'd experienced, she couldn't drag her gaze away from his enrapturing eyes, precision-trimmed stubble, and magnetic smile.

Then, the guy waiting for her on the A-road shot into her mind, and the dreamy Mr Sándor's safety became paramount.

"A hotel might be better," she advised. "People are looking for me and I don't want them to visit your house."

"Would you feel secure in a hotel? If they find you alone… Come home with me, Miss Rae. Where I can protect you. Where I can easily do that. Trust me. Because I'm not afraid of them."

~

Swindon-bound, an anxious Addison worried if going to a hotel with the sexy, dark-haired VVU officer was the right decision. As he talked, she relaxed. Her surprising hunger to know everything she could about him led her. She felt like a fish on a hook and sank into his mellow tone, hanging onto every word. His electric presence bewitched and drew her. It made her regret choosing the hotel over spending time with him at his house.

She glanced in the wing mirror, clocking the headlights behind, but remained attentive to Laszlo as he talked. He seemed a genuine guy. He said he had no wife or children and he'd been with the charity for two decades. His father, who had worked for Hungarian Internal Affairs, died two years after Laszlo was born, prompting his mother to move him and his older brother to England.

Headlights still beamed from behind as he explained the iron-absorbing syrup he would prescribe her, its fast-acting effects, and the lessons he intended to give once she settled in at the hotel. The hypnotherapy sessions sounded the worst. Wary, Addison bit her lip, glad Laszlo couldn't see it, especially as she felt so at ease in his company. For whatever reason, she trusted and believed his concern. It wasn't just because of his allure. Something else lingered, a confidence in the circumstances. She didn't fear him or her safety with him. She felt as if she had the skills to protect herself.

The car behind them was a different story. The occupants could be an unpredictable threat, and she didn't actually possess the skills to protect herself. It hadn't turned off in twenty minutes. Her breath quickened. Had they found her while watching Marsha's house? She tried to remember if she'd seen any cars parked on the street, but could barely recall arriving.

Paranoid, she looked over her shoulder, then at Laszlo while he watched the road. What if he had told them?

"What's wrong? You look worried."

Despite the uncertainty, she voiced her erratic, and lately, unreliable, thoughts. "I think we're being followed."

He checked the mirror and shrugged. "There's been a car behind us since we left, true. Doesn't mean anything. This is one of two main routes into Swindon."

Addison glanced back. The driver could be on their way home from a night shift. Her gut said something was wrong. Was it warning her about the car or Laszlo? Maybe the sickness was playing with her, giving her paranoid delusions of grandeur that she was important enough to be chased. Or could it be instinct alerting her to more danger?

Deciding to deal with the immediate issue first, she said, "I'd feel better if they just went on ahead. Will you turn off?"

"The hotel's right here." The indicator clicked for the roundabout exit.

"No!" she blurted. If the arsonists were following, they would know where he was taking her. "Keep going."

He glanced over, confused, then flicked the indicator off and took the next exit. Addison watched the hotel disappear and the headlights behind joined them.

She swore. "Please turn off."

"I'll do one better and lose them. I used to do this to my brother all the time." The flash of his eyebrows encouraged her. "Watch me work."

Gravity pushed her back into the seat as the car gained speed, her eyes widening at the rear of a lorry fast approaching. Laszlo overtook it without breaking a sweat, then killed the lights and slammed on the brakes as they neared a turning. He skidded around the corner, and Addison squealed when her shoulder hit the window.

"Sorry. I'm not used to jumpy passengers."

He drove through back roads and residential estates, each turn cementing her trust in him. Why thread the streets intent on losing their tail if he wanted it to follow? The uneasy feeling vanished now they were alone on the road.

He pulled over on a quiet street. "My house is only minutes from here. Another hotel is around fifteen. Your choice, but I can assure you, you'll be safe with me. And, if I'm honest, I'm afraid to leave you on your own."

Addison feared it, too, although she refused to let it show. She tried to forget how close she'd come to death on Friday night and how easily it could happen again if she stayed on her own. Laszlo had done everything she asked. He'd taken her to a hotel and then recklessly driven along residential streets, pandering to her unsubstantiated accusation. Her doubts about him were certainly uncalled for, and she felt safe with him—or safe *from* him. Either way, because of him, she felt protected.

"Okay. I'll go with you," she whispered, still unsure if it was for the best.

Five minutes later, they parked on the drive of his detached house. The outside looked ordinary, but inside it was spectacularly posh. Paintings adorned the white lounge walls. A huge, mounted TV faced light furnishings and a glass coffee table with silver legs. A conservatory, rich in wicker and pine, led off from the lounge. The monotone décor ended at the kitchen, where deep red cupboards contrasted with white walls, copper utensils, pans, and wrought iron shelving. The pans hung from a rectangular frame above the island unit, and woven through the black bars were threads of synthetic English ivy. Such colour and detail. Odd when the other rooms were so plain.

"Have a seat. Hungry?" He rolled up his navy shirtsleeves to wash his hands and gestured to the row of breakfast stools.

Addison shook her head, looking around and listening for people. "I haven't had an appetite for days."

She pulled out a stool, surprised by the weight of the wrought iron and the comfort of the plush red velvet seat. They must have cost a fortune.

"What's your favourite food?"

"Lamb."

Laszlo laughed and rolled mischievous eyes as he opened the fridge. "Something ordinary which might be in my house."

"Chicken nuggets?"

His offended face peered around the fridge door and Addison looked away, grinning.

"You insult me now," he replied, amused.

"Sorry. What do you class as ordinary?"

"Chicken breast, salmon, tuna steak, vegetables, pasta, rice–"

"I like creamy pasta sauces."

"Chicken and prawn? Garlic?"

Addison's mouth watered for the first time in days. She licked her lips and smiled, feeling calmer now they had arrived. "That sounds really good."

A minute later, he'd piled all the ingredients onto the quartz worktop. Addison raised her eyebrows at the portobello mushrooms and Spanish onion. She would have opened a sauce jar from her cupboard.

"Can I help?"

"Best not. I'm obsessively fussy."

Before she could say it was only chopping, he pointed to the wine rack with the tip of his fillet knife.

"Third down, in the middle, is a Soave. Do you mind dry white? It goes better with the food. Swap it for the open Sauvignon in the fridge. We'll start with that. Glasses are over there."

Addison opened the cupboard to a display of all kinds of glasses. The perfect vessel for every type of drink. Shot, brandy, champagne flutes and coupes, crystal…

"Other side," he replied.

She spun around, eyes wide, and pointed to the selection. Laszlo laughed.

"What? That's for sherry, that port, the one on the end is a nosing glass in case I want to sniff the wine first, and the wobbles on the end are for *wobbling* brandy."

Nosing glass?

At her glazed expression, he laughed again. "Other side."

She placed the two largest glasses on the island, earning a wink from him.

"Glad you went for the big ones."

"Reckon I need it after the week I've had." She opened the fridge, surprised not to see Coleman Farm packaging. Had she imagined the contents of hers leaning in that direction?

An eruption of snarls outside stalled her heart, and she slammed the fridge shut with a quiet shriek.

"It's only cats fighting." He set down the knife. "Relax. No one knows you're here. The car behind us was a coincidence. It didn't follow, did it? You're safe. Besides, I have excellent security." His face contorted. "Saying you're secure in a stranger's house probably won't make you feel any safer, but all I'm doing is cooking you food."

Her shoulders unwound. The prowling men didn't know she was at Laszlo's house. Trusting that, she squashed her fears. They wouldn't find her, and if the handsome Laszlo intended to cause her harm, he would have done so already. He'd given her no reason to doubt him.

She poured the wine with a steadier hand and sat on a stool, awed by his dexterous skill as he chopped vegetables and griddled chicken pieces like a pro chef. It relaxed her, and the alcohol warming her heart sidelined her troubles. Watching him make a roux at four in the morning without a recipe or measured ingredients was mesmerising.

Sexy.

Laszlo scanned the island for the open wine bottle. Spotting it beside her, he reached for it, slower than the pace of the rest of his cooking. He wafted his aftershave, a rich woody tone with a citric top-note. As he drew back, he turned, inches from her, blue eyes searching her oval face. Her heart thumped. Mere seconds felt like minutes.

He cleared his throat and moved away, bottle in hand, before asking, "What sort of music do you like?"

She breathed, coming down from the bizarre electric moment, and gathered her composure. "I prefer the old stuff. Seventies to early nineties. I also like tracks from the twenties and forties. Then again, I don't know if that's true anymore."

"Shall we find out? Alena, play the Charleston." He tossed the whisk and caught it as music trumpeted from the living room.

Despite her aches, she slid off the stool and started dancing, steps almost perfect if not for the two glasses of wine she'd consumed and sore blisters catching on her socks. "Ha, yeah. I still like it."

"Wow! Impressive. Where did you learn that?"

Her face fell. "Something to do, I think. My heart feels heavy to think about it."

She saw herself at fifteen, sad and empty in the Jockey, practising the steps she'd learnt from the video at home. But deep inside, another hazy recollection lingered. Hadn't her like-a-sister best friend, Chloe, bought the dance lessons so they could learn The Charleston together?

Polka-dots teetered at the edge of her memories.

"Alena, play random top hits from the 70s and 80s, volume six." Laszlo turned to Addison. "You know how to stir, right?"

"I'm sure you'll tell me if I'm doing it wrong." She gave him a sarcastic smile.

As she came alongside him, he elbowed her gently in the ribs. "Cheeky." He handed her a whisk.

"Stir, you said. That's not a spoon. You might know your glasses well enough, but utensils not so much."

Laszlo laughed, put a firm, warm hand over hers, then took it to the pan. "We're thickening. *Stir* with the whisk while I make pasta."

He dumped flour on the worktop, cracked a couple of eggs, and poured olive oil and salt on it. Addison watched in horror, wondering if he'd ever heard of bowls.

"You make your own pasta? It's four in the morning! Who makes fresh pasta at four in the morning?"

"Me, apparently."

"Don't you have dried?"

"Don't swear at me!"

She laughed. "You're tiring me out just watching you chase runny eggs around the worktop."

Laszlo almost lost control of the mix, but soon the gooey dollops of pale-yellow stickiness became a dough. "Thanks to you, putting me off."

"That's right. Blame it on the trainee stirrer."

He pressed the button on a food processor to drown her out. "Sorry, what was that? I couldn't hear you over the sarcasm." When he flashed her a smile, eyes sparkling with amusement, she couldn't help her laugh.

While the machine kneaded the dough, he topped up their wine and took over the sauce, adding the remaining ingredients. She leaned on the worktop staring, dizzy from wine and intoxicated by the aromas soaking the air. She had never watched a man cook this way. Perhaps it was why she felt a strange connection to him. No one other than Mason ever made her dinner, and he was more of an oven-chip chef.

Laszlo brushed against her with a whispered, "Excuse me," wafting a tea tree scent from his hair. He reached into the cupboard above her head. Sparks erupted. Their magnetic chemistry gripped her. She took a breath, cheek to cheek with a stranger she knew little about, while his breath tickled her ear and drilled into the base of her spine. Nothing but the present moment seemed important.

"Who taught you to cook like this?" she stuttered as he placed a pasta shaper on the counter.

"Me. I'm obsessively fussy. I like restaurant quality dishes, so I learnt to make them." He threw the spaghetti into the pan.

"Regular sauces are nice too, you know."

"Oh, please." Minutes later, he handed her a steaming bowl and pointed to the stool. "Try this and see if you can say that again."

Creamy. Buttery. Garlicky. Perfectly balanced flavours rolled over her tongue. The chicken fell apart, the spaghetti was bouncy, and prawns popped in her mouth.

"It's the most sensational thing I've ever eaten."

"Nah, sauce is a bit iffy. I blame the trainee. You let a skin form, didn't you?"

This time, she elbowed him, and she wasn't as gentle as he'd been. Laszlo groan-laughed.

As they ate, she noticed one thing missing, but kept quiet. She wouldn't want him to whip out the bread maker if he didn't have a garlic baguette in his freezer.

She smirked unintentionally.

"What's so funny?"

"The song. It's been a while since I star-trekked across the universe."

Addison thought she heard a muttered "Not as long as you think," but he said it too quietly for her to be sure. "Pardon?" she asked.

"I said, I need another drink."

He refilled her glass. She pondered if Meatloaf had ever made an album because none of his songs had played. When Yellow Polka-dot Bikini came on, Laszlo groaned and peered at her.

"I'm in hell." His pleading eyes made her laugh.

"Alena, play the most popular stored playlist." Soft piano began, and a familiar melody flooded from the lounge. "I don't listen to classical music, but I recognise this. The pianist is something."

"Chopin's Nocturne. Pieces of his work feature as background music in all sorts. This tune is in the movie Firestormers. Have you seen it?"

"Oh, yes. I saw it with Mason last year." She giggled at the recollection of her brother throwing popcorn into the air and not catching it. One time, it bounced off Mason's chin and into her mouth while she yawned. She didn't know whether to laugh or gag.

Then she realised the memory wasn't real and, like a person with Alzheimer's setting a plate for a dead spouse, she rediscovered mourning all over again. Defeated, a tear rolled down her cheek.

Laszlo laid a gentle hand on her back. "It will take time to get control of this. But we will. Together."

She looked up, watery eyes swimming with the island lights. "I don't know if I could stand it either way. The sadness of not having a brother or missing the one I knew."

"We'll finish the dinner, sleep, then begin. Okay?"

Though nodding, she wasn't convinced she wanted to remember. Or forget. She preferred to fall asleep and wake to a normal life again. Whatever normal was. At least she would know if it were true.

The rest of the meal was awkward. He kept rolling his chin, irritated, and she wasn't sure why. She stayed quiet, suddenly wary of the stranger she had found so perfect until now. What confounded her most was this growing attraction to the mystery of him. Kind, sparkling eyes with a hint of stringency and defiance burned into her fossilised soul, melting the once-saturated knots of hurt and self-doubt. Stoked and amplified by the several glasses of wine she'd knocked back.

Laszlo gathered the empty dishes. "You ate well, considering you don't have an appetite."

"It tasted too good to leave," she replied as normally as possible. Though cautious, she couldn't help desiring him. She sipped her wine to hide it.

"Sorry I went quiet. The music helps me think, and I was deciding where to begin tomorrow."

"You look annoyed."

"I am, but not with you. I'm frustrated. You're a nice, decent woman who doesn't deserve this."

"No one does."

"No. But this conversation is for later. Now, I reckon you need to wash your feet. You're bleeding through your socks."

"Oh!" Addison inspected her heels. "The plasters have come off my blisters."

"Come on. I'll show you where everything is."

Following a man upstairs always tickled Addison. Every time, no matter who it was, she would think, *'Please don't fart.'* Laughter came out as a breath. Addison pressed her lips together to fight the consequent threatening squeak as she rounded the corner and into a handsome grey and white wet room. Then they popped open, her mirth frozen inside a deep breath.

"Wow."

Seven rose-gold shower heads sat on slate grey tiles in the far corner. Three on one side, three on the other, with a generous rainer in the ceiling. Their nozzle positions reminded Addison of a decontamination unit, and she wondered if part of the floor spun around.

"Don't you bath?" she asked, intrigued. Didn't every house have one?

Laszlo laughed. "Who has time for a bath?"

"By the looks of your shower, you don't have time to rinse either."

"I'm done and dressed in four minutes." He pointed at the nozzles. "Setting one is the middle one, obviously. Seven is all of them, and that switch is the dryer."

"Dryer? Will robot hands come out and wash me as well?"

"How lazy do you wanna be?" he teased, rolling his eyes. "I'll fetch you a towel in case you bottle it. In here will be your room."

Down the hall, he opened the door to a brilliant white bedroom. Pure and heavenly. Addison made it dirty simply looking at it.

"Reckon I'll decontaminate myself before I go in there."

He laughed. "You're funny, ain'tcha?" He walked into another bedroom, returning seconds later with a folded red t-shirt.

"I don't have much in the way of pyjamas or clothes for you, but this is sufficient for tonight."

As she moved from the bedroom, she collided with him coming out of the bathroom. His hand caught the small of her back, the other cradled the back of her head. His palm provided a softer landing than the wall.

"Careful." He pulled her to his chest. Faint citrus aftershave lingered under his shirt.

Tipsy, and afraid to inhale his divine scent, she stepped away, mumbling an embarrassed apology.

He hesitated at the door, biting his lip as if he contemplated something, but instead, said, "I'll leave you to it. I put your things over there, and you'll find what you need under the sink. Get some sleep and we'll catch up when we're refreshed."

Fifteen

16th April 2023, 11:45 – The New

Sleep was fitful. The Laszlo in the coffee shop scooped her onto a table and pulled her head back, kissing her throat. It made her insides liven with lust. The Laszlo on the helicopter hauled the ladder all the way up and she climbed on top of him, eager fingers undoing his shirt buttons while kissing his chest. A burly Laszlo standing in Marsha's doorway, or cooking in his kitchen, or climbing into her bed. Every face was his, and every thought ended in sex.

Sleep was fitful.

Addison padded downstairs to the inviting aroma of bacon, but it wasn't why she rushed. She hurried to watch the mesmerising Laszlo cook again, while her stomach knotted with worry over what the first day would bring. She hoped for more than a dementia app.

Shopping bags littered the floor. Some empty, some set-aside. A few tunics hung on the door. Addison's size.

"Excellent timing. Brunch is ready." Laszlo smiled and poured her a coffee from the cafetière.

"Smells lovely."

"Sleep well?"

"Yes, thank you. What's all this? Did you shop for me?"

"Not exactly. A local I know runs a clothes swap. She donated them when I explained about the fire. I guessed you're around an eight, ten max. She also helps at the night shelter, so she added new underwear. I picked these toiletries up at the supermarket."

Addison flushed.

"Sit. Let's eat. I want you to give me four days. No distractions. All communication switched off. Just me, you, and the memories. We have enough food for a week. Plenty of wine. You'll likely need that for the history lessons."

"History lessons?"

"Robert Naise isn't dead."

Strange that she remembered the event so well. "So I discovered. The creep."

"Do you accept? Four days. No world other than what I show you."

She lifted her chin. Could she trust him? That was the biggest question. Her mind in his hands. What did he have to gain but Addison's recovery? And he was the only one offering to help her. At least he understood her experiences.

Eventually, she nodded.

~

For two days, they had watched, learned, and listened to classical music. She appreciated the wine while she sped through historical facts, not knowing if they differed from The Real. It became laborious. They cooked, talked, and laughed, and when Addison cried over her memories, Laszlo offered a word of encouragement. She enjoyed the time to reflect—something she was rarely inclined to do.

Reflection, however, only unearthed more memories of Mason as she curled on the sofa with a coffee. She grew to despise them. Laszlo welcomed them, often suggesting seemingly valid alternatives.

"I made him dinner to take home when he finished work. I always did, but if he never existed, then

Addison pre-Wednesday wouldn't have cooked him food. So, why was there an extra plate in my fridge?"

"You had leftovers. It's a coincidence. Or maybe you make yourself two or three meals at once, so you don't have to cook every night."

She smiled and shook her head, amazed at his acumen. It sounded like her. Cooking for one was why she didn't mind Mason's custody terms.

Her face fell as she considered that again. Then she remembered Sting grieving over a scent he shouldn't know.

"Sting!" She put her glass down in surprise and noticed Laszlo's confused pucker. "My precious boy."

"You've a son named Sting? The records didn't say."

"No. My dog. He's mourning Mason, too. But he shouldn't. Should he? Sting wouldn't know his flat or be looking for his scent. But he is. He should be comfortable being at home on his own. But he isn't. None of it makes sense!"

"It's all right, Addie." Laszlo leaned over and took her hands. "It'll take time."

Thinking of Sting made her remember his strange behaviour on Wednesday morning. "What about the dogs barking right up to the moment this weirdness happened?"

His mouth opened and closed, face neutral as he considered his reply. "*If* it happened, well, dogs sense vibes. They also hear high-frequency sounds. But it's irrelevant."

"Sting yearning for his daddy isn't. Mason is the only thing consistently stabbing at the roots of what we're trying to achieve."

Laszlo's eye twitched. "I'm aware of that."

"I remember living a life with a brother I don't have. There are so many things about him. New memories keep surfacing."

"New?"

"Rekindled, then. Though, memories recalled for the first time are new. Sometimes unrelated things remind me of him."

"What if they're not true memories? What if the reason you haven't recalled them is that your mind is making them now?"

"They have to be true." She slammed her cup down on the silver coaster, stubbornly clinging on to having a brother as if it was the only thread of truth she had left. "I have a life of memories. I was coming into my teenage years with a four-year-old sibling to babysit. His first day of school, and his little face as he said goodbye to our mum. He hated school, always did from day one." She laughed again. "Do I go on? Christmas plays, show and tell, football matches, sports day, high school, puberty–"

"I–"

"How isn't it true? My life is somewhere else, and nobody seems to believe me."

"I believe that you believe it. But I know different things. I have read about it and had the misfortune of watching the grainy CCTV footage. I won't put you through that, but in this folder, you'll find the media headlines and police reports."

Twenty file thumbnails. One previewed with the headline 'HIT-AND-RUN FOETICIDE'.

Addison's eyes bunched up, her heart sinking further into darkness as Laszlo summarised the truth. Then, discovering she had been a witness at the roadside shocked her into speaking.

"I wasn't there. I'd remember it."

"Perhaps this is the trauma at the root of your dementia. How long has it been feeding? Have you never remembered, or did you forget recently?"

"All I know is that on Tuesday, I had a brother!" She wiped the tears caressing her burning cheeks.

"It's all right. I understand." His calming voice was an instant distraction. He had fast become her rock. "I've been in similar situations before. Though never as personally involved as I have become with you." Embarrassed, he looked away with a heavy sigh.

The fabric of her red tunic bounced to the rhythm of her pulsing heart at the thought of touching him. She took his clenched fist in her hands. "You've kept me together. You're a welcome distraction."

"You're not supposed to be distracted." His gaze penetrated her repressed soul. She hadn't felt this way since she fell for a two-timing moron who, for three years, cheated on her with several women.

"I can't help it," she whispered, wetting her lips and leaning towards him.

Firm hands clasped her face and pulled her closer. Soft, hesitant lips touched hers. Winter played, and his tongue swept like silk across her bottom lip. Hungry kisses lowered her onto the sofa as his chest pressed against hers. He tasted sweet, his aftershave adding a citrus tang. Her fingers wove through his floppy, black hair, trembling breaths betraying her excitement. An incredible craving simmered inside her.

Without breaking the kiss, he pulled her to her feet. His hands drifted under her top, sweeping along her shuddering spine and gathering the fabric to pull it over her head. His thumb brushed her breast as he tossed red cotton onto the floor, then lifted her to his hips, his intentions pressing hard into her thigh. As she linked her ankles, his lips moved to her jawline, tongue trailing.

She didn't know or care where he sat her, but it was the perfect height for him to bite across her collarbone, lean her back and bury his face into her ample breast, leaving his hands free to roam there, too. Gasps and quiet moans accompanied his expert touches as her fists clutched his polo shirt.

Then his lips went limp, and he growled, head rolling against her breasts. He straightened her bra before resting his hands on her shoulders.

No, don't stop.

He must have heard her thought because he kissed her before pressing his forehead to hers. "We can't do this. I'm your Vulnerable Victim support worker. It isn't professional."

He retreated, trousers bursting and arousal fading from his sexy eyes. He placed her top in her lap and disappeared into the kitchen.

Hands shaking with adrenaline, she dressed and crept to her room. Though she understood the circumstances, she felt ashamed to be rejected by this perfect man. One who knew exactly what to do, where to touch her and how, as if it wasn't their first time. No one had aroused her so significantly and made her feel so desperate so quickly. It was as if he'd correctly judged a sequence of controls he couldn't possibly know.

~

A gentle knocking disturbed Addison's fourth memory authenticating dementia lesson. She closed down the app as the door opened and Laszlo's awkward face peered in, unable to hold her disenchanted eyes.

"I made dinner."

"Be right there. Thanks."

"Can I get you a drink?"

"Do you have any vodka?"

He nodded.

"I'll have a strong one, please."

She wanted to use the bathroom, but didn't think she could brush past him without hanging from his neck and kissing him. Unsure of how close she could get without his salacious magnetic force sucking her further in. She waited for him to leave before moving.

Downstairs, a vodka with ice and a slice sat beside a plate of butterfly chicken. Laszlo perched at the island with his hands in his lap, food untouched until his guest arrived. Next to her fork was another dose of the iron absorber to protect her liver and help sort out her life. She swallowed the bitter syrup with a two-mouthful vodka chaser. As she ate, she glanced at him now and then and noticed he only picked at his food.

Halfway through, he rubbed his face, frustrated. "Addie, I'm truly sorry."

"I'm not."

"I overstepped my position, your trust, and my rules. It won't happen again."

Deflated, she inhaled a shaky breath as shadowy threads of abandonment wrapped around her like barbed wire. It was utterly ridiculous. She hardly knew the man, but he had become a salve for her insecurities.

"Excuse me," she whispered, putting down her cutlery and rising from the stool.

Laszlo caught her wrist. "Wait. Please. Tomorrow, you should liaise with your insurance company and organise temporary housing while your house is fixed. I'll see you're transferred to another support worker."

Addison's trembling jaw opened in surprise. "You promised four days. We agreed."

"That was before I took advantage of you."

"Oh, get off your high horse, would you? You're not superior to me."

"You are my patient!"

Right now, she would become whatever he wanted to stay and feel safe. Huffing, she raced from the promise-breaker back to her room and flopped onto the bed, a rush of baby screams echoing in her mind. She huddled in a foetal position, gripping her ears to shut them out, and sobbed, mourning everything she had lost. Even Sting had a temporary new home. Addison missed companionship—with him or her brother. She had never felt so alone.

Hours later, as her blank eyes stared into the darkness, shuffling sounds paused outside the bedroom door. A loitering Laszlo, hesitant to knock. Fearing his knuckles would never meet the door, she offered a helping hand.

"What do you want?"

The door brushed the carpet as it slowly opened.

"I wanted to check if you were all right."

"I'm fine," she replied, keeping her back to him.

Laszlo sighed as he snapped on the lamp. "I don't think I am."

"I'll leave in the morning."

The bed dipped. In the silence, she could feel his longing as if it tapped her on the shoulder.

Overruling her stubborn decision not to turn around, she rolled onto her back and looked at the ceiling. In the corner of her eye, she saw him staring at the carpet, arms resting on his knees.

His hungry blue eyes looked up, stirring her pot of petering desire. "I don't like breaking my promises, and I don't want you to go."

He pushed the quilt over her hips, fingers trailing down her legs. She trembled, abandoning the shame of wearing a scanty pair of cotton knickers under his t-shirt.

He removed his polo shirt, revealing thick, rounded shoulders and a smooth chest. Then he pulled off his jeans.

Heart pounding, she grasped the sheet as his lips played around her stomach. "Don't do this again if you're about to change your mind."

Eyes determined, he levelled with her face, rubbing himself against her groin. "I won't change my mind. I can't," he mumbled as their lips met.

The way he loved her made her feel as if she mattered. They moved in unison, with an intimate connection she'd never experienced before. What would have been insignificant touches with anyone else, aroused her to peaks of ecstasy beyond her imagination. Over and over. How, between the enviable shower, restaurant-quality food, and incredible sex, would she ever leave this house?

The next morning, her body ached as she climbed from the bed. Halfway to the door, a sharp pain seared the back of her head, and her stomach swirled as the ground undulated like the sea. She collapsed to the floor with a thump, cheek bouncing and blood spattering the carpet. Blinking, she glimpsed Laszlo's socked feet before another spate of baby screams took her into a blurry darkness.

~

"No hospitals, doctors, or police, I said. Just you, me, and the memories. Do you still agree, or do you want to go to the hospital?"

Addison shook her head. The bedroom ceiling greeted her when she opened her eyes, a damp cloth over her forehead, and the quilt tucked under her chin. "I still agree."

"Marsha said you blacked out before. How many times?"

"This is the second. Why does it keep happening?"

"How long for the first time?" he asked, ignoring her question. Didn't he know?

"Three to four hours."

"Only an hour today, not so bad, but you wouldn't even wake with smelling salts that could rouse the dead, and I've practically frozen your lip. You bit it when you fell."

"Why do I keep fainting?"

"I don't know. I haven't come across it before. You haven't been eating much, and you're under a lot of stress. Maybe it's your body's way of resetting."

Her mouth was dry and her lip swollen. She swallowed. "Can I have some water?"

While he went to fetch it, she assessed the ground before getting up to use the bathroom. Except for a sore lip, she felt well, as if nothing had happened. On her way back, she met a concerned Laszlo at the top of the stairs, eyes now slinking down her legs.

He laughed. "I'm not sure which question to ask first."

"I feel fine. What's the next one?"

"Didn't you have some pyjamas?"

Cheeks aglow, she returned his impish smile. "I quite like wearing your t-shirt."

"Your water." His expression was more serious as he handed it to her. "Are you alright?"

She nodded and gulped mouthful after mouthful, enjoying the cold liquid sliding down her parched throat.

"Ready for breakfast?" He must have caught the naughty glint in her eye because he laughed and kissed her, avoiding the place where her teeth had gouged her lip. "I meant food. Something light. Scrambled eggs?"

Addison's growling stomach agreed, and while he made breakfast, she dressed, gaining hold of her spinning mind before she joined Laszlo in the kitchen. He'd changed into tan trousers and a hunter green shirt that hugged his muscles. She wore a second-hand pair of jeans and a white t-shirt and looked a fright.

In what was now becoming a habit, she swallowed the prepared medicine before sipping the coffee beside it, all the while watching him finish the eggs.

He peered over his shoulder. "Stop staring at me."

"I can't help it. All I can think about is last night."

"Well, that's too bad. We have work to do today." He handed her a loaded plate.

The juicy eggs smelled delicious, and she moaned in delight as she swallowed the first mouthful.

"You're an excellent cook. I don't want to leave tomorrow. I've never been so spoiled."

He finished chewing and washed his mouth with juice. "We aren't as far as I planned. After this morning, I'll be taking things slower than I intended. I'd like to keep you another day."

She contained her delight. Only the leap in her stomach could give her away. "I'm not complaining."

"I want to try hypnotherapy. Four half-hour sessions throughout the day. We'll shake the pot and see what comes out."

"But will I think of anything else but you?"

"You'd better or there will be no more of me."

"That'll just make it worse."

Laszlo chuckled. "Eat your food, you whore."

Though she laughed, the fact he was better at controlling his desire raised suspicion. Addison only wanted to be hypnotised by his caress. She stared, eyes raking over his stubbly face, down his thick arms to the muscular legs he'd rocked her on for pleasure last night.

"I can feel the lust rolling off you." Laszlo smiled and leaned in to kiss her. As her lips parted, heart thrumming with anticipation, he shoved a piece of toast into her mouth. "Eat your food. We have work to do today."

"Ow!" She pulled it out, minding her lip, and stroked his fingers. "Can't we just…?"

"Later. If you deserve it."

"Spoilsport."

He winked and kissed the nib of her nose. "I have things to set up. Finish your breakfast and join me in the conservatory. The sun is beautiful in there this morning."

Addison chewed her toast, trying to dilute the tendrils of gripping arousal as the breathless reminders crept behind her eyes. Thinking about her treatment was more important, but she couldn't shake off how he'd made her feel last night. The need to be with him overwhelmed her, and the yearning was more than lust. On top of her already confusing thoughts, she had feelings for her support worker. Was a life with him just a dream? A whim?

What future could they have? Why would he want a woman who couldn't tell what was true from the past? She breathed miserably and poured a fresh coffee before joining Laszlo in the conservatory.

Sixteen

18th April 2023, 09:15 – The New

A sweet smell with a citrus kick wafted from the sunlit conservatory. Laszlo had opened a recliner ready for her. The machine beside it had a dangling wire.

"What's that?" Addison asked, worried.

"It's just to measure your pulse."

"You don't need to know how fast that is right now."

"I hoped you'd be more relaxed." He plucked the cup of coffee out of her hands. "Let's lay off the caffeine for a bit. Okay? Sit. Lie back. Shut your eyes."

"What's that smell?"

"Aromatherapy. My own special blend. Shush."

She made herself comfortable and closed her eyes, nervous but intrigued. She had never tried hypnosis.

Squashy headphones slipped over her ears, and a monotone male voice soon bored her into submission. He mentioned beaches and sea sounds, rustling trees and running trains. Swishing sounds and soft clickety-clacks flowed into her ears. Safe sounds. Safe places. The voice asked her to choose one, but she was leaving those sounds behind. Now, she zoned in on the irritating background noises—quiet pings, drills, and sharp knocking sounds. Before long, she couldn't hear the boring man describing paradigm chambers and storage boxes in her mind. The tinier sounds had led her to her own paradigm chamber, an empty cavern.

Empty but for Laszlo waiting with his hand out, vowing to guide and protect her. Telling her she shouldn't fear what came through the doors.

The plain cylindrical wall swiftly adorned itself with red handleless doors, and she felt a sharp sting between her toes. Addison hissed, unable to lift her heavy socked foot. Her control drifted into oblivion amidst a chaos of sounds and brown, whirling surroundings.

"Focus on me," she heard as she fell further away from its echo. A warmth rushed from her ankles and nestled in her stomach where soothing vines spiralled. They coated her face, reaching into her throat and calming the blurry red base of the whirring cavern.

Laszlo's arms reached around her stomach. Secure and tight, his scent surfing the vines down to her heart.

"Focus on me."

Slowly, the cavern stopped spinning and the red doors came to rest. Warmth radiated from within, hot to the point of discomfort, but peaceful. And heavy. Its tranquillity fashioned a comfy chair, the same pastel-green shade as Palowa's logo used to be. But the thought fizzled. She was exceptionally cosy, sitting on Laszlo's lap with his arms tight around her.

As they sank deeper into the cushions, she realised she couldn't move, though she didn't mind so much when the armchair felt like springy clouds. Then she flushed too hot, tongue sticking to the roof of her mouth and itchy patches she was too tired to scratch flaring across her body.

Vanilla and sweet orange lingered. At the side of the chair, a new table holding a fruit bowl brimming with green, knobbly fruit had materialised. Bergamots, one sliced in half with regimental vanilla pods standing in its flesh.

"Addie, behind these doors are your favourite things."

"I can't look. I can't move. And there aren't any handles."

"Do you know what might be inside?"

Sting, Mason, the Jockey, Chloe (Mason's ex-girlfriend), reading, holidays…

"Let's focus on Mason Rae for now."

A door on her left opened, and a swirling yellow and lilac light sucked her in. She could see Mason climbing trees and playing football, taking his infectious excitement wherever he went through his smile, laugh, or gaze. Mason fighting in the park or receiving another detention lecture from their father. The time he got caught shoplifting a bar of chocolate, a dare gone awry. The memories multiplied—dinners and dog walks, house moves, cinema visits…Jumanji.

Fragments of the movie sequel unfolded. Alan holding his abandoned childhood toy soldier in his old makeshift shelter. A giant pink flower almost eating one of his children. The soldier in a beige suit and bulbous helmet, hunting for them in the jungle.

The fragments splintered, and Addison found herself back in the springy armchair, Laszlo's arms still tight around her. He hadn't let go yet. Not once. Her rock.

Another door opened, this time without a swirling light to take her anywhere. Could it be Laszlo's door? She was reluctant to find out what lurked behind it, afraid he would discover how obsessed she'd become.

Still hugging her tightly to his chest, he kissed beneath her ear. "It isn't time for me yet. What about Sting?"

Several doors opened, each spinning her through life with her precious boy. The puppy visits and his first night home. The training and custody agreement. All the long walks she loved and hated in equal measure. The time she and Mason took him camping, and the bonfire freaked him out. He barked until they put it out.

"Did you let Sting go because you planned to burn your house?"

Addison recalled the fire, voicing each step of her near demise and clever escape. She saw Laszlo's familiar face pulling up a ladder...

The cosy warmth crisped into talons of anxiety hooking into her veins. Frozen inside his tightly wrapped arms, Addison's memory changed. Now, the fire tore through Mayor Robert Naise's house like a Roman Candle.

Shouting, she fought the safe arms that had fast become her prison.

"Addie, now it's time to be free. Hide these doors to forget everything you have seen. After a countdown of five, you'll wake bright and perfectly well. Five, four..."

The doors drilled into the cavern floor and beads of crumbled basalt rock bled from the wounds.

"Three, two..."

The ground reset as if the doors were never there.

"One."

The blinding sun appeared above her and she blinked. A million sunspots occupied her view. She sat up, surrounded by Laszlo's sun-soaked conservatory windows, wondering where her coffee had gone.

"How do you feel?"

"Thirsty. Can I have my drink back?"

He kissed her cheek, whispering that he'd fetch one. When he picked up her empty cup, she frowned, confused, sure she hadn't drunk the other coffee. She was still blinking the annoying spots from her eyes when he returned and handed her a full cup.

"How are you feeling?"

"I feel weird. Light. We did the session, yeah?"

"Yes, and I want to do a few more today, much the same as we've done already."

"I don't remember anything."

"Good. It means it's working. Tomorrow will be different. You'll face the truth, and I want to prepare you for it. Mostly, I don't want you to be afraid."

Addison laughed, scornful at the suggestion. "You don't know me very well, do you?"

"I know you're clever enough to build an escape in your chimney. Why do you have it?"

"Insurance."

"For what?"

"In case of a threat to my safety."

"Is there? Why?"

Addison's forehead creased as she tried to remember, thinking she'd discovered something, but nothing else came. She glanced at the plants on the shelves. "I don't know."

"You seemed confident just now, or why would you say insurance?"

"I built it so I could escape should an expected threat come against me. Though why it should I can't remember."

"Something to do with the government? You said you wouldn't surrender to them."

Though something flickered in her mind, it was dim and distant. She shrugged.

"Okay. That's enough for now. Work on the app for a while. Ask if Robert Naise is dead."

"Mayor Naise is dead? When?"

Laszlo smiled. "Just ask. It will give you his public history."

~

Sitting in silence was Addison's new pet peeve, and while the memory authenticity app quizzed her new knowledge on the now not-deceased Robert Naise, she hummed to smother the constant baby screams. They faded in, haunting her, then melted away, leaving a lingering echo imprinted on her cochlea. Lingering and preparing to mingle with the next one.

By the time the third hypnotherapy session finished, she had adjusted to the app work. She enjoyed it, even preferred it to the sessions, and it became a godsend after the fourth instalment. The app focused her confused and weary thoughts. Broken thoughts. Sometimes she'd find herself blank staring, and only the app beeping because time had run out, or Laszlo talking, drew her out of it.

Addison favoured the staring over endless baby cries which, by mid-evening, hadn't quietened even after drinking a glass or two of wine. Instead, the alcohol exposed surprising things, like the memory of swinging a sledgehammer at her chimney wall with some vigour. The toxic emotions she'd released seethed with hatred for the British Government, but why she should feel this way was beyond her. She only saw the grubby, mouldy beanbag inside the Jockey.

The tablet with the memory app disappeared from her hands.

"That's enough for today."

"I need it."

"You shouldn't overdo it." Laszlo switched it off and set it on the bedside table.

"It centres me. I need it."

"Why?"

"Because I can't concentrate. There's nothing in my empty head." She rubbed her eyes, noting her speech was slower than normal.

"Give it time–"

"And I keep hearing a crying baby. It's quieter when my mind is busy, and then I don't hear the drums."

Eyebrows raised, Laszlo queried *drums*.

Addison shrugged. "It started yesterday afternoon."

"Okay." He flicked through the channels on the gigantic wall TV. "We'll find something to take your mind off it."

He opted for a popular romantic comedy that he didn't know Addison would hate. She didn't mind as she curled beside him, thinking of friends who had raved about the film. Unfortunately, she couldn't recall who they were. As she sipped her wine, playing with the end of Laszlo's finger, she didn't care.

What did it matter, anyway?

Two-thirds into the movie, she giggled at the characters getting frisky.

"I feel bit drunk."

Laszlo pointed at an almost empty bottle of red wine. "Well, that was the second bottle."

"Oh," Addison replied. "That then that's why." She laughed again, grabbing his shirt and trying to look at him. "I like you, Laszlo. You make me feel fizzy."

He laughed and stroked his thumb across her cheek. "You mean fuzzy, and that'll be the wine."

"Thas walla said. Fizzyyyyy."

Laszlo flung her arm around his shoulders and pulled a groaning Addison up. "I think you should go to bed now."

"Are you taking me to bed?" she asked, giggling.

"Yes."

"Are you taking me to bed…bed?" She stumbled over his foot.

"Most definitely."

He scooped her into his arms and carried her up the stairs, tolerating the sloppy kisses washing down his cheek until he plopped her on the sheets with an overzealous bounce. He pulled off her trousers with a playful growl and then drew the quilt up to her nose to hush her giggles.

"I'll be up in a minute." He kissed her forehead.

She was asleep before he left the room.

~

A blinding headache on top of screams, drums, engine roars and bright lights was not the best welcome to Addison's morning. She approached the kitchen blinds and shut them before settling on a stool and pressing her face to the cool island surface.

Laszlo dropped bread into the toaster. "Dirty hangover this morning?"

"Headache."

"Fry up?"

"No, thanks."

"A filthy hangover then. No more drinking for you, Missy. I didn't realise you were such a lightweight."

She stuck out her bottom lip. "I'm not, usually. I don't remember drinking so much."

"It might be the hypnosis. So, no more alcohol."

"Then you'd better ply me with lots of hot chocolate."

With a roll of his eyes, Laszlo agreed, then he grinned as he shoved a mug of strong coffee into her hands. "I'm failing already."

"Only if I don't get paracetamol with it."

Already prepared, he held out the tablet box with the bitter syrup on top. She downed the liquid and slurped her coffee to dilute the vile taste it left, then took out a strip of tablets. Her eyes focused on the red cross logo on the box, her vision blurring into a larger, hazy version of it glowing in a shop window. The thick red 'X' had a thin white stripe running through it and standing regally in the centre were two black lines. Black's Pharmacy. Addison recalled looking at the hair accessories in the window, reluctant to obey her mum, calling her away. Baby screams turned the harsh corner, growing louder as a car accelerated.

"Addison?" Laszlo sounded impatient, as if he'd called her more than once.

"Hmm?"

"You zoned out."

"I remembered something." She squirmed, feeling disconnected, as if the memory came from another life. "I'm in the street and a baby is crying. I think it comes from the car that knocked over my mum. The driver is a dark-haired boy, and the crying stops when he drives away."

His eyes bulged and his lips peeled apart, mouth silent.

"It's proof that I don't have a brother." A tear slid down her cheek. How could she remember a person and a life so vividly? Her tears soaked into Laszlo's shirt, his juniper scent washing her with comfort. "Did I create an imaginary friend to support my sad life or…"

"Sometimes mandala dementia sufferers fill in the gaps with things they wish they had. I planned to work on truths today. Now I'm not sure how to go about it. I intended to show you the CCTV footage, hoping to dig out what you were hiding from yourself, but as your memories appear to be returning, I shouldn't interfere with the natural process."

If Mason had appeared because of mandala dementia, then what were the real memories?

"I still don't recall everything. What about the double drum and cymbal I hear with it? I want to see it."

"Maybe not while hypnotised. And not before, either. I want to see what else surfaces without inspiring it." Laszlo waited, eyes wide and eyebrows high. "I want to start now while it's fresh."

"Can I at least brush my teeth?"

"I don't care about your coffee breath."

"Well, I do! I haven't had my good morning yet, and—"

Luscious lips, hard and rhythmic, smothered the rest of her argument, and feeling unclean, she tried to pull away, but his hands held her jaw, fingers cupping her ears and refusing to let go. Listerine flavoured her mouth as his tongue dipped in and tickled hers.

"I don't care about your coffee breath. Good morning. Now, let's go." He pulled her off the stool and led her into the conservatory.

She sat in the recliner, not expecting him to tug the lever at the side, and she screamed when the seat stretched out.

"You're so impatient!"

"I'm excited to see you well." He smiled. "Ready?"

He kissed the corner of her mouth, and she groaned in pleasure when his lips caressed to the base of her ear.

"In puncto reflexionis," he whispered.

Unseen fingers rubbed her cheek.

"Are you in your paradigm chamber?"

Brown cavern walls built around her, fruit scents strong, and a heaviness descended upon her the moment she saw Laszlo sitting in the armchair, tapping his lap. Addison sat without moving and turned her face to kiss his neck.

He trailed his fingers down her arms and took her wrists, bringing them to cross over her body, then wrapped his arms around her. "Today will be tough, but I'm right here. You are safe. The doors you show and the things you remember can't hurt you now. Ready?"

"Yes." She added a serious nod. The shiver rippling through her made her doubt herself.

"If you're cold, make a fire. Your chamber could do with a little heat."

Stone crumbled in the wall. A sharp piece must have struck her foot because it stung between her toes again. Her leg twitched, and she curled her toes. It felt too familiar. A pattern forming.

The stings were regular.

Then the roaring fire threw out tongues of heat that chased the sting and cold out through the crown of her head. Flushed and heavy, Addison relaxed against Laszlo's soft and springy body, his arms strapped over hers.

"Do you have a fire in your house?" he whispered.

"No. I have a cupboard."

"Everyone has a cupboard."

"Not one that can take you to the roof!" she replied with a proud smile.

"What do you need that for?"

"None of your business."

Offended, Laszlo huffed. His tone crisped. "Why did you set your house alight?"

"I didn't."

"The arson report says the fire was deliberate and police evidence confirms you were at home around the time it started. But you weren't there when they put it out. Did you start it?"

She scrutinised the empty cavern space for data, but no response lit. No door came. Nothing sounded but the soft crackle of flames and Laszlo explaining how she had let Sting go. Whoever they were, they weren't at the house when it burnt.

"I don't remember any of it. Why don't I remember anything?"

"Ssshh," Laszlo breathed into her ear. "I'm here. Relax. It's all right. We'll come back to it." His stubbled cheek brushed hers. "Where did you go after the fire?"

"There hasn't been a fire!"

"Where did you send that dog?"

She vaguely recalled a yellow Labrador jumping the neighbour's fence. "To the Jockey."

"Then what?"

The freezing waters of Horseshoe Lake surrounded her. "I went swimming."

"I think you've forgotten something in between," he said.

But there was nothing.

"I must've blacked out."

"Perhaps you aren't aware of doing it."

"I guess that might be true."

"Do you remember any scary hospital visits?"

A blue door appeared, then swirls of yellow and red sucked her in and threw her out onto a plastic chair, emotionally detached and unsure of what was happening.

Machines beeped. Her mother lay in a bed with a flatter stomach and tubes coming from her mouth. Her blank father stared at the view from the hospital window as Addison's gaze flitted from the back of his head to her mother's ashen face.

No baby lay with her.

Then, the car accident, the root of trauma, sped through her thoughts like an express train. The double-drum thump of her mother, first hitting the bonnet and then the windscreen of a black car, drilled into her soul. The cymbal of a wine bottle smashing on the road sent a shudder down her spine.

Agony tore her heart. She couldn't breathe. Laszlo loosening his arms changed nothing. She felt restricted and pressed upon, and the pain was excruciating. Tragic. Addison screamed.

"They didn't catch who did it. Did they? They couldn't see the driver on the cameras. They couldn't identify the car."

The memory rolled on. The piercing scream morphed into another's standing inside the pharmacy door, replacing the baby's fading ones as the car revved away.

She glimpsed the empty space of the dark-haired driver's face and replaced it with the lovely Laszlo grinning at her.

"Laszlo," she whispered, nestling deeper into the armchair and kissing his neck. Inappropriate memories rushed, playing out on the cavern floor. Her breath quickened, the jarring shift from trauma to Laszlo ignored.

"You keep thinking about me, just like you did in the session yesterday. Maybe you should put the thoughts behind a door and label it, so it's easier to find later. You wouldn't want them to get muddled while we recover the others."

"A nice big door." She grinned at the unvoiced *My Perfect Man* label swinging on the front.

"Why did you say no to a date with Orlando? Didn't you want to go?"

"Yes, but I couldn't get home from the cinema, so my mum said no."

"Your mother wouldn't fetch you?"

"My father took the car when he left us." A tear rolled down her cheek.

"Addie, now it's time to remember. Anchor these doors to your chamber walls. Robert Naise. The house fire. Your mother's accident and your parents' divorce. After a countdown of five, you will wake bright and perfectly well. Five, four, three, two, one."

~

Sunspots plagued her vision again, yet it was cloudy outside, and no lights shone. Her head thumped, her mouth was dry, and she had a hole the size of London sitting in her gut. She sighed, melancholy and missing something she'd never had.

Laszlo's tender comfort soothed the brittle edges of it, and the next few sessions cleansed the pustules of dark confusion.

Addison never had a brother.

Always so thirsty after a session, she guzzled the water Laszlo brought and thought of the Jockey. And not for the first time. Though why the tatty eyesore should keep flicking back, she didn't know. Or care. It had served its purpose. Now she didn't need it, and Laszlo didn't need to know about her childhood insecurity and abandonment issues or the childish keepsake box she saw hidden under the floor beneath the beanbag. If it opened, she would likely find nothing more than swimming badges and a shabby teddy.

She hid the Jockey memories behind a small door with a tiny label and locked it.

"The curry is ready."

Pulled from her thoughts, she breathed, nauseous and not hungry, but the candlelit spread he'd laid out touched her heart. He'd gone to so much trouble. She would force the food down if she had to. He'd set out samosas, bhajis, lamb rogan josh, and keema naans in dishes beside an unhealthy helping of pilau rice.

"Are you hungry?"

"Not much, but I'm gonna try. You made all this?"

"No trouble. It's only twice as much."

Addison rolled her eyes and laughed. It should have been hearty but it came out breathless and weak.

"The sessions were rough on you."

"It's working. I'm doing all right." When she looked up, Laszlo was giving her a quizzical stare.

"I rattled you today. Who are you, Addison Rae?"

"What do you mean? You would know more of what's true about me than me right now."

"I mentioned the mirror and the cupboard you saw, and you told me to mind my own business."

"Ooh, the plot thickens." She laughed before shoving a piece of lamb into her mouth.

"And where did you go on Friday night?"

"To the shop," she answered, still chewing.

He said no more. She devoured the delicious lamb and was looking for more when she noticed Laszlo staring through his plate as he chewed. Addison's puzzled gaze broke the spell, and he grinned, eyes brightening.

"Mmm. The curry has a *sting* in it, doesn't it?"

Addison frowned, finding something familiar in his sentence, but nothing came to mind. "Don't you mean bite?" She glanced over the amazing food as she ripped off a piece of naan. "I will miss this. I don't want to go tomorrow."

"Well, I wasn't about to kick you out at five o'clock. You can stay another night." He kissed her gently, his breath spreading over her bruised lip. "You can stay until your house is ready." Another kiss. "Then, maybe we'll…"

What…? Did he want her to move in? Already? Did she love him? Beyond an addictive infatuation, she didn't know.

"What is there to return to?" he asked.

"Not much, other than a job I'm not sure I have anymore."

"Addie, with your healthy bank account, you don't need to work. Neither do I, really. I just like it. I clean up people's problems. That's what I do. It's what I'm good at."

"Like cleaning mine?"

He smiled. "Yes."

They finished the food in companionable silence, and as Laszlo cleared the plates, he winked and suggested she shower. Although she thought she ran, it was a power walk at best.

She closed the bathroom door and collapsed. A sharp pain sliced across the back of her head. Confused why it kept happening, she breathed through the pain, sickness, and sea-like floor. Convinced the blackouts were making her better, she embraced it, needing to forget the things she used to think were true.

Seventeen

20th April 2023, 05:30 – The New

Darkness enveloped Laszlo's bedroom as he lay staring at the ceiling, expecting the sun to rise at any moment. He'd already waited twenty minutes, preferring lying in bed churning things around in his head to pacing the living room carpet.

The last few days had been difficult, and on occasion, his cover had almost unravelled. But luckily, Addison hadn't queried how he knew about her healthy bank account. It meant her psyche was right where he needed it. Trusting him and assuming she'd mentioned her family inheritance.

Twice since her arrival, he'd carried her into the spare room. Twice, he'd uncoremoniously dropped her on the bed. The first time, she was too drunk to notice and fell asleep before he left her. Yesterday, he found her on the bathroom floor, conscious, but weirdly distant. Yet she sensed his impatience and kept apologising.

Today, he would need to reinforce his *feelings* for her again, having cleverly avoided sex since Monday night. Even though he'd always intended to make her fall for him, he'd hoped to leave the physical for as long as possible. He only backed down because he feared she might sneak off in the middle of the night. Now she would question why he hadn't followed it up when she was so willing.

It was difficult to be honest with himself. Hard because he liked her. Sarky and funny, and sometimes she showed an attractive dark side, but she was too flaky to be relationship material and he hated deceiving her. Monday's premeditated rejection was painless. Thinking of Lorrie excited him. Thinking about Addison didn't. Therefore, the dismissal had been easy. Eating his meal before bringing her down for dinner so he could pick at another and pretend to be nervous about asking her to leave, was genius. Although it was wasted when she didn't notice the strain he'd tried to portray.

The tormenting voices were waking. He sighed and got up. Yes, he knew it was his fault that Addison didn't notice. Yes, he'd injected a vulnerable, confused woman between the toes with his own blend of DMT, a hallucinogenic drug that distorted her view of reality. And yes, he'd also played a few blinding tactics to ensure she looked only to him for stability. Easily achieved once they lost Trainer-Guy in Swindon the other night. Laszlo recognised the car number plate, prompting a call to Ross Barnes while he shopped for Addison's things.

His mind regurgitated the same old taunts while he prepared coffee, hiding the stress behind his sullen eyes. Stress he would also have to hide when he called Barnes with an update. If the impatient message Laszlo received last night was anything to go by, it needed to be soon, before Addison woke.

His stomach whirled. Was it the upcoming conversation making him nauseous or the impending morning sex?

Despite his feelings, or lack of, he would need to play it well. Addison would spot a ruse. Bringing her home to meet the true Laszlo, at least, the man he would be with a spouse, had proved to be the perfect tactic to convince her of his sincerity. What better way than to tolerate a coffee-breath morning kiss? Although she'd stunk, he didn't feel as dirty as he had after strip club Debbie.

Offering his home also kept Addison close and leagues away from Barnes, Coleman's crew, and furious politicians. On Sunday, his call with Barnes to explain the helicopter snatch had shown Laszlo just how careful he needed to be. It began with shouting and ended with Laszlo hanging up. He'd spent the rest of the day on alert for company.

No one came.

He poured himself another coffee, now ready to tackle and reason with Barnes. With wisdom most of all. Laszlo didn't want it known that he cared if Addison lived.

"Where have you been?" Barnes hissed, impatience in every word.

"Locked down. I told you that on Sunday along with, 'I'll be in touch—"

"You haven't."

"—after four days.' Are we a little anxious?"

"You have no idea. You need to come in."

"Why?"

"We want to see you."

"Why?"

"You ran off with the mark, Laszlo. It hasn't gone down well. My excuses on your behalf are wearing thin. As is my fucking patience!"

"I needed her to trust me! To feel safe," he spat. Then winced. Addison slept in the room above the kitchen. He moved into the lounge. "It's why I chose to lock us down for a while. My plan is better. It's working. You don't need to kill everybody."

"You do what we ask. Aren't you supposed to be a professional?"

"I kill criminals for criminals, not innocent women who wake up one day—"

"A woman whose name happens to be Addison Rae! The sister of the child you killed, I believe. You see how it looks. Come. This morning."

"I can't just leave!"

"You will. You'd better, Laszlo. I won't be the cushion taking any more hits for you."

Laszlo threw his phone and watched it bounce across the sofa cushions, his lip curling. He detested being their call-girl. They called, he went. Like a dog. Like a Lassie dog. The name rekindled a familiar anger which pricked his throat, only calming as he prepared breakfast.

A floorboard creaked. Addison had roused. He hid the phone inside his coat pocket at the same time she reached the bottom stair. She looked rough, but her kind smile diluted the grey in her face.

He closed the cupboard and kissed her cheek. "Morning. How are you feeling?"

"Rubbish. But better than yesterday. And for once I'm hungry."

"It's not surprising when you eat like a sparrow. Breakfast is cooking. Rest up on the sofa."

"Actually, I prefer your kitchen, if it's all the same."

His kitchen had saved many lives. Heading for it provoked a genuine smile. "Me, too. Still, some find it too dark." His brother, for example.

"I think it's the place where you show your personality," she replied as she sat on the stool.

He paused pouring the coffee, evaluating how perceptive she could be. It was an attractive trait. He felt dark. A black soul. Empty, and devoid of real worth. What else had she discerned and stored away? He knew little about neurodivergence, but research suggested she would make patterns and associations. Had hypnotherapy done enough to break any of them?

He placed her coffee on the island. "Sorry about yesterday."

"You stayed. It was good enough."

He had crept to his room the moment she settled.

"Besides, what could you find attractive about me right now? No make-up or clothes. I don't even have nice knickers!"

"The no clothes part sounds interesting, and your knickers wouldn't stay on long, so…" Although he forced a smile, making her feel loved for a while wasn't such a hardship. Addison was pretty, and he couldn't deny he liked her, but she was also his job. He didn't use women, so he hated that, romantically, she meant little to him. His mother would smack him if she knew. Laszlo's deeds might be controversial, but he was mostly honourable. Plus, he didn't want to kill her. However, deception reigned, despite knowing Addison would forget all about him. Safety first, of course. His need for anonymity was imperative.

He served breakfast, feeling brighter for having prepared the groundwork for that. Though not knowing the name of the door Addison created to hold her memories of him irked him, he could still bury the thoughts stored inside. He only had to say the words.

As they ate, he studied her, flicking his eyes away when she sensed it. Then he would glance and smile as if she'd prompted the exchange.

"No syrup today?"

"Not until you've had another blood test. I wonder if it's causing the blackouts."

"What about sessions, any more of those?"

He shook his head. "You've done in two days what we usually do in five. So, no more sessions."

"But I don't remember anything."

"You will naturally. I can't help with the personal things, but they'll return. Like when you met Sting, or your first day at Palowa, or what it was like to live through your parents' divorce. I can only tell you what I know is true. That Robert Naise isn't dead, Palowa has always been yellow, and you are an only child."

She slipped her fingers through his with a sheepish smile. "Thank you for helping me. I appreciate everything you've done, but I should contact my insurers and apply for temporary housing."

Judging by her constant, shameful apologies last night, he had been expecting it.

"I was going to suggest you contact them while I go out today. The sparrow needs food and I have business errands to run. What I will ask is that you consider staying with me."

"Why?" Her brusque tone confirmed how much he needed to reinforce his *feelings*. Doubt darkened her eyes. "What do you find attractive about me after two embarrassing blackouts since Monday night's tryst?"

He detected the shrewd Addison of Past Two and pursed his lips, sensing her silent questions. The last six days would hardly form a romance, and his game needed to be flawless to keep her in the ruse.

"I quite enjoy your company." It wasn't a lie. Most of the time, he did. "Look, I can't make you stay, or explain my reasons for wanting you to, when I don't fully know myself. You've somehow hooked me." He leaned in for a kiss, his mind going to Lorrie to make it feel like it meant something. He lingered on Addison's lips while he remembered her.

Breath now rushing, he withdrew, collecting his empty breakfast plate. "*But*, as much as I don't want to, I do need to go out. You'll have a few hours to yourself. Will you shower before I go? Just so I know you won't knock yourself out and drown while I'm gone."

Addison raised her eyebrows, amused, and when she rose to leave, he planted another sultry Lorrie-kiss that didn't appear to have the same effect as it had at the beginning of the week. She didn't respond and drew away.

At the door, she turned. "Even if the inside isn't, at least let me get clean on the outside before you do that again."

Laszlo evaluated the messy kitchen as she went upstairs. He sighed, and leaned on the worktop, knowing he had to get the job done and willing himself to keep up the pretence. If he shut his eyes, he could be loving Lorrie.

As he cleaned up the dishes, he surfed old, but not faded, memories of that wild week. The second night had started with Lorrie demanding a shower after her shift, teasing him and making him wait for her. He repaid it, and she loved it. Just like Debbie did. Just like Addison would.

Hopefully. Because now, he was readying to re-enact that favourite memory. He stripped to his shorts, left his clothes on his bed, removed his dog tags as he had every time, and loitered outside the bathroom, waiting for the right moment to enter. He tried the door, not knowing if it would open. If it didn't, he was losing her.

Addison hadn't locked it and didn't look surprised to see him as the last of the soapy bubbles rinsed down her legs. "I hoped you'd come."

"I decided if my charm, cooking, and tender loving care aren't persuading you, then this is all I have left. And I've this needling desire to make you wait."

He stepped under the spray and pressed her wrists to the shower tiles. Her eyes swam with needy anticipation—a look he had seen before in other women. It was like watching pupils dilate with every skipped heartbeat.

He crushed her lips with an urgent kiss, pleased she'd brushed her teeth this time. Then he put her hands behind her back, pressed her to the tiles, and lifted her hips. "Business errands and shopping have suddenly slipped in my priorities."

~

Palowa came into view at two minutes to twelve. Still morning, so Barnes couldn't complain. Laszlo's lateness wasn't deliberate, even though he'd shopped first ...after spending an obscene amount of time with Addison.

A rather enjoyable time.

And one that had ended without having to pretend. The feelings sprouted from his gut. From deep down inside. Emotions he didn't want, or have the space to navigate, yet they wouldn't leave. Neither would the memory of her responding to his touch. Then he almost collided with Marsha Law coming out of Barnes's office.

"Mr Sándor. What a surprise. How is Addie doing?"

"Morning, Marsha. I came to give you an update and reception directed me here. She's doing great. The treatment is proving very successful."

"That's a relief. I told Ross how grateful I am for you and the Vulnerable Victims Unit."

Ross, huh? Not Barnes.

"When can I see her?"

"Whenever she wants. She hasn't asked. Sorry."

Marsha's smile fell. "Thanks for updating me," she said before walking away.

Barnes stood at his desk with steely eyes behind his glasses, angrier than Laszlo had ever seen him. He shot an expectant look over Laszlo's shoulder. "Where is she?" he growled, impatient fists resting on the desktop.

Unfazed by the pantomime scare tactics, yet stunned that Ross expected Addison to be there, he considered his reply. "Obviously, I haven't brought her. She's in no state to go anywhere. She's blacked out three times since Sunday, and every time she forgets something—or rather, embraces the memory of this reality and not the last. I'm giving her an iron inhibitor and DMT. I've hypnotised and retrained her, but she isn't fit. Yet."

"How long are you gonna keep this up? How long do you think they'll let it go on? And they are letting it go on. You know that, right?"

"I guessed when no one came to raid my house."

"And whose lap have they left it in? Temporarily, anyway, seeing how they're acting on my advice to kill her. Why is she so special? Are you planning to marry her or something?"

Laszlo laughed. "She'd probably bite my hand off if I asked. She does whatever I say if she thinks it will make her well. So, I'll make sure she gets better, and then you can leave her alone."

Barnes's fists tightened. "So, you want me to tell Anton and Robert that you'd like a honeymoon period? Before we shoot her anyway, because she knows you?" He rolled his jaw and calmed his shouting. "You want me to tell them that?"

When Laszlo matched his fierce stoop over the desk, Barnes flinched. "I suggest she stay with me until her house is habitable. So, get the builders on it, double time. A month. Max. Then, when it's done, I'll make her forget ever meeting me. She won't even recognise me in the street. I will hand her back fully cognisant and accepting of the current reality. All fixed." He returned to his chair. "Tell them that. And then say they've different fish to fry. I discovered some things. Oh, sit down for goodness' sake, Ross."

Laszlo threw a memory stick onto the desk. Its clatter unstiffened a dazed Barnes, who shoved it into his computer.

"Who are these people?"

"I'm interested in the one calling himself Jon Wells. It isn't his name, but I'll let you investigate that. He spent Friday night with Addison Rae. Or rather, she spent it with him. She also said she sent her dog to *the jockey*. It must mean the Lechlade local shop. On Saturday, it closed twice, which I thought was strange, and this Mr Wells was acting...off. As if he tolerated me. I wish I'd listened to my instincts because I knew something didn't quite fit."

"He named himself community spokesman on Monday and harassed the police for updates," said Barnes. "We gave Marsha's story. Addison went into counselling voluntarily and would be in touch when she was ready."

"She was frank with me about being chased and someone burning down her house. Now she accepts she might have done it herself and blocked the memory. But back then? She would have told him, and judging by his behaviour, he must know more than he's letting on."

"Then get Jon Wells. Let's have him in for a chat this afternoon."

"Tonight. He'll be running the shop until it closes at ten. I'll get him while he sleeps. But before that, there's another thing needling me. Addison's dog." He cocked his head as he sat forward. "How can it remember Mason Rae if he doesn't exist here? The dog shouldn't know she had a brother. I wonder if he, and all the dogs, surfed the turning point as well, because she describes them frantically barking right before things changed. What do dogs have?"

"Good point. I don't know. They have a fantastic neuro set-up, because don't they see spirits or something? Barking dogs haven't trended in any other dementia statement. One account doesn't make it true."

"Ross, lemme tell you. It doesn't add up. You should explore it—once you've dispatched the boys to grab the other man on the memory stick. His research is a threat to all this." He rose to go. "Meanwhile, find me somewhere to take Wells because I need to get back to

Addison. I don't want to leave her alone for too long. Not that she'll run, but she is a prisoner and still my target for now. I will say this. Murdering her will be my absolute last resort, and I'll protect her from you if you make me."

Ross laughed. "Then you'll die. Because you won't see us coming. Tell me why we should wait?"

"Because it's working! The hypno sessions were deep. And rough. Addison fights in her sleep. She lost her bedcovers three times."

"Let's hope it's all she lost."

"I'll conduct the best psychological approach to save her from you, and I have a month to complete it. Why clean up her dead body when I can wipe her mind, which I am succeeding at, as I told you? We buried much of the old Addison. Now we wait for more of the new to emerge, for her to discover the life this Addison lived. She will take her rightful place. With nurturing, trust, and encouragement, which I have built, she'll get there. So let me take it the full course."

"Just don't get her pregnant, or you'll have fat chance of making her forget you."

"I'm forty-five years old. Well, technically, I'm seventy. I think I can avoid that. The important thing here is that she knows Mayor Naise isn't dead and there was never a brother. The rest can be explained away."

"I'm in awe of your talent, Laszlo. If you're feeling compassionate, other wormhole-surfing candidates have surfaced."

He laughed. "I don't think so."

Ross raised an eyebrow to show he wasn't joking.

Dismayed, Laszlo's brow furrowed. Encroaching on Addison's vulnerable mind and then using her body to ensure she dangled nicely for him was sickening enough.

"No, Ross. I won't do it again."

"But you're good at it. And you said yourself you'd rather clean minds than bodies."

"I WILL NOT do this again." The dark, teasing voices sparked behind his flinty glare. He was usually too subtle to reveal his hand and rarely showed this side of himself. He leaned on the desk, feeling the old, Past One murderous anger swelling and meeting with the years of 'call-girl' resentment. His feelings must have been clear because Barnes recoiled in fear. "Don't push it!"

Laszlo wouldn't do it to another person. Ever.

Addison's mother was partly responsible for his emphatic rejection. Truth be told, if not for that day, he would have treated Addison as he had the last pretty woman he cleaned. So, was it deception? Admittedly, an inner attraction to Addison had sparked this morning. Still, no matter how he skewed it, they didn't have a future. Sex would remain a mere transaction. He used it. He used her.

Laszlo slammed the door on his way out. The rattle of the blinds clanged against the window. Addison was the lucky one. Soon, she would forget him, like all the other things he'd buried for her.

He would remember it forever.

~

The moon cast a dim light as he made his Lechlade road trip. He left a peaceful Addison sleeping. She wouldn't wake and find him gone overnight. Especially as he'd told her to help herself in the morning, as he had an early start. To ensure she stayed asleep until a reasonable hour, he'd slipped a sedative into her bedtime drink. The cup was empty when he checked on her.

Finalising the delivery location caused another clash with Barnes. Laszlo threatened to take their guest to

Ross's garage if he failed to come up with a solution. They agreed on an outbuilding in between Lechlade and Burford. It would be off road, but no matter how much Laszlo loved his baby's suspension, he didn't relish a nighttime drive to Henry Coleman's Surrey HQ as an alternative.

He parked on the pavement outside the Lechlade shop, aware of the camera above the sign. He pulled up his hoodie, tightened his leather gloves, and popped the boot, keeping his face turned from the CCTV before picking the lock of the flat above the shop.

Halfway up the dark stairs, he heard a dog growl. Not just any dog, but one who would recognise his scent.

Addison's dog.

Time stood still while his hatred for canines multiplied.

A thick lump of snarling black shadow raced from the living room. Laszlo backed into the kitchen, raising his arms as it soared and arched down with hefty front paws and a sharp jaw.

Sting thudded into his chest and knocked him on the floor, claws piercing his hoodie and teeth bearing down, gripping the flesh of his defending arm. Screaming, Laszlo kicked and fought, but the snarling Sting held on, eyes round and feral, tugging on Laszlo's arm as if he were a sturdy rope toy.

His sleeve dripped with blood. The snarls vibrated into the muscle of his forearm, adding to the agony. It wouldn't let up, and Sting wouldn't let go.

He rolled onto his hip, feeling his skin tear inside Sting's mouth. His gun dug into his side. With a soundless scream ringing in his mind, he gripped it with his free hand, pushed the barrel into the soft yellow fur at the dog's throat, and fired.

The shot echoed in the quiet flat. Sting's jaw slackened and his furry weight felt heavier on Laszlo's chest. Further along the hall, light filtered as a door opened with a creak.

A pale, sweaty Laszlo loosened the dog's teeth. Red slime around its muzzle seeped into his wounds as he pulled out his arm, hissing at the horrendous pain and having a silent tantrum about having to tackle Jon coming down the hall—awake, aware, and ruining the element of surprise. He scrambled up, ready to fight if he must. It couldn't end here like this.

Arm at his chest and weapon raised, he staggered to the wall beside the door as the light flicked on and Jon stepped in, arm still in the air as he took in the bloody scene. Canine blood pooled, and Laszlo's had spattered over the cupboard doors.

Blanking out the excruciating pain in his forearm, he shoved the Beretta into the distracted Jon's neck with an echoing click. "Stop. Don't make me pull it twice."

Jon's shoulders drooped, and he exhaled a long breath. It was a second before he raised his hands. "Won't it be the same result in the end? I wondered if the local mystery would eventually reach their ears."

With a callous flick of his Beretta, he forced Jon down the stairs, content to let him believe his past had found him. At the open boot, he pulled out a syringe and swapped the gun for a needle prick just as Jon elbowed him in the stomach. Even with his muscles tensed, he felt the impact. Seconds later, Jon fell shoulder first, rolling into the boot so perfectly that the restricted Laszlo only had to tuck in his legs.

He slammed the lid shut and thumped it, annoyed at leaving his blood and DNA at a crime scene. Both would be dribbling down the dead mutt's throat. Awash with fury, he pounded the steering wheel. There shouldn't have been a crime scene. All because of his loathing for dogs.

That was Izsak's fault for breaking into an MOD storage facility in Gloucester. Laszlo had followed, curiosity building as he watched him searching files. Laszlo later discovered they were his old Sandhurst files. His crimes had roused Izsak's suspicion. In avoiding him when he left the facility, Laszlo met with six black, demon-possessed Rottweilers, snarling and dripping goo.

Running from that mess was hardly the same as leaving this one. Once he delivered his catch, he would go back to the shop and do the swiftest clean.

Oh, how vexed Barnes would be about babysitting their captive alone.

~

The late-morning sun flitted through the trees and into the car like strobe-lighting, worsening Laszlo's headache. He pulled up outside his house, glad the job was over but still anxious. How could he look Addison in the eye after he'd just disposed of her 'precious boy?' Explaining his bandaged arm, bleeding and unbearably painful even after a shot of morphine, would also be a challenge.

His phone chimed a convenient delay...until he answered it.

"Laszlo Sándor?"

The smarmy voice brought a memory of the mocking name "Lassie." Michael Butler may be posher these days, but he was still the slimy Mario Spinzer underneath.

"You came recommended. Very highly recommended. And for this contract, you need to be."

Laszlo hung up. He knew how the call ended... "What's your opinion of the current Mayor of

London?" In Past One, Sprinzer had asked in person at his club. Now, he wouldn't give him the chance to ask. He switched off his phone, rubbed his face, and shook off the irony of another wasted twenty-five years. Inhaling a deep breath, he channelled the shock to get through the next delightful call-girl job.

Finding the house empty therefore was another unwanted complication.

Eighteen

20th April 2023, 11:30 – The New

Serene, smiling and still shuddering thirty minutes after Laszlo had left, Addison lay naked and almost paralysed on the bed. Physically, she could stand and walk to the bathroom. Mentally, she couldn't even string the thought together. Only the last two hours floated in her dreamy head, wrapped in Laszlo's arms with the showers spraying wherever he pointed them. Little penetrated the ecstatic replay, except for the growing urge to snoop around his house while he was out.

Then another image intruded. The Jockey kept flashing into her mind. She growled and got up, pleasant moments dissolving inside rotting wood and a mould-stained beanbag. Again and again, they came back. Each time, the floor opened, and her hands hid a metal box.

Her brow furrowed. She took notice of her hands. Grown hands. Not young and hiding childhood keepsakes. Her heart thumped, instinct bubbling. Or was it mere curiosity? What had Addison New hidden, and why did she need to remember it?

She threw on her clothes, eager to look, but stumped by how to travel there. Would hunting for fare money be a satisfactory reason to pry into Laszlo's personal things? Why not get to know his life while she looked? He rarely mentioned his family, and she hadn't seen a single photograph.

She snooped.

The lounge and kitchen drawers, pots and boxes in the cupboards, and shelves in the conservatory, were all shy of banknotes. She checked the freezer, behind the radiators, and inside books, wondering why she'd think of such obscure places to keep a bit of change, as if she expected to find a hollowed-out book full of dodgy dealings. Addison New might expect that, but after flicking through Laszlo's chosen autobiographies and finding them fully paged, she looked under the paintings—the fishing pier facing rolling hills her favourite. She found nothing tucked behind the frames, no surprise safe in the wall.

Addison climbed the stairs, reluctant to enter his bedroom. Her hand hovered on the handle, torn over doing something she knew was invasive. Laszlo hadn't taken her to his room for a reason. It was private.

Exactly. It would be where she would find his life. And with any luck, some spare change. Decided, she opened the door for a little peek.

Pistachio-green silk sheets and matching curtains, with a deeper shade on a feature wall, brought flashes of a green front door and garden gate. Her heart fluttered, then ached with an unmatchable sorrow. Sighing, and dragging her eyes from the décor, she glanced at the glass shelf under a flatscreen TV, and saw a sleek, silver notecase.

Addison's toes sank into a thick cream carpet as she entered. Feeling like an intruder, she wiped her hands on her jeans and scooped the notecase up to view the swirly pattern engraved on the top. It came open in her fingers and several crisp fifty-pound notes stared at her. She debated taking one, to borrow, not steal. Laszlo would understand. He would have helped if he'd known this morning, and she *really* must visit Lechlade. Specifically, the Jockey. She needed to find what Addison New had hidden.

After stuffing a fifty into her jeans, she raced down the stairs and called a taxi, then wrote a note on the pad beside the kitchen phone in case Laszlo returned first.

As she put the notecase next to the IOU, she noticed an inscription written on the bottom.

'Laszlo, this holds ten £50 notes. I challenge you to fill it. Izsak xxx'

Laszlo appeared to have fulfilled that challenge, and Addison had stolen it. Borrowed it, she corrected herself, but debated if she should take it at all. She pulled out the polymer note, curving and wavy, but not creased. It wasn't as crisp as the others, directly out of the cashpoint and each facing the same way.

Beethoven's fifth *da-da-da-da* rang from the doorbell, startling her. The taxi had arrived with its meter running. She placed the notecase back on the centre island and left.

~

Approaching the Jockey gave Addison the oddest of butterflies. Reluctance. Anticipation. Shame. Deep inside, she knew she hadn't been here emotionally in so long. The hard part of her heart was happy to use it as secret storage. The empty part mourned its worth. An unremembered best friend.

She imagined Sting sniffing and chasing wild rabbits through the trees. An unfamiliar cosiness tingled in her stomach, though why was a mystery. She rarely brought him here and never stayed long enough to watch him so lovingly. The hazy picture replayed, along with an even stranger vision of excavating something red from brown cave rock.

She shook her head. It had been one heck of a week.

Tossing the mouldy beanbag aside revealed a small hatch with a fingerhole in the floor. Only mud was underneath. Deciding not to ask Farmer Cotter for a spade, she said goodbye to the rest of her fingernails as she prepared to burrow with her hands, rolling her eyes at the irony of digging up red objects in her mind.

Her fingers pressed into the unusual soil. Soft. Squidgy. Synthetic. Vibrations tingled her fingertips, carrying the pulse of something shifting under the floor beneath her knees. The mud covering moved, exposing a metal box. It weighed more than she expected, and she dropped the heavy secrets onto the Jockey floor with a thud.

Strange. No keyhole. Addison ran her fingers around the back and sides, feeling for a switch, but felt only smooth metal. Fully secure. As she tilted it to inspect the front, her thumbs pressed on two cold, black squares at each end. The box beeped and opened.

Thumbprint entry.

Her thumbprints.

Her eyebrows rose with a hint of fear. How had she come by a box like this? It must hold more than childhood secrets.

Curious about its contents, she lifted a file filled with documents and photographs. A memory stick bearing the name Anton Jarvis fell into her lap. She frowned, sure she'd heard the name before. Wasn't he a politician? Her fuzzy head couldn't think clearly, but then the memory app session, when Laszlo had suggested she ask if Robert Naise had died, pushed through her sticky thoughts. London Borough Labour MP, Anton Jarvis, was a friend of the mayor.

Interesting.

She flicked through the papers—financial statements, official government letters, copies of emails, and transcripts of phone calls. Far too much to examine now, but the highlighted sections centred around a weapons manufacturer in Zimbabwe.

Next, she scooped up photographs of four men. Three of which she recognised. One she saw regularly. Ross Barnes. Why would her boss be in her box of 'treasures' along with Anton Jarvis, Robert Naise, and a fourth man she couldn't place? The old man looked familiar, and it pointlessly niggled. How valuable would the recall be when she couldn't trust her memories?

A wad of rolled-up twenty-pound notes and identity documents lay at the bottom of the box, including a passport, for a woman named Melody Bishop. Each bore a photograph of a long-haired Addison. She laughed at how ridiculous she looked, grateful she'd kept it short since her late teens.

Finally, she pulled out an old diary. The corners were bent, the cover faded, and its title, 'where it all began', was in her handwriting. Ink smudged. She flicked through the meagre, sometimes food-stained entries. On the last page, she found the name and postcode of a man who, according to previous entries, she'd known and valued for over a decade. Vishnu Patel. They'd started as lovers but realised they were closer to siblings.

Addison didn't even remember him.

Bewildered, she stared at the walls, her mind familiar with the Jockey's wooden knots and veins. In the shadow under the shelf, she thought she saw something etched into the wood, but it rubbed smooth under her fingers. She looked through the plastic window and sighed, feeling as if something was missing.

The emptiness was abhorrent, and her eyes burned with tears. She threw the diary onto the floor, frustration bleeding from her crackled scream, and let the tears go, unsure who or what they were for.

Rap-rap-rap.

"Addie. Is that you?" a female whispered. It wasn't Marsha.

Addison sniffed, rubbing the salted emotions into her cheeks. "Yes."

The Jockey door scraped open and a lady with rampant dyed mahogany curls entered, arms outstretched. They enveloped her, wafting a lily of the valley fragrance.

"I heard about the fire and was so worried about you."

Addison stiffened, unsure if the face was familiar, but the smell certainly was.

The stranger must have noticed because her hug relaxed. She let go and shied away, eyebrows furrowing. "I've been here every day hoping you'd turn up looking for that." She nodded to the box. "Where have you been? Are you alright?"

"Who are you?" Addison asked.

"Addie, it's Jennie Durham. We've been friends since high school."

Friends? Addison remembered a Jennie with braces being mean to a boy much younger than them, and because Addison cared for him, she hadn't liked the girl after that.

"You were mean to Mason once." The words popped out unbidden.

Jennie shrugged. "Who's Mason?"

"A boy I used to know. I think." Her gaze trailed out of the window, and pellet guns sprang to mind.

In her imagination, dimly lit brown rock shook, and more red headstone-shaped items rose.

"I'm glad you're in one piece. The group's on amber alert because of you. Where are you staying? Are you safe?"

"Why wouldn't I be safe? What do you know?"

"I know the men in the photographs are likely behind your house fire. I know we're getting too close, and they hate it." Her eyes drew to slits. "I know you should know this already. What's going on?"

"Getting too close to what? Is that what all this is? Proof?" She spread her arms towards the treasures of her metal box.

"Some. Some of it's just straw. We're tracking people who manipulate and profit from the future. Those like Anton Jarvis and Robert Naise. We'd mostly focused on them. Lately, thanks to you, Henry Coleman hit our radar." Noticing Addison's frown, Jennie continued. "I relayed your concerns about Coleman Farm monopolising the market. Turns out, he owns far more than we thought. And not just in Britain. He exports. And imports. He owns international orchards, European mills, and rice fields. He almost single-handedly controls the world's food supply."

Addison remembered her fridge. Then Laszlo's. Coleman wasn't controlling his food supply. "I don't remember having any concerns. I…" She dropped her eyes to the abandoned diary. "Who is Vishnu Patel?"

"The answer to your problems, I hope. When did you start to forget? It's never happened suddenly before."

"What hasn't?"

"A change to one's reality. Usually they've always known."

"Mandala dementia? I've been having treatment for that. Things are coming back to me. My mother got knocked over and lost her baby. Other insignificant things linger in my empty head. All hazy and not making any sense. Now that the root of my trauma is out in the open, Laszlo says my memories will come back."

"Hypnosis?" Addison nodded and watched Jennie shove the papers back into the box, then caught the wad of notes she threw. "You might need these. And take these as well." She tossed Melody Bishop's passport and driving licence at her. "Wherever you go, you use her." After hiding the box, she took out her car keys. "Come on. Let's go see Vish."

~

A thin, gangly man with shiny black hair and oak-toned skin answered the door. His reluctant expression morphed into a wide smile that lit his eyes as he ushered them inside, locked up, and slid across three extra bolts.

"I'm so glad to see you." He took her arm and dragged her into his spacious kitchen.

"Vish," said Jennie. "We've got mandala issues."

His delight plunged into a deep swallow at her sombre expression. "Treated?"

Jennie nodded.

He turned to Addison. "When did it start?"

"Last Wednesday. Things around me were different, but I forget what they are now. I guess that's the point. I'm recovering."

"No, Addie. They're covering it up. And the longer it goes on, the less you'll recall. Did you keep track of the inconsistencies?"

Addison nodded, a frown creasing her brow.

"Did they test your blood?"

She dropped her eyes, and when Vishnu asked if they had given her medicine, she nodded again.

He sighed. "Your ferritin levels will be low, then. How many hypno sessions?"

"Eight, I think. Over two days."

Vishnu whistled. "Wow. Were you drugged?"

"No, of course not! Laszlo wouldn't. He isn't like that. There's no way he's drugging me to cover anything up. He cares about me. I don't believe he's part of all this or knows what's really going on. Besides, none of that worries me. What haunts is me being trapped in some kind of cavern. Sweaty, tired, and digging up curved, red objects from the rock. What the heck is that about?"

"It's your subconscious telling you they buried your life inside a mind palace. One they helped you to build."

"A paradigm chamber," interjected Jennie.

"Same thing."

A cavern with blue doors and a cosy fire came to mind. Warm, protective arms curled around her—

"Do you remember your trancing phrase?"

—and Laszlo's provocative voice in her ear, sweeping his breath across her neck with his words.

"Addie!" Vishnu shouted. She flinched, startled back to the present.

Jennie laid a hand over hers. "We need to undo it."

"No. Stop. It'll make me confused again." And Laszlo would be furious. Though she didn't voice it, she could picture his aggravated rolling jaw.

Vishnu settled beside her, scratching his short, black hair. "We don't know how it happened, but we're sure it isn't time travel. I arrived here twenty-five years ago. And, like so many others, I remembered being this age then. Can you imagine being twenty-five inside a nine-month-old body?" He shuddered. "The 'hospital' treated me for years. I was a genius at first, then labelled crazy until they diagnosed me with mandala dementia. It took me as many years to correct what they did, but it taught me how to help people like you."

"No. I don't want to remember. The memories aren't true."

"But you do want to. You should, and you must. You wouldn't be digging up doors otherwise. At least let me undo the control they have over you. Do you remember your trancing phrase?"

Addison shook her head. Having been under hypnosis at the time, she couldn't answer this or the follow-up questions. It eventually persuaded her to allow the expert Vishnu to access her mind. After all, he'd reversed hypnosis for other people. She didn't have a reason to doubt him when her diary confirmed their friendship and that they'd worked together several times. She cared about him, though in what way? Her emotions were unclear. It was as if she trusted someone else's recommendation.

"What do you hear when you first see your paradigm chamber?" Vishnu asked, as an incredibly relaxed Addison sank to lower planes.

Immediately, the cavern surrounded her.

"In puncto reflexionis," her impulse replied. Hearing the words paralysed her, and took her to a less springy chair, this time, without the moreish warmth pulsing from her stomach.

And without Laszlo.

"What colour is it?"

"Brown."

"How do you feel?"

"Heavy."

"Have you ever felt heavy before?"

"Once. I had an operation."

"What colour is that?"

"Violet," she replied.

A pause.

"Our brains allocate colours to everything we think about. When hypnosis triggers, like in puncto reflexionis, are associated with something else, for example, assigning it another colour, its power weakens. Allow it to change. Match that heavy feeling to your violet operation. You're in control, not the words or their assigned colour. It's your paradigm chamber, not theirs. And certainly not Laszlo's. It's your memory, and they have no right to steal or alter it. The thoughts were true once."

The cavern walls stretched and distorted. Radiant red one second and silky green the next, then rugged-rock-brown again.

"Don't force it. Just…let."

Slowly, the brown trigger colour blended into a strong purple, resembling the one assigned to the anaesthetic woolly-head. Addison followed Vishnu's instructions, repeating the trigger phrase and colour transfer several times to secure it. She had the tools to shield and break the strings of hypnotic hold and combat future covert attempts.

Vibrations shook the violet cavern, disturbing the flames in the idyllic fireplace. Red doors broke free, coming to rest above the blue doors, all wide open and beaming colour. From them, pictures formed and swirled around the cavern, blurring into a vortex. Afraid of being sucked in, Addison gripped the chair's arms, digging in her fingernails and fighting a dose of nausea.

Six more doors formed. Pale purple ones.

"You are in control of these doors. Only you. Nobody else can hide them or force you to hide them. And if you're ever asked, you deny they're there. Keep accessing these new doors. They will show you where the memory belongs, side by side with the counter ones."

"The Real and The New," whispered Addison, as she rediscovered its meaning.

"Exactly. Both are true. Both are realities. Now, bring yourself out. Get up from your chair, put the fire out, and open your eyes. This is your key. Get up. Douse the fire. Open your eyes."

Surprisingly, the expected sunspots were absent as she blinked. Addison thanked him for that, and Vishnu shook his head, muttering to Jennie about how they'd done a number on her.

"You've also had blackouts. How many?"

"How do you know?"

"Sub-conscious resistance unrelated to hypnotherapy. How many?"

"Three. And I came round once, forgetting I'd thought I'd seen a movie."

"I can't tell you how it was done, but I can confirm that some things have changed. This isn't the life I lived before. Yet, in some respects, it's better. I carried my knowledge through school and excelled in my studies. I was relentlessly bullied and shied away from everyone, so I could secretly develop my only passion. My dream, in this life and the last, is time travel. I want to be The Doctor."

She raised an eyebrow. "Good luck with that."

Vishnu laughed. "It works, but the machine isn't powerful enough to send us back twenty-five years. I can't go back to undo it. We can't. You can. You've only just come. But we don't have long before the blackouts make you forget naturally. They aren't making you better, Addie. They're bringing your memories into the New."

Jennie gasped and took his arm. "Are you sure?"

He nodded. "We should do it soon. It makes sense for her to go back. If I go back a month, the reality is the same. If Addison goes back a month, she returns to the true past, where she can stop all this. Jennie, once she remembers everything, from then and now, she can prevent it. She hasn't lived here for as long as we have." He turned to Addison and the excited sparkle in his eye almost had her convinced. "It needs to be soon, though. It won't work if you return without the right memories."

"My brother is there. Mason is dead here, but he isn't there."

"Which won't matter if you forget him."

There would be no chance of forgetting him. Memories burst from a purple door that didn't hold any blue ones. A couple kissing on the beach, waves lapping at their feet, Sting weaving through their legs, impatient for a thrown ball. Sting loved Mason and Chloe.

Mason...

Baby cries. A thump. Thud. Crash. Screams surging from the shop doorway.

Her least favourite blue door opened, bleeding out its reality into a purple one labelled Mason, and the emotions separated instantly. Mason was alive in her world.

~

Declining Vishnu's offer to stay in Faringdon and suggesting he loan her a phone so she could leave didn't go down well. Addison defended Laszlo's intentions, refusing to believe he played a part in this nightmare. Persuading Vishnu took too much time. Stubborn and still phoneless, she huffed and walked out, following the street until she found a bus stop. She waited to catch the next one that came along, wherever it was going.

Jennie pulled in and opened the car window. "Addie. Get in. We can talk about this."

"There's nothing more to say. I won't let you judge him. He's been brilliant."

Jennie rolled her eyes.

Addison could guess what she thought. The assumptions bored her now. "Laszlo believes in what he does. You don't know him like I do."

"You've known him less than a week."

"Longer than I have you! If he burnt down my house, then why would he be taking care of me?"

Jennie looked away and sighed. Was it in frustration or defeat? Spotting a bus coming, Addison asked one last time.

"Lend me a phone. I know what I'm doing. I like him, Jennie. Vishnu's given me the tools I need to protect myself. So, what's the problem? Drop me off at the end of Laszlo's street."

She assumed Jennie would reject her request when her lips made a hard line, so it surprised her when she threw a phone onto the passenger seat.

"But you're to be on high alert," she said as Addison opened the door. "You don't tell him anything, or give him reason to be suspicious, and you say nothing about the Jockey storage. No one can see what we know."

Didn't she realise Laszlo was just a support officer? A therapist, not some... criminal mastermind.

"You research at night when Laszlo is asleep, and it's safe."

She means private, surely?

"And be prepared to leave The New at a second's notice."

For most of the journey, Addison stared out of the window, listening to Jennie recap the things that Addison New already knew. Though attentive, she mostly focused on the hypnotherapy triggers she'd learnt from Vishnu, and the coloured doors finding homes in her understanding.

They parked in Laszlo's street, and when Addison reached for the door handle, Jennie took her hand.

"Just in case. It's only a sedative." She let go, leaving a capped syringe in her palm, and then handed her a gun from the glove compartment. "Take this as well. For goodness' sake, hide them well."

"I won't need them, but if it makes you feel better." Addison pocketed the syringe and hid the revolver as best she could inside her coat. It felt heavy under her arm, yet the weight seemed familiar.

"Stay safe." Jennie smiled. It didn't hide the worry in her eyes.

Addison nodded and rushed off, keen to start her research online through Laszlo's rather snazzy internet TV, but within moments of hiding her secrets under the chest of drawers in her bedroom, a distant and monosyllabic Laszlo appeared. Instead of switching on the screen and learning, she spent the afternoon on edge, untangling memories and constantly reminding herself to think, *blue doors, blue doors, blue doors,* to ensure she said the right things. Despite everything, she couldn't shake the intoxicating hold he had over her heart. One sensual kiss, dripping with want, had once again lured her into not caring.

What mysterious cover-up?

That evening, she watched him make dinner, toying with the idea of him being part of the conspiracy. His grumpy and quiet mood lingered. Something had infected his thoughts. Addison feared it might be because she had gone out. Although it wasn't forbidden, was it?

Regardless, it illuminated her guilt for going behind his back.

Shaking the imprisoning thoughts away, she sipped her wine and glanced at the silver notecase now containing only nine £50 notes. "Are you sure you don't mind about the money? It's just that your mood is…a little brooding."

"You had legal business in Lechlade and no other way. It's unfortunate that I went shopping and into work. I would've liked to have gone with you, but it's fine. Take it. It's only for emergencies." He kept his back to her. Did he mean it?

"But there was five hundred quid in there!"

Laszlo shrugged. "To quote my brother, 'how do you know how much an emergency might cost?'"

"Touché."

Mood shifting, Laszlo fingered the inscription and sniggered. "I used to be rubbish at saving money. Izsak gave me this for my eighteenth birthday. It was full before my next one. I always fulfil a challenge."

She raised her eyebrows, and he laughed.

"Every. Single. Time," he said, with a kiss between each word. The last lingered a moment.

He returned to the dinner, and Addison to her wine, again thinking *blue doors*.

Throughout the meal, red door memories swelled and melted her heart. Mason. Her not-absent father. Her best friend, Chloe. Sting. But then the blue doors bred New memories of a teenage Addison rejecting her newborn half-sister, Rebecca. She was twenty now, and they were enemies. Rebecca's littlest brother, Shane, was a nicer child, and although a fragile relationship, it was a connection for Addison all the same.

Flickering memories of Jon erupted, shooting an urge through her that Addison Real had become accustomed to with Laszlo. They entwined with the rest of Addison New's feelings of rejection, abandonment, and envy of her father's new family.

"Why did you want to see my bedroom so badly?" Laszlo asked, snapping her from her thoughts.

She compartmentalised the memories as she took her plate to the sink. "Curiosity. What else?" It wasn't to snoop through his bedside drawers. She wouldn't do that.

"Scanning for what to thieve?"

"Maybe I was tired of waiting for you to take me." She smiled.

"You want to go to my bed?" He walked over, his tongue licking his bottom lip. The enticing spark in his eye made her stomach leap. It was the first time she'd seen that. His hand circled her back, fingertips pressing into the curve and sending tingles sailing up her spine. "You only had to say."

His hands lowered and lifted her, lips brushing her neck and his consent pushing hard into her abdomen. "It'll be a night you won't forget." Though he sounded sincere, the spark dampened in his eyes.

Addison ignored it, instead running her fingernails to his top shirt button. "Another one," she replied, undoing them as he carried her up the stairs. She pushed it off his shoulders, face buried in his neck, and when he laid her on the pistachio-green sheets, his dog tags swung from his neck like a pendulum. Impatient fingers tugged at his belt while he removed them.

"Wait."

"Can't. Don't wanna." She stripped to her bra.

When he grabbed her wrists, the corner of a condom wrapper dug into her skin. "Stop. That's my job," he grumbled, taking over and hastily finishing it with expertise. He straddled her, still wearing his shorts. Addison wasn't having that. While hot, zealous lips met hers, she hooked her toes into the waistband and dragged them down his legs.

"Patience."

"I don't have any," came her breathless reply, "and I'll hate you if you do the same as last time." The teasing had been both the best and worst sex of her life.

His lips lowered, breathing a chuckle. "I want to hear your climactic squeak again. That was damn hot!"

She dug her heels into his buttocks, drawing him inside her, surprised he didn't take control and stop it. Amazed he didn't do his usual and pull her into more lustful positions. Missionary might be uninspiring to some, but right then, it was intimate and tender, and the first time it felt like he loved her with such passion. It was more than sex. They shared themselves like soul-joining lovers.

Nineteen

21st April 2023, 09:45 – The New

Addison's deep sleep was devoid of snores, as was normal lately. Dreams of doors plagued her, capturing specific moments of The Real and New, surfing both timelines in perfect unity behind the purple doors. Timelines that blended emotionally, bringing a hard-hearted Addison New into a loving and innocent Addison Real.

The thrill was explosive.

Desire sparked. For Addison Real, it equalled love, but combined with Addison New, it fired with a fierce heat. The purple Laszlo door appeared and the 'My Perfect Man' label swayed on a bulky nail as it swung open. She surfed the memories, the chosen favourites flowing first, most of which were sex. Cooking, music and laughter were wholesome, but then she reached the dark corners where coffee shop guy laid her on a table, and the fantasy of straddling the Laszlo on the helicopter. She dreamt of their last sexual encounter, connecting swinging dog tags to the moment she hung from the helicopter rope ladder. The dog tags had swung then, too.

Why hadn't she noticed it before?

Addison squirmed under the covers, desperate to escape. Her dream took her to another dark corner, where Laszlo's lovely smile replaced the young hit-and-run driver's face. It now morphed into the true face. The very much younger version of Laszlo Sándor.

Heart pounding, sweat pouring, Addison woke screaming, purple doors shutting with a loud thump.

Closed doors didn't stop the thoughts, though. One by one, they clunked, timelines coming together like cogs and breaking Addison's heart. Had he knocked over her mother and killed her brother? Was it really Laszlo on the helicopter chasing her? Were the others right about him? She didn't know what was true anymore.

She sucked in a shaky breath, determined not to cry. If Vishnu and Jennie were right, and Laszlo wasn't helping her, what did he want?

Groggy and with a nasty taste in her mouth, she looked for water. The only thing on offer was the crusty remnants of a sickly smelling hot chocolate. She went to the bathroom and splashed her face, drying it as the itch to research what she'd learned yesterday motivated her down the stairs. While fixing coffee, she plucked up a sticky note. *'Help yourself to anything.'*

I will.

To research uninterrupted, she hoped his business errands took him all morning. She searched the internet for articles on hypnosis, then spent hours devouring them, practising the hypnotic block guidelines. If she were ever to remain in control of her paradigm chamber, she would need to disable Laszlo's tactics. Realising they might be tactics both devastated and hardened her. Mastering that had taken priority over exploring the politicians' crimes, but at least she could be confident of outplaying his next move should the need arise.

The trigger phrase 'in puncto reflexionis' led her to those people in high places. The phrase meant turning point in Latin. But what flummoxed her was the Greek translation 'convolve.'

Ross Barnes must be involved.

She scrolled the convolve results, finding the same web pages repeated until she found Shikari.com. A fascist opposing dark website. A community of 'big game hunters.' Predators of predators.

Radical. And instantly familiar.

The name Soothsayer Shikari comforted like a blanket but meant nothing to her. She shoved her hand into her back pocket, feeling and then remembering the memory stick from the Jockey. Her curiosity revived, and she set it to play on a fifty-inch screen. A distorted film of a naked Anton Jarvis having brutish sex in some kind of strip club wasn't what she expected to find.

What was Addison New doing with it?

Her Big Game hunt started with Jarvis, the public man who was always so friendly and reliable. Happily married with three children and serving his country—his passion since he left school and moved into civil service. No one saw him putting a step wrong. Just like Mayor Naise.

Poncy Robert was a miscreant to Addison from the start, but as sickening New memories surfaced, she realised he was worse than she thought. She read about charity drives, school openings, and third-world aid schemes, then remembered finding evidence of secret soldier schools, human trafficking, and the weapons trade, and storing it at the Jockey in a metal box.

Who would have thought it of such an innocent politician?

Her last search centred around the day of her mother's accident, her heart crushing at the headlines vying for attention. An abduction had occurred just hours before the hit-and-run.

Having seen the car hit her pregnant mother first-hand, she read up on three-month-old Mario Spinzer. Although they never found the child, good had come from it. His parents formed a charity.

Addison accessed the browser settings and deleted her search history, frowning, and then laughing at herself for covering her tracks. A laugh that flattened when she realised it would be what Addison New would do. One that froze on her lips when the history list refreshed.

Jon Wells. Jackson Lowe. Michael Butler. Mario Spinzer. Vishnu Patel. Names searched on government pages and associated shared databases. Records of which revealed secrets Laszlo knew how to find.

Baby Mario Spinzer was not missing. The name led to a stock market trader called Michael Butler. Laszlo had left a bookmark titled, 'Butler is still an arse', and commented, 'In any reality, even after living two completely different lives, Mario is still a knob.'

He knew. Laszlo knew!

Surely, she…this wasn't…? Had she been the idiot who had fallen for a conman?

She delved into the other names to see what else she could expose. Butler and Vishnu had attended the same boarding school in Burford, though both were day students. The records noted two fighting incidents between them, but nothing more. She thought of Vishnu's jovial smile. He had hidden the harassment, as well as himself, from the world.

The next refreshed page was Laszlo's 'stay logged in' email account. She found connections between Anton Jarvis, Robert Naise, Henry Coleman, and her boss, Ross Barnes.

The thread involving Laszlo and Barnes contained a name she knew, and their recent exchanges yesterday had included the other three as recipients.

'Vishnu Patel could have the capacity to undo all of this,' Laszlo had written.

'How do you know?'

'I've been following him for some years. He was bullied at Burford School.'

'Butler's school?'

'Patel's experiments got smashed up before he could display them at science fairs. After a while, he quit trying to show them. Now, he's an introverted agoraphobic who has rather explicit items delivered to his house. All relative to his passion for discovering time travel. He rarely does anything else.'

'Has he?' Barnes had replied, with an eager eye emoji.

'Wouldn't know. I'm not his friend. But the equipment is certainly interesting. It's worth a visit considering the excess energy he uses. More than the average daily amount, and therefore, a reasonable excuse for the government to demand an inspection.'

'I'll get back to you. The research is worth a look.'

Addison sank into the sofa cushions. Ross Barnes was undeniably involved. The pieces aligned. He and the Palowa coffee shop Laszlo knew each other in The Real, too. Were they in the car that knocked over her pregnant mother? Had they been stealing a baby at the time? She recalled the screams as the car turned the corner and sped away. Perhaps the Real Mario would have grown up in Bristol to terrorise a different boy. Laughable really, because his abduction and re-homing ripple effect had come to their aid…the bullied Vishnu could get them all home.

She grabbed her phone, absently letting her eyes scan back up the history results on the TV. Near the top was Jon Wells. She opened it while waiting for Jennie to answer, and her face drained. Sting's temporary guardian and the owner of the Lechlade local shop stared back at her.

Stunned, she didn't respond to Jennie's hellos at first. Tingles of a longing for Jon that she didn't know she carried were heavy in her heart. Strong. Were they Addison New's feelings?

"Jennie. They know about Vishnu, and I think my friend is in trouble. I need to leave. Now. Come meet me where you dropped me off. I'll be there waiting because I can't stay here a minute longer."

She deleted the latest history search, collected her things, and locked up, pocketing the key.

~

The low sun's glare on a wet road flashed in Addison's eyes as they crossed the picturesque Halfpenny Bridge into Lechlade. The River Thames rushed by, fields behind it, and a riverside pub renowned for its food and local history stood proud. This perfect scene distracted her from thoughts of the past week living with the man who had chased her from the beginning. Last night's dreams had installed another Laszlo Sándor. Jennie said the charity-funded, Vulnerable Victims Unit didn't exist, and that Addison had received the standard treatment for mandala dementia, but from an unregistered practitioner. She also said the team had found Vishnu's place all messed up, but empty. She couldn't decide if that was better than death. They'd be on dangerous ground with Vishnu in enemy hands—him and Shikari. Laszlo's doing. Again.

The more she thought about Laszlo, the deeper her anger burned. She squeezed the edge of the car seat, close to losing control, and berated herself for being so stupid. It felt like two sides of her were circling, one not knowing the other. Addison Real had never been this angry. Addison New had never felt so unbroken.

Lechlade was already full of visitors. Finding a parking space was impossible. Addison guided Jennie through the side streets into a back alley, where they abandoned the car behind a pub and took a walk-through to the high street.

"Any news on Vishnu?" she asked as they approached the shop.

Jennie shook her head. "They'll call when they know."

The fraught Saturday staff were a man short. Jon hadn't shown up for work or answered his door or phone. When Addison explained that Sting might be upstairs alone, a flustered Zoe looked inside the till for Jon's spare key and handed it over with a note. Addison unfolded it, surprised to see Marsha's name.

'I've tried reaching out, but Laszlo fobs me off, even to my face when I saw him at Palowa yesterday. He said you didn't want to see me. Please contact or visit me. I have news.'

Addison hid it in her pocket—one thing at a time—and entered the flat. She expected Sting to come running the moment she opened the door, but even her whistling as she ran up the stairs didn't rouse him. She scanned a lounge littered with Addison-charity bin bags and boxes, Jennie on her tail. Jennie went in while she turned towards the kitchen.

Uber clean.

It even smelled clinical.

New bowls for Sting were on the floor near the door, one licked clean, the other half filled with water. She ran her fingers over the table where she'd drunk hot chocolate, numb to Jon stripping her of wet clothes. She saw him wink while he unloaded a crate of vodka and accidentally-on-purpose leave a bottle behind as he wheeled the crate away on a sack truck. The Jon who carried her to bed when she hurt her ankle and didn't once overstep the mark. Then she saw Jon fiddling with her Christmas earring and leaning in for a kiss. She'd almost relented, but stayed strong enough to step back and leave.

Addison New memories. Her feelings. Jon had often salved her tortured heart.

Jennie poked her head in. "The flat's empty, so I'm off to check the security cameras."

The distant Addison scarcely heard. Her mouth filled with water, stomach whirling, floor undulating. She crouched, palms flat to the floor, breathing through it and trying to gain control of a transition happening inside. Warmth flooded a cold heart like a spring in dry lands. A collage of endurance, but the challenge unmet. An offer she could never say yes to. Her dangerous life and suspicious nature had prevented her from ever saying yes, even though she wanted it so badly. Jon's persistent date requests were flattering to Addison New.

Blue doors formed, and New memories of Jon rushed. One snatching her attention above the others because of a painful sprained ankle. He'd cared for her in a way no one else had and left her self-respect intact. If he'd leaned just a little closer as he placed her on the bed, staring with eyes like the nutrient earth, she would have met his kiss.

Shaking, Addison stared between the kitchen chair legs, half-noticing something on the floor under the table while filtering the memories of the New into order. She didn't black out, but her psyche was conforming to the New reality.

Jennie's hands were all over her, trying to pull her up, but Addison needed a moment to adjust.

"I'm okay. Stop."

"At least sit in a chair!" Jennie hooked her arms under hers and prepared to hoist.

"Wait. What's that?" She pointed to a smooth white item lying against the skirting board. Intrigue piqued, she reached under the table, neck crooked and face crushed into a chair leg as her fingers blindly searched. Feeling it, she teased it into her palm just as Jennie switched on her phone's torchlight. In her twisted position, Addison caught a glint from under the cooker. Jennie went to look while she unravelled herself from the chair legs and peered into her hand. A long, slightly curved tooth.

A dog's tooth.

Sting's t...

The scene around her fell like a soggy painting, dragging colours into a diarrhoea-brown mess. Only the tooth on a blush-pink surface was crisp enough to see. Like a lens, she zoomed in on the gleaming point, brushed with a red smear, then the bloodstained root.

Jennie placed a round tag the size of a 10p piece next to it. Sting's tag, the link ripped open.

"Jennie. Where's my dog?" she asked, not breathing. Not daring to think the worst. It didn't stop her hands from shaking as she got to her feet, glancing around the spotless kitchen. The answer dawned, and her whisper was barely audible. "They've already been here."

"They must have Vishnu as well. No one has called because Shikari hasn't found him yet. How do they even know about him?"

"In summary, Laszlo was tracking another boy from Vishnu's old school. An unlucky entanglement."

Her reply was robotic, and while Jennie phoned to update their friends, fury built inside Addison like an inferno, coating her face hot-pink. Laszlo. The brother killer. The firestarter. The con artist. The sex fraud. The–

"I know where he lives and I'm going back there to drag it out of him. And if he doesn't tell me, I'll grab hold of his tongue and pull it, until all the words line up down his throat."

"I like your style, Addie. But we regroup at HQ."

"That won't help us find them."

"But it will keep us safe. You don't have any idea who we're dealing with, do you?"

Addison smiled, contrasting the hate in her eyes. "Neither do they. And Laszlo is mine."

"If that's what you want. But we regroup at HQ. Luckily, the politicians haven't found Vishnu's lab. Because then, you wouldn't be going anywhere."

~

Shikari HQ turned out to be the front room of a fifty-year-old man from Cheltenham whose eyebrows puckered when Jennie introduced him as merely Mr D. His soft face sharpened at the insinuated danger, and a professionalism seeped in. Addison could tell she was suddenly a stranger to people she was supposed to know.

He shook her hand and turned to Jennie. "How bad is it?"

"We don't know. Depends on how far the roots go. Vish cut some puppet strings but…" She shrugged. "We won't know how effective it is until…"

"He tries the hypnosis trigger again," Addison replied on her behalf, knowing they were discussing her dementia treatment. "And don't talk about me as if I'm not here."

Jennie sighed. "Sorry. We're cautious because there's a freedom of speech issue now."

"I don't care about your secrets. I only want Jon and Vishnu back, and revenge for what Laszlo has done."

"Jon?" Mr D asked.

"Addison's new friend."

"We don't have outside friends. It puts them in danger." Anger darkened his chestnut eyes.

"But I didn't know that!" She massaged the tooth in her pocket, suddenly regretting ever going to Jon's flat. Surrendering to her ripping heart, she dropped onto the sofa with a deep wail. Genuine fear for what might have happened to Jon and Sting mingled with a strange self-hatred. She'd allowed herself to feel such torrential sorrow again. Her sadness fuelled a vindictive vendetta while listening to Jennie explain their morning discovery. Addison revelled in dishing out its justice, her imagination a rushing river until it dammed with the TV footage of Vishnu's house.

"He's one of the guys hunting me. I saw him in a photo taken from the shop security camera." She pointed to the man who had also waited for her on the road to Highworth.

"They disabled the cameras at seven this morning. We can only assume they took him."

"By the direction of the emails, it's likely. Did they take Jon as well? I want to know which of them killed my dog so I can crush his throat!"

"I know you love Sting, Addie, but anger only fuels failure, not success."

Jennie cowered from her fiendish glare. "I'm beyond angry. And Laszlo and his friends are going to feel it. Play the shop footage."

The night-time black-and-white image angled at the main road towards Burford played. Dim lights glowed, casting a stream of white onto the pavement.

A car pulled up, and a shady figure stepped out, securing the hood of a jumper tighter around a face already hidden in shadow. The gloved hand opened the boot as it passed, then accessed Jon's flat so fast it must have held a key.

When the door closed, Addison studied the car, and her heart sank into a cesspit of turmoil. "That's Laszlo's Audi. I know it, despite the fake plates."

Laszlo killed Sting. He…

"Jennie. Take me back to Swindon. Now."

~

Mood typhonic, Addison's hands bounced on her knees, throat constricting as the car passed Laszlo's house. His black Audi was on the drive, displaying the correct plates. A red Nissan had parked beside it. Whose car was that? With furtive steps, she approached the front door. Finding it ajar, she crept inside.

Muffled, angry voices seeped through the lounge door.

"Why can't you admit it? For once! Admit it was your car."

"We've been over this, Izsak."

"Repeatedly. Which is why I'm done with you unless you have the guts to be honest. I'm ashamed."

Laszlo's impatient sigh accompanied a cup banging on a coaster. "Because a detective questioned me about owning a car like the one linked to a string of crimes? Again, that's a stretch for being guilty."

"Is it?"

"Yes!"

Keys jangled as Izsak's voice neared the door. "I did my own digging. Reckon I can trust my judgement."

She froze, unsure if she was ready to be discovered by Laszlo's brother. The handle dipped.

"Wait."

The sound of brushing fabric disturbed the electric silence. Izsak's curt tone followed it, less muffled now the door was ajar. "Was. It. Your. Car."

A longer pause.

"Yes."

She heard more rustling and the sounds of a scuffle. Laszlo grunted.

"Why? Why hide it and why lie? To me!"

"The last time we spoke, I didn't lie," replied Laszlo.

"Do not start that."

"I already told you. You didn't believe me. And I don't have any other way to explain it."

"Will it outshine the fact you murdered some random man because he killed me in the past? Because, if not, don't bother." Izsak laughed. "Because he obviously didn't."

What? She frowned. Laszlo was like Vishnu. Reeling, she sat on the bottom stair with a light bump.

"Will it explain your sociopathic tendencies, or why I'm married, with three children, and you live alone like a blacklisted movie character? Will it–"

"Why are you still digging? After all this time."

"Because you killed a man! On a whim, or dream, or whatever mental episode you had. And I've always known it was your car involved in the other two."

"I killed him to protect you!"

"It was still because of me. The result is the same. I live like a ghost of the man I might have been because I walk in another man's place."

"The man was a cretin, and I killed him anyway. It was just months later–" *and in another life.*

Izsak's snort reminded her of Laszlo. "I can't even be bothered to work out what that means, but whatever it does, it is still months he should have kept."

"To do what? Hospitalise his girlfriend to the extent she goes on the run to escape him? After lying and giving him an alibi for your stabbing, by the way."

"In your world, Laszlo. In mine, you killed an innocent man."

Laszlo was arguing about his world and Frost's crimes when Izsak interrupted.

"Why the baby? What did Spinzer have to do with it?"

"This is where I don't know how to tell you."

"Did you commit a hit and run in your battered-up black Renault? It's your reg."

"It was a duplicate reg."

"Did you knock over a pregnant woman and kill her baby?" Izsak confronted with a hiss.

A dumbstruck Laszlo stared as Addison opened the lounge door.

"Did you?" she asked.

"No," replied Laszlo at the same time.

An irritated Izsak spun around. She gasped at how much he looked like Laszlo. "Who's this now?"

"The dead baby's older sister," she snarled. Her anger stewed in a bubbling pot. She couldn't take her eyes off Laszlo's stunned expression. "And you've some explaining to do."

Twenty

21st April 2023, 16:15 – The New

Pain was written across everyone's expression. Disbelief, frustration, and guilt. Addison was expectant to the point of tapping her foot, utterly in control of the unfolding car crash memory. It played in the background behind the image of Laszlo killing Sting, and maybe Jon and Vishnu, too. She breathed, turning the heartache into vengeance, and pressing on a wobbling lid. It was the only thing stopping her from running to him and breaking his face. That and anticipating his imminent confession.

Laszlo's eyes bled apologies, his mouth quiet while the room carried a tetchy buzz. Addison could almost hear him figuring out how to talk his way out of it.

Izsak lifted his appalled chin and ran his hand through his charcoal hair. "Sister? You're unbelievable."

"Izsak, please."

He huffed and rushed out. His car door slammed, the engine roared, and tyres skidded off down the road, while Laszlo watched from the window.

"Are you going to explain?" she asked. He continued to stare as if he couldn't hear her. Eventually, she pushed through his blank stare by grabbing his arm. "It was you. Wasn't it?"

He recoiled from her tormented expression and threw up defensive hands. "I'm sorry you had to witness that, but it was not my car."

Liar!

She felt the heat splash across her cheeks before Laszlo noticed it.

"There isn't a coincidence," he argued.

"There is, because we conveniently know each other."

"I didn't conveniently give you mandala dementia just so I could help you recover. Ergo, making myself feel better about a twenty-five-year-old crime I didn't commit. They questioned me because my car matched the description."

She bit her lip, recalling how she'd subconsciously replaced the driver's face with Laszlo's. She'd tried to tell herself who the unknown boy was all along. How stupid had she been to fall for a *coincidental* infatuation?

Her heart hardened, as though there were no emotions, scruples, or toxic veins from last week corroding the polish of her armour.

He turned his back to the window and faced her. "How much did you hear?"

"Enough to know your plates, your car."

"They look like my plates because I had a fake duplicate set made to hide me."

"How convenient." She stepped around the coffee table, nearing the door.

"When I heard they were looking for *that* Renault, I changed mine back to the legal ones before the police arrived. Izsak knew the duplicates, so it's natural he thinks what he does. I'm sorry you had to hear the accusation, but it wasn't my car."

Liar!

Hiding her true feelings made her cheeks dimple in protest.

"Where did you go? I was worried."

"Aren't I allowed out?"

Laszlo frowned, tilting his head. "Of course. I didn't mean…" He sighed and moved into the kitchen.

She perched on the edge of the sofa like a stranger, knowing she didn't belong but unsure how to fake it.

Unsure how to behave when on the inside, she wanted to torture him. Soothsayer Shikari knew how. Addison New was becoming a part of her, and she wanted to smile as she made him bleed.

Addison would make him talk. Prepared to ensure that he did, she used the ruse of going to the toilet and grabbed her protection.

Laszlo had opened a bottle of red and filled two glasses. She sat laughing inside at his cheesy tactics. She wouldn't be drinking any of that. Not with him, and not tonight. Tonight was playtime, and she would play him at his own game.

"Not for me, thank you."

"It wasn't my car."

"So you keep saying, and I've no choice but to take your word for it. Fast forward to when you said you didn't conveniently give me mandala dementia."

His face paled, the wineglass halfway to his mouth. Her words had conjured the right response.

"You added 'just to help you recover'."

"Riiight." His frown deepened.

"Why are you?"

"Because it's my job."

Addison signalled to her surroundings. "This isn't your job. I am not your job. I'm an hour a week at best. A number."

"You are more than that."

"Not to a medical practitioner."

"Which is exactly why I stopped us on there on Monday night." He pointed to the unit beneath a stunning watercolour of a Venetian bridge.

The reminder stoked the embers of a dying fire, stuck in a vacuum behind a wall so tall only an unchecked blue door could allow it access. His kisses. His caress. His natural smell with a hint of tea tree wafting from his hair. Addison couldn't get enough of him from the moment he brushed up against her while reaching for the pasta maker.

"If this isn't some kind of recompense, then why offer your home? Who am I to you?"

"On Monday, you were my patient. I confess, your past influenced my motive to counsel you. Saying that, the current circumstances are unique. Now it's complicated. We shouldn't be lovers, but we are. We shouldn't be living together as patient, counsellor, lovers, but we are. I'll be fired if we're found out. Fired if I register a relationship with you—even if I do transfer your case to another therapist. Then I'll probably face charges for taking advantage of a VVU patient. Even if she is worth it."

His wicked laugh, alluring smile, and mysterious eyes were enough for her to get lost in his gaze. Even from the other side of the sofa, she could feel his hot lips on her neck.

Lies. All lies.

He was as wicked as his laugh, as corrupt as his smile, and his gaze a deadly, evil game.

Addison slammed the blue door shut and reversed the 'My Perfect Man' label. She loathed the desire she couldn't help feeling for him. He was good, she'd give him that, because she had fallen in deep, without a clue or her guard up. Only Vishnu could uproot the Laszlo strings. First, he had to stay alive long enough to be rescued. Before that could happen, Addison had to survive this encounter. There would be nothing to uproot if she were dead.

Clocking him watching her, she forced a smile, but it wasn't as good as his performance. He beamed and regarded her as if there was something true about his feelings.

"I could resign."

She held back a simmering laugh. She couldn't risk ruining her bluff. "Yes. That sounds like a reasonable option."

Laszlo finished his wine and placed the glass on the table.

"I rather like the idea of you being here as my filthy little secret." His finger ran up her leg.

Addison snatched them, careful not to squeeze too tight, willing her impatience not to snap his bones. "Ground rules."

"Really?" He chuckled and nibbled underneath her ear, sending shivers and a burning ache to the bottom of her spine.

She breathed off the nausea that followed and held up a warning finger. "Yes. Really."

Ever the gentleman, he sat back. "Do we get to have a chart?" he asked, eyes wide like a child's.

Despite herself, she laughed. "Good idea. I'll draw something up." She made a mental note to adorn his chart of activities with thumbs-down-you-failed stickers.

He placed his folded hands in his lap and waited patiently for the ground rules.

"You know me inside out and upside down. I know hardly anything about you. Tell me something nobody knows."

He winced. Something hurt. "That's a condition, not a rule."

"The rule is you let me get to know you."

"Surely that comes with show, not tell."

"Which is why it's a rule."

"Okay, a thing nobody knows…I don't love easily. Two women, my whole long life. The pain of that is enough."

"So, this with you and me is what, if not a seed of love?"

He pulled down the corners of his lips, thinking. "It means something to me. I want to see you get better, and I'd risk everything to protect you. You mean something to me." It sounded so genuine it was frightening. "Sex is immersive and supremely personal to me. My mother taught Izsak and me to respect love. Women. Monday was a lustful desire. Thursday, it meant more to me because I knew more about you."

His face contorted. Whatever sped through his mind was obviously painful. Addison didn't care. Hardened, she continued her ruse.

"There you are then. You just proved the point of my first rule. I would like it to mean more to me when I know more about you."

Her smile was genuine. Addison welcomed confession when she could reveal knowing him enough for it to mean much, much less. She listened to his coming of age in a single-parent household story. Schooling in Reading, a volunteer in the army reserve, and travelling. If any of it were true, Laszlo had led an interesting life. He shared how he missed having a father and added to the Hungarian Internal Affairs detail he'd given when she first met him.

"My dad endured an unpleasant death when they caught him spying in Russia." He teared up, and when Addison didn't move to comfort him, he inhaled and smiled, embarrassed. "Is that enough for at least a first-base kiss?"

Addison crawled across the sofa and straddled him, letting his hands circle around her waist and pull her towards him. "It's a start, but I think we can do better than that." She put her arms behind her back and thrust out her breasts.

Predictably, his hands slid under her top as hers slipped into her back pocket. *If the bastard is lying, and if he has been drugging me, then I'm about to return the favour.*

She popped the cap from the sedative Jennie had prepared. To proceed with her plans, she'd need Laszlo asleep. She leaned forward, bringing her hands to the back of the sofa, and primed him for the strike by stealing another semi-desired kiss. And hating every disgusting moment of it. She traced her lips across his cheek, then down his neck, denying the power of his scent while his hands roamed.

Then, his neck stretched as she ran her tongue along the muscle, exposing the soft tissue she needed.

Laszlo flinched as her nails dug in, disguising the pinprick. The strike was so professional it surprised her.

A minute later, his hands slid off her back, and his lips slackened. He was heavy, unshiftable, and staying on the sofa until Jennie came to help carry him. She sent a message to confirm success, trusting Jennie had retrieved the box from the Jockey, then added a request for a strange stationary order.

While she waited, she lumbered up the stairs with one of the wrought-iron breakfast stools and prepared her place.

~

Cable ties fastened Laszlo's ankles to the stool foot rim and his elbows to the backrest. His wrists were drawn behind and handcuffed. Only for effect, because he likely knew how to escape them. Still, he couldn't get away. Addison had confidence in how secure he was. If he pulled an unexpected stunt, she'd unravel that bloody bandage, a wound she now assumed came from Sting's teeth, grab hold with both hands, and twist his skin— away from her with one hand and towards her with the other. With any luck, he'd pass out from the agony of the friction burn. Wishful thinking perhaps, but the image made her smile.

Keen for him to wake, she grew impatient, tempted to switch on the rainer above his head. Only, he sat on a folder that she didn't want soaked. Instead, she breathed and looked around the bathroom, double-checking her other preparations.

A dressing gown hung curtain-like across three hooks, the perfect size to cover what she'd pinned to the bathroom door. Excitement for its reveal grew, but she would need to wait until Laszlo woke—it had been more than an hour already.

The thumbprint-secure box from the Jockey sat in the large basin with a stylish silver tray on top. On it, looking classy against the dark grey tiles, rested Laszlo's most expensive red wine. A 2011 Romanée-Conti collectors' bottle, breathing beside a tumbler and a shot glass. Opening it had been a diabolical act, but justified considering his deeds. In six days, he had taken more than fine wine from her.

Inside the mirrored cupboard doors were pictures of Sting and Jon, courtesy of Laszlo's high-tech, super-definition printer. When the right time came, she would show them, letting Laszlo know how much she knew. He'd fulfilled the first ground rule. She had learnt everything she needed to know about him, and he'd gone too far for sex to happen again.

On the stool beneath his corrupt butt, sat the folder she did not want to get wet. It contained Laszlo's internet search history, thick with evidence, and hot off-the-press while he slept.

He couldn't lie his way out this time.

His echoing rhythmic breaths slipped into a drawn-in nasal one as he woke.

Addison switched on the versatile lamp from the conservatory, its bulb angled directly at his face with a too-bright light that, no doubt, had also given her sunspots during the vulnerable hypnotherapy sessions. Even more vulnerable when she'd discovered how light distracts the mind. Did he flash it on and off for her? Did he bring the bulb so close to her face that she would feel the heat of it through her eyelids? Were her eyes even closed the whole time?

"What's this?" he asked, groggy and squinting from the light. He tried to lift his arms to shield his eyes.

"This is ground rule number two. Role play, where I get to be in control."

Laszlo half-smiled, probably wondering if she was as serious as she sounded. At the same time, he jiggled the handcuffs and tugged the ties at his elbows to see how firm her control really was.

"I promise to play nice. Look. I brought wine." As she poured some into the tumbler, the wrong glass for the obsessively fussy Laszlo Sándor, it spilled.

He shut his eyes at the tragedy, his lips forming a thin line. "That's a 2011 Burgundy! Twenty grand a bottle!"

"Oops. My bad? Sorry. Oh, well. It's open now." She shrugged, and with a sly smile, swallowed a large mouthful. "It's really good." After dribbling some into the shot glass, she angled it at his reluctant lips. "Go on. You don't want me to drink it all by myself, do you? Never having a sip? You must have wanted a taste from the moment you bought it."

She held his chin and poured it into this mouth while his suspicious eyes bore into hers.

"What's going on, Addie?"

She wanted to yell, *"Don't call me that! You are not my friend!"* Only shouting it would reveal her intentions. Instead, she bit back her anger and unhooked the dressing gown. She placed it on the chair with a clunk. Another piece of protection in the pocket, should the need arise. She replied without a care. "I drew up the chart you wanted."

The elegantly scripted reward scheme taped to the bathroom door had three columns. The second and third were empty, but the first had a comprehensive list of gold-star-worthy topics.

Addison held a zip bag Jennie had brought. "I have stars, too. Lucky you. Are you still excited?"

"I'm alarmed, truth be told. Perhaps a little intimidated."

"Aw. C'mon. Humour me. Don't you trust me?"

Laszlo raised an unconvinced eyebrow. "Not at this present time. But if I'm to play along, shift the light. I can't see my good boy chart."

Ignoring the sarcasm and eager to share its delights, Addison pointed the lamp at the door. "First on the list. Manner. Let's see. How have you struck this week? You've been honest and transparent. Kind. Keen to help. Positive. Charming. Someone confident that I admire. And during the scary times, your calm grounded me."

She peeled off two gold stars and stuck them where she had written 'manner' in flowery script.

"Next. Personality. Well, you have pizazz, and enough mysterious roguishness to make it sexy. You've great style, though a little bland in places going by your décor but, overall, not bad. You're intelligent, but not judgemental, ambitious and daring. I mean, you did offer to have a stranger stay in your house. Affectionate and caring. All through my recovery, you were supportive, always kissing me and making me feel wanted. You're meticulous, even down to the glass you drink from. Which reminds me. I owe you two."

She poured wine into the shot glass and fed it to him. Then she poured more for the second gold star. She swallowed another large and uncouth mouthful herself and raised the tumbler. "For me, it's just a vessel."

"What game are you playing, Addison?"

"Role play. Aren't you listening? You had four hours of my uninterrupted, undivided attention. Now it's my turn. So, to finish, you are devilishly funny and can always make me laugh even when I am loath to."

She placed another two stars on the chart and poured more shots for the good boy. He rolled his chin, not enjoying the childish praise and reward.

"Oh, now. Look. Home Economic skills," she crooned with a beaming smile. "What can I say but kudos to the restaurant-quality food. Sensational. You even made a curry with my favourite meat. Choice wines. An appliance for every need. Impeccably clean. A man who doesn't cut corners, even for emergency four a.m. snack stops. I'd have to admit, it must be a genuine part of you. That sort of commitment isn't fake."

Laszlo frowned at the insinuation, but she smoothed a sticker and moved on before he could argue.

"Leadership skills. I can only say you showed great guidance. You took my confused hand and brought me under your wing, giving decisive and dependable instructions that were flawless. You're persuasive, motivational, and probably morally stable. I'd say that shows great leadership!" She grinned and smoothed another gold star before pouring more wine.

"I don't want a drink. Let's skip to the part where you add up all the stars and tell me what I've scored, and then what I'm allowed to do to you."

Couldn't he allow his ego to consider she'd found him out, or was he faking his calm to test her?

"Patience, honey." She ran her tongue along his bottom lip to confirm his assumption. "There's so much more to come. I promise the rewards will get better." Let him think it was a sex game.

He drank the wine.

"Swimming progress? Uh, I don't know. Uh, do you have any badges?"

Laszlo laughed. "Not since primary school."

"Oh. In that case, sorry." Addison dipped her hand into the zip bag, loosened a thumbs-down-you-failed sticker, and stabbed it to the chart with her finger. "Never mind."

"I can swim, though."

"What's next?" Unable to help herself, she giggled. "Ah, yes. Bedside manner. The art of loving. Well, if only I had a bagful of red-hot stars for this category." She waved her hand. "Because you are hot stuff. How do you know exactly how to excite me? It's as if you can read my body like a street map."

"Come here. Let me show you. It's more fun."

She approached with a scheming twinkle in her eye, rather enjoying the charade. She leaned on the backrest, allowing her top to fall forward and reveal her breasts before she let him kiss her. Seconds later, she pulled away and swigged her drink to avoid vomiting in his mouth.

"Often the persistent and patient make the best lovers," he murmured, then laughed.

"What's so funny?"

"I'm reading the rest of your list."

"Don't jump ahead," she snapped, moving in front of the chart.

"But the next one is 'hunting prowess'. Unless it's about bargain shopping, then it's going to be a thumbs-down. What else do I hunt?"

"Your problem-solving potential is phenomenal, and the prowess you displayed in hunting clothes for me and being a competent size-guesser wins you a star. For always wanting to make me feel comfortable."

He waggled his head in acceptance of the suggestion.

"Undercover lying skills? Ha, have you shown any? I guess you'd be savvy enough! Murdering capabilities? Again, another thumbs-down. You're looking like suitable husband material so far, Laszlo."

"I hoped I'd get there, eventually."

"Ever been close?"

"Once. A long time ago. I was staying at The Babbons in Swindon. Must we have this discussion tied up? It's losing its appeal."

"Yes. Because this is where the game gets really interesting. Manner–"

He groaned.

"Let's see... You lowered a rope ladder for me to escape a burning fire. Then stopped my vulnerable self from venturing out of Marsha's house and into that perilously cold and dreadful night." Her glare pedalled hate-filled, sharp claws that slashed at his face.

With all threads of confidence and security shredded, his concerned eyes sharpened. "In puncto reflexionis," he whispered.

The effort barely brushed her, and she continued without faltering. "Then, you creepily offer a confused woman a bed in your home. I can't believe I fell for the grooming."

She smoothed a thumbs-down sticker onto the third column and pressed the bottle to his lips. She tore his head back and poured as soon as his lips parted to decline it. He choked as wine ran down his neck, staining his shirt. "Now we aren't having glasses."

Twenty-One

22nd April 2023, 00:49– The New

Concentration was impossible, thanks to Laszlo's worried swearing. The constant scraping of plastic as he tugged on the cable ties around his elbows grated like fingernails on a chalkboard. He favoured his right arm more than his left, and both his legs tensed, tugging at the ankle ties, but he couldn't get the traction needed to snap them when his backside slipped on the folder he still hadn't noticed. The trouble he was in became clear in his eyes.

When the opened handcuffs landed with a heavy clink, they startled her, although knowing how to free himself didn't surprise her. The resulting rush of adrenaline fed her anger. She called him out with a shaking voice.

"Your honesty is disgusting. The arrogance and cunning are a turnoff. You're detached, alone, and unsociable. I haven't seen a single visitor except for Izsak. We'll get to him later. If there's time. For now, let's move on to Home Economics and the captivating way you used a four a.m. dinner to impress me. But then it was supposed to, wasn't it?"

"Yes. I wanted to impress you." Laszlo looked confused, but his answer seemed honest enough. "What's wrong with that?"

"Nothing. On its own. When the plan is nefarious, angled at my mental health, there becomes a lot wrong with it. Was the food and drink used to subdue me? Did you drug it?"

"No. Don't be stupid. What do you take me for?"

"How am I to know?" she yelled, her cheeks burning with rage. With the bottle of Burgundy in her hand, she closed in, his furious expression bouncing off her temper. "I only have your word. You took hold of me and led me on a merry dance. That calls for superb leadership skills because Addison New isn't easy to crack. Then again, your sexual tactics when I was at an unfair disadvantage only helped you, and that's an 'uh-uh' worth six bedside manner thumbs-down."

Addison didn't bother with the stickers. She forced-fed him more reward wine, and again spilled more than he drank.

"You didn't show empathy for my feelings at all last week."

"How do you know?" he spluttered. "You make assumptions, but you know nothing!"

"I know you can swim. I saw you jump from the helicopter to hunt me at Horseshoe Lake." She angrily slapped thumbs-down stickers onto the poster. "What would have happened if you'd caught me? Would I be food for tree roots?"

"Don't be ridiculous."

"Pigs then? Then again, your impulse for cleanliness is a bit much to go near pigs. Ha. You're too clean."

Frustrated, Laszlo sighed and lolled his head to peer at his lap. "How can anything be too clean?"

"Jon's kitchen is too clean. Clinically, in fact." Addison shrugged when Laszlo's head snapped up. She slugged another mouthful of wine and then topped up her tumbler, noting the bottle was nearly empty.

Grabbing it, she turned, ready to fill his throat again.

"In puncto reflexionis," he said, loudly. Authoritatively.

The cavern surrounded her immediately, his voice cushioning her like a warm and comfy quilt. A fire burned beside three rows of doors. The red ones on the bottom row looked battered and tatty. The blue doors above them now had keyholes, and the purple memories flowed freely in their correct slots. Cavern walls changed to violet, while Laszlo encouraged her to cut the cable ties now that she'd put down the wine bottle.

The springy armchair jabbed into her body as if she sat on a bed of pins. Sweat trickled down her face. She stood up, doused the fire, and opened her eyes. Vishnu's shield against hypnosis, and her personal training to combat the triggers, meant his words only captured her for a moment.

She breathed, green eyes staring him down. "Your undercover lying skills are excellent. A convincing savoir-faire. The diplomacy to say or do whatever is right for the occasion. Shame, though. You didn't clock this one, did you?" She stuck on a batch of gold star stickers for the con and a thumbs-down for not detecting her deceit. "Problem-solving, hunting prowess, and murder capabilities go together. Don't you think? You come across a problem, find a solution, hunt down that solution, and murder them. And you're so house-trained, you clean up after yourself. Oh, and let's not forget the extra points for putting the toilet seat down."

Affronted, Laszlo pushed his tongue into his soft cheek, and she laughed. Was this how he responded to sarcastic praise? She opened the cupboard doors one at a time to show off the pictures of Sting and Jon.

"I discovered the deeds you've been sitting on and covering up." She reached for his crotch and he flinched, buttocks dragging as she yanked the file from underneath him. "I don't have the stomach to touch you. It's why I haven't castrated you. So, save it." She placed the folder on the vanity top beside his toothbrush. "Thanks for the use of your printer, by the way. Extremely helpful in producing the evidence I need. But actually, I've changed my mind. Let's do this first."

"What you playing at?" he growled.

Ignoring him, she moved the silver tray and opened the thumbprint-secure metal box. "I must say, I'm in awe of the company you keep. You have friends in high places! Respect."

"I don't have many friends."

"I wonder why."

"By choice."

"Theirs, by any chance?"

With an impatient sigh, he shook his head. "Will you get to the point of all this?"

"I will. First, I want to discuss your friends. Did you know they create secret soldiers and fund human trafficking? They make poor families super-rich by buying their children. Then they expect those children to pay off the debt. Slavery of all kinds. Usually, at once. You get me, don't you? They're somewhat broken and institutionalised by the time they've bought their freedom. By then, they're too used and can't work anymore."

"That's disgusting and untrue."

"But it is true. Shikari has the proof. You must've heard of us."

Wide eyes met hers. "Us?"

Addison laughed as more of Addison New revealed herself. "Oh, yes. You picked an upper-level member of the resistance to draw into your lair. If only you knew who you had in your clutch. Would I still be free? Alive?"

"Who do you think I am?" Laszlo yelled. He tugged the cable ties, a muscle twitching at the angle of his jaw. Fear flashed in his eyes. "In puncto reflexionis."

"Haven't you worked it out yet, Laszlo? It doesn't work anymore. The thought of your voice nauseates me. Your touch crawls with maggots, and your smell is like my dog's farts. My paradigm chamber doesn't belong to you. It's mine. And my rules."

She glugged another mouthful of wine. The memory of Sting smarted with shards of bitterness dragging down her throat. Pictures of perfect love battling with the acid in her stomach. Even the pulse in Laszlo's tense neck didn't ruin her flow.

"What would your mother say? Is she proud? Do you even know what love is to treat me like that?"

"I've already answered—"

"You said you fell for a woman at a hotel. What happened? Did she discover you were a fake, too?"

Laszlo's eyebrows puckered. "Fake?"

"Tell me about the woman at the hotel."

"Why? There's not much to say. A whirlwind week with a lady I would have married. But I had to leave. She couldn't come and she didn't wait."

"Is this a New memory, or one from our lives before?"

His lips parted with a clop.

She reached for the dressing gown hung over the back of the chair and pulled out the revolver Jennie had given her. Addison Real had never held a gun. Addison New seemed to know how to release the safety clip.

"Were you jealous that I spent the night with another man before I met you? Is that why you stole him and killed my dog? Or is it still about you covering up what all of you have done?"

"What the hell are you talking about? Why have you got that?"

"Let's rewind to your conversation with Izsak. You didn't know I heard it all, did you? Fancy killing a man for committing a crime in the past, one that doesn't actually exist anymore! Your brother couldn't get his head around it, could he? But I did."

"I think you may have misunderstood—"

"Please don't insult me. Admit you killed my brother, admit you've lived two pasts, admit you remember it, unlike most of the rest of the world, and then admit you're covering it up!"

Addison placed the gun in her waistband and gazed wistfully at the picture of Sting. A tear rolled down her cheek and dripped off her chin. She kept her back to the murdering scumbag while he thought about his response.

Sighing heavily, he replied, "I lied because it's easier to believe the narrative than for you to be confused about the truth. It's easier to accept one line of truth than muddle through two pasts like you had to. I expected Soothsayer Shikari to mention and even battle the conspiracy about mandala dementia, but you didn't know about it. I was, am, trying to keep you out of hospital and prison."

She rolled her eyes. "Yeah, yeah."

"Addie, you don't realise the trouble this has brought you."

"Stop calling me that! You are *not* my friend! I don't need you to worry about me. Cover your own ass. It's what you're good at. Tell me how to undo it. How did you go back? Because a time machine is so cliché."

"Not a time machine, exactly. They're called turning points which technically manipulate time, but not in the way you think. It's more like we slipped into a reality behind ours."

"Twenty-five years behind?"

"Yes. Robert Naise couldn't stay dead, and I was forced to help reverse it."

"With Jarvis, Coleman and my boss?" Laszlo frowned again. With an impatient sigh, she opened the folder, throwing pages at him while she spoke. "An email. Another email." She turned to the metal box.

"Evidence of what I've just told you, along with weapons dealing with a Michael Butler, aka Mario Spinzer. The baby you kidnapped on the day you killed my brother!" She pulled out the revolver and prodded his temple as she emptied the box over his head with a heart-shuddering, "Then, my dog."

"Jarvis made Ross Barnes my handler. I like it less than you do. Do you think I've enjoyed this? Being their call-girl for whatever they want? I made the best of being used by using them right back."

"They kept a good eye on Butler for you and shared in his dealings in Europe. Expensive, billion-dollar deals. The transactions aren't even in pounds sterling."

"What deals?"

"War weapons, Laszlo. Bombs and heavy artillery. That kind of thing. You left a bookmark comment on your browser. 'Butler is still an arse. In any reality, even living two completely different lives, Mario is still a knob.' Your words."

"More so now. He called me asking for my services to assassinate Robert Naise again."

Wait. What?

"Again? Did you do it the first time?"

He flicked his eyes away and nodded. "I'm sorry. If only I could go back and undo it. I would use the knowledge to the world's advantage."

"Guess what? I can."

"Maybe in two years, when Convolve fully understands the turning points."

"Convolve…pfft. In Greek, it means turning point as well."

Laszlo looked surprised, and she used this to specify another interrogation highlight.

"Where are Vishnu and Jon?"

Addison hoped it would distract and stump him, but instead, he sniggered. "I was right, then. Vishnu Patel is ready. I considered using him when I realised what he was building, but couldn't face *another* twenty-five years if it went wrong. I'm technically already seventy."

Addison blinked, stunned, needing a moment to swing her focus back to the point. "Did you kill them?"

"No."

"Then where did you take them?"

Silence.

"Okay. Why did you take them?"

"Mostly to protect you, Soothsayer Shikari. Barnes wants information. Sometimes I save it for when it suits me. Sometimes, I use it to distract him from pushing orders I might not want to honour. So, I used your friends as a distraction. Did you know there are dubious records under your avatar name? You're right. If only they knew who was right under their noses. Soothsayer Shikari made the secret service wanted list via a request from Jarvis and Naise."

"Are you trying deflections on me now?"

"What would be the point?"

"A for effort. But let me tell you how it is. You tell me where they are and make this easier all round. I promise that when I return to my proper life, I won't hunt you down and shoot you in the face. Dammit!" Addison stabbed the gun into the soft part of his cheek, breath ragged and willing to go as far as she needed to get what she wanted. She was angry enough.

"An outbuilding on the way to Burford," he mumbled. "My car's satnav history will take us."

"Us?" Her eyes widened as she turned to view her beautiful Sting's face. From the corner of her eye, she noticed his shoulders slump.

"Then do it, but first, let me share something. There is no going back once you kill. It changes nothing for good and the voice of conscience is never silent. So, if you're going to…shoot me, do it, and be prepared for the consequences. Then go. Here, I have nothing but a brother who hates me. There, no brother, but at least I had Lorrie."

"Where did you take Sting?" she whispered shakily, battling the tears stinging her eyes. Then, with spit peppering her lips and grief salting the words, she hissed, "Why did you kill him?"

"Because he attacked me and almost chewed my arm off!" he yelled. Compassion twisted in his expression. "I didn't know he was there—I wasn't prepared. I would have…"

"What? Prepared what instead?" She bent over to look him in the face.

"There are other ways."

"Like what? Poisoned meat?"

His eyes twitched, adding to his fearful gulp. "Fresh meat. A taser. Drugs."

Treacherous tears ran down her face. She grabbed his arms, gripping harder on the right. He jolted at her touch, and his yell of pain gave her respite. "Where did you take him?"

"To the crematorium incinerator."

She remembered the heat of the flames rushing up her chimney, and her temper blazed as bright. "You burnt him?"

Laszlo closed his eyes, his neck muscles taut. "Yes."

"Aren't you glad I made you drink the wine? Because it's your last."

The trigger spring strummed as she fired the revolver.

Twenty-Two

22nd April 2023, 03:18 – The New

Murder. That's what it was. The simple, stark truth. As Addison approached the parked car at the end of the street, her conscience ran riot. Taunted. Jennie started the engine before Addison climbed in. She grabbed Jennie's arm to stop her from pulling off and shook her head rather than disturb the on-speaker call with the head of Shikari, Mr D. He spouted worried theories about the politicians and what they might know since they'd caught Vishnu.

Jennie wasn't so polite and talked over him. "What? Isn't it done?"

"Isn't what done?" Mr D asked. "Is she back? Addie?"

"Hi, Derek. Yeah, it's done. They're being held somewhere on the Burford road. To know exactly, we'll need to take the Audi." Addison jiggled the keys and faked her smile, not feeling as jubilant as she'd expected. The memory of finding his car keys haunted her. Fondling a dead man's pockets would have been hard enough, but Laszlo's were torture. While her fingers searched, she had flashbacks of undoing his belt as she lay on his pistachio-green sheets. When his head lolled forward and blood trickled from his temple, tea tree shampoo wafted—taking her back to him reaching for the pasta maker. There, her tears froze. She'd done what she had to do. Only the image of him tossing Sting's carcass into an incinerator could dampen the repulsing fact that she had pulled the trigger.

With ears still ringing from the gunshot, she tuned in more attentively to Mr D…or Derek, as she now knew him. The life of Addison New revealed itself more and more. Derek's name had fallen off her tongue as if she'd always known it.

"I'll update Travis. They'll follow you. They're in the van around the corner."

Jennie unbuckled her seatbelt, but Derek continued.

"Listen, I can't physically help you, but please, make it work. Because being here from the age of seventeen, without my sweetheart from primary school, is unbearable. One morning, Celia didn't know me. When I kissed her, she smacked me in the mouth and reported me. I ended up with a criminal record. Nobody believed me, even after many suicide attempts. So, please. Get Vishnu and sort it. Right?"

Addison's heart filled with compassion. Derek had suffered these feelings for twenty-five years. How many others carried a similar heartache? Humbled, she was glad not to have endured the turning-point consequences for as long as them, but it didn't lessen her mourning.

Nor did it help to remember some of Addison New's past and how tragedy had choked her childhood. How she found it hard to trust people after her parents parted. It happened the day the garden centre delivered the Jockey to Mr Cotter. Addison New ran home, excited to surprise her father and ask for his help putting it together, desperate to spend time with him. Instead, he'd already packed a bag and left, leaving her mother to weep in her bedroom again. The constant crying had been the catalyst for Addison ordering the shed. She'd needed somewhere to escape the sadness, somewhere to magnetise a little joy to her heart, but solitude only hardened it.

"I will sort it, Derek. It needs to end. Soon. Because every time I black out, I forget something. I want Mason and Sting back, and your version of Addison wants Jon, even though she always said no to him. So, let's fetch them, and do it for her too."

~

The Audi and van pulled off the A361 at Broughton Poggs. They followed Laszlo's satnav across a field towards premises that looked more like a disguised business than an outbuilding. The shutters were closed and security lights blazed from the rear. They parked behind a patch of trees, moonlight dappling the ground.

Derek's right-hand man, Travis, forty-something and greying around the edges, knocked on the car window, and Jennie opened the door. "I've sent the coordinates. We wait."

Addison grimaced. "How long?"

"Until we've an idea of what we're dealing with," he replied. "The layout of the premises. What the dangers are. Not being funny, you should know this."

"I do. I'm just impatient. They could be doing anything to them. They might already be dead. I need to know."

"Derek's on it now. He'll only be a few minutes."

It seemed like a decade before Travis summarised the details of Derek's email. "It's listed as an outbuilding, except it's an illegal chop-shop. They'll have machinery, welding equipment, and nasty, harmful tools to use as weapons. Be vigilant."

Travis and his two teammates chambered a bullet, as did Jennie. Addison left her gun in the car. She had killed enough today. It already suffocated her thoughts. She didn't want to add more faces to her guilt. Recent ones, anyway. She closed her eyes on the dead strangers flooding her memories. Were they Addison New's victims? This version of her was fast infiltrating her psyche.

Jennie tapped her shoulder, and they followed Travis through the trees, strategically approaching the back from the north. Silent. Professional. Focused. No one knew how many enemies were inside, or how skilled they were, and no one wanted them alerted.

A silver BMW parked at the rear entrance had a familiar registration plate. Although aware of Barnes's involvement, it shocked Addison to see his car there. She pointed to the tyres and nodded at Travis, her grin widening when he loosened his knife and stabbed every one of them. As he stood, he hooked his fingers under the boot lid. It wasn't completely closed.

Addison put her hand to her mouth, holding back a scream and swallowing the bile in her throat. The woman folded inside, wearing a lime green dress, was unmistakably Marsha. Her shiny eyes were staring and she had a strange smile, but her neck didn't sit right on her shoulders.

All Addison could picture were the two motherless children, but then the taunts began. Her stupid mouth was to blame. She shouldn't have confided in Marsha or gone to her house and revealed things about a daughter she didn't have. That reminder took her to the note left at the shop. Didn't Marsha say she had news? Had she finally believed her and discovered something worth a broken neck? Broken by Barnes? It had to be. Marsha was dead in the boot of his car.

His motive had to be Addison. If only she had known, like Addison New.

Anguished, she turned away, letting the self-condemning guilt follow as they crept into the chop-shop. The team paused in the corridor connecting the workshop to the utility rooms. Muffled voices floated from the office. Haunting screams came from the shop floor. Addison recognised Ross Barnes' deep voice and signalled right. Travis directed his friends to the screamer while pointing at his eyes, a cautious reminder to stay alert.

Addison's heart thumped at the enormity of the mission. Playing with politicians meant playing with fire, as Marsha had discovered.

Bosses, however, were thumpable.

With Jennie and Travis beside her, she approached the voice droning behind a closed door.

"You know something, community spokesperson," Barnes teased. "Shall we have another go? Attack a few more ribs?"

A brief scuffle developed. Then Jon yelled out in frustration. "I told you. Addie was confused. She said things that are physically impossible and then took off. I don't believe the police or medical reports, or her so-called retreat from society to get well. Because I know she'd want to speak to me. She'd want an update on Sting. She would definitely want one now."

"That was a shame. I hoped to run some tests on him." Barnes sighed. "Still, plenty of other dogs. Canine neurology and biochemistry are probably much the same, and their senses are remarkable."

Veterinary tests might explain why dogs barked when nothing appeared to be there and why Sting remembered Mason. Did they have a sixth sense? Sting's behaviour certainly suggested so.

She swallowed a wave of grief and opened the door, scanning the room for her former boss. Jon captured her immediate attention. They'd tied him to a chair and his face and chest were bruised, his lip and nose bleeding. The sight cracked her heart. He was alive. A small mercy.

Clocking their entry, the men on either side of Jon sprang into action. Addison left them for Jennie and

Travis. She marched up to Barnes and snapped his stunned mouth shut with a swift jab. He banged his shoulder on the table as he fell. A silver metal suitcase toppled and landed with a thud. It almost disguised the shot fired from the shopfloor where Vishnu had stopped screaming.

Barnes stumbled to his feet, holding one of his teeth.

"Eye for an eye. Tooth for a tooth." She pulled Sting's from her pocket and showed it. "What do you get for single-parent killings?"

A red mist covered the image of Marsha's pleased, dead face. Addison punched Barnes again, this time with her other fist, hoping to knock out a matching pair. It caught his right temple.

Fury kept the punches coming. Barnes stood in the way of her going home, and the longer she stayed, the more blackouts she'd have—each one cementing her deeper with Addison New and causing her to forget life in The Real.

That was *their* fault. Them and their stupid resurrection games. She harnessed the hate and rage, yelling, "Why is Marsha dead in the boot of your car?"

Barnes cringed on the floor, his ego shattered.

Travis hurled one of the minions over the desk. He landed in an awkward, twisted heap. The other minion cowered in the corner under Jennie's loaded Glock.

Barnes stayed down, stuttering an incoherent answer.

"What was that? I couldn't hear you over your wobbly teeth."

Jennie sniggered.

Barnes didn't reply.

When it became clear he wouldn't explain, Addison closed in, bristling with resolve. "I'm going back to undo this. And guess what? It'll be my turn to know everything." She stabbed her finger towards his face. "And you won't have a clue that I know anything at all."

He paled, his lips parting. He looked vampiric as blood trickled from the corner of his mouth.

With the threats neutralised, Addison turned to a shocked Jon. As she sliced through his ropes to free him, she blurted, "I'm sorry I didn't trust you. I should never have let this happen to you."

"They killed Sting."

"I know." A tear fell. "It's not your fault. I'll make it right."

Free now, Jon grabbed her shoulder and spun her around. "I knew there was a reason I wanted you. I'm not even going to ask."

Strong hands held her and his bristly face neared, eyes begging for more than permission. Then, his rough lips pressed hers with a passion-driven kiss. Her heart leapt. Confusingly, she liked it.

Addison New liked it. A long-awaited moment of sentiment and relief built inside her.

Jennie pulled them apart. "Save it for later," she moaned as a sallow, bleeding Vishnu appeared at the door hanging on the shoulders of his comrades. He was missing a finger, and a spatter of bloody wounds stained his grey t-shirt.

"Van keys! Now!" Jennie caught them when they arched through the air. She turned to Vishnu. "Looks like we're going to the hospital."

"You, too." Addison pushed Jon towards the door. Without argument, he followed them out, holding his ribs.

Only Travis stayed as Addison's support. He guarded Jennie's minion on the floor in the corner. Barnes had snuck around the desk, trying to wake the other one by tapping his foot. It was pointless.

"You duped me. Dr Collins was very persuasive. You burn down my house, chase me, hound my brain into believing your diagnosis, and take away my life! Then you killed my dog!"

"I didn't do that," he rounded the desk to face her.

"Yes, you did. Just as Mayor Naise and Jarvis did. Just as much as Laszlo did."

She lifted her arm and blocked his surprise punch before she registered it. She intercepted two more and retaliated, smacking him on the nose. "You used me for an experiment as much as he did."

"I did not," he snarled, grabbing tissues to soak up his nosebleed. "And as it turns out, neither did he." He spat out a mouthful of blood with a frustrated growl. "Laszlo likes you. For the record, he prevented us from taking you out, because you still being alive wasn't our intention."

"Why? Because I woke up one day and thought Palowa was green?"

"I think you know it's more than that."

"What? Like Soothsayer Shikari?"

He stopped tending to his bloody nose and looked up.

"Nice to meet you," she said with a smug smile.

He laughed, mumbling a disbelieving, "All this time," under his breath.

His lack of shock irked her. "You're nothing but a pimp."

Barnes laughed again. "Saved your life, though, didn't it?"

"What a shame Marsha didn't have her own schmoozy sleazebag to save hers. Oh, I forgot. She did. *She had you.* So, tell me. Why is she dead in the boot of your car?"

"Because you aren't! And you told her about a daughter she doesn't have. I had to shag that ass until she admitted she believed you. So, what you and Laszlo get up to is between you two. I made it quick. She didn't know it was coming. And for your sake, I hope Laszlo is still around because you're gonna need him. They'll come for you, and they won't make it quick."

"Laszlo is dead. Did it myself."

His eyes widened, and he whistled. "You killed a narcissistic assassin? Respect. Then I offer my condolences, because it makes you easy prey. You're next."

His head jolted with the crack of gunfire, and she sucked in a startled breath as he crumpled to the floor.

"No, she isn't." Travis returned his aim to the minion tied up in the corner. "Aren't you the lucky one to survive? Chair. Now."

The man took Jon's place, relieved to be restrained and not killed.

Fighting the urge to vomit, she looked away from her boss's empty eyes. Another face to add to Addison New's pictures book of victims. Violence didn't dampen *her* sentiments, but her ambidextrous fighting skills surprised Addison Real.

Travis dragged her away. They followed the sporadic blood trail to where the van was speeding off. Jennie ran back to the car when she saw them coming.

"Get in! C'mon!" She popped the boot for the silver case Travis carried.

Addison glanced at Barnes's car as she passed. Whoever arrived for illegal work first would find Marsha and the others. She mumbled an apology and climbed in beside Jennie. "Did you take photos of Marsha?"

Jennie secured her seat belt. "I have everything. Is Barnes ready for the police?"

"Does 'everything' include Naise and Jarvis and the other crimes they should pay the price for?"

"Everything. And when we release what we have, the evidence will be open to the public. They'll find them guilty and demand justice. Even if the politicians hide this murder to protect Barnes, they can't cover up a media explosion."

Addison laughed. "Yes, they can. They did."

Travis grunted from the backseat. "Barnes is dead. He threatened Addie and made it personal, but she's still a target. Release the info now. Give the politicians something other than her to focus on while we fix up Vishnu and end all of this."

"If I'm a target, is it wise I go with you? Vishnu, too. What if we're recognised? Which hospital are we going to?"

"The nearest Shikari one," replied Travis. "Salisbury. We can hide that we were ever there if we have to. You should know this."

"I know. Glad that I don't though. I don't like it here. No offence, it's been horrible."

Jennie smiled and nudged her arm. "Jon doesn't think so."

"Jon loves her. She loves him. Me? I get bits of her, flashes of him in a memory that shouldn't be there. Along with her grief mingled in with my own."

For Mason. Sting. Marsha.

For Laszlo.

Twenty-Three

22nd April 2023, 15:15 – The New

Excited chatter about the documents they leaked to the press filled Derek's lounge. Jennie leaned on the shelves under the window, shuffling the papers for the next titbit to share. At the flimsy table in the corner, Travis counted the money inside the silver briefcase. Was it Laszlo's pay or a bribe to silence Jon? The conversation halted when Jon entered. The bulbous radiators creaked as they warmed. It broke an awkward hush. Derek left. Travis and Jenny continued their tasks in silence.

Back from Salisbury just an hour ago, Jon's delectable glances had been as exciting as they were discarded. It was hard to separate the feelings circulating inside his purple door. Those that were Addison's, and those that were Addison New's. Addison Real didn't know Jon, nor was she in love with him.

She shouldn't be in love with Laszlo. But she was.

Addison sighed, her heart grieving for the man who killed her brother and her dog. Grieving for his kiss and the effortless touch she found so damn satisfying.

Somewhere underneath the Laszlo spell were flickers of burning desire and memories of the same gaze Jon held now. The one where the rugged Jon was in the shop and not Arnold, with his date wine and breakfast milk, leaning forward wafting an intoxicating musky smell as he said, "But you're the only one I ask out."

At least now she knew Shikari was the reason Addison New always said no to him.

She glanced over at Jon wincing as he rose from the brown leather sofa. Standing must be more comfortable than sitting.

"So, Vinny Jones. What's a man like you doing behind the counter of a country shop?"

He held his bruised ribs and laughed. "Maybe, if you'll have dinner with me, I'll tell you."

"Dinner it is."

He looked away, tongue poking his cheek. "Better make it quick, because when Vishnu returns tomorrow, you'll be gone."

"I will. She won't." Addison rose and glanced at Jennie. "Will she?"

Jennie pursed her lips. "In theory, reality will return to how it should be. What it should have been before we turned. Shikari might not have a reason to exist. Who knows? For you, the world will be as you remember, six weeks before the turning point, and there will be two versions of you for those six weeks. You and Addison Original. Two, right up until you reach the day we all turned. Then…" She sighed. "Things will go back to how they should be."

What wasn't she saying? Addison stared at the grains in the wooden floor.

Gentle fingers held her chin and Jon looked tearfully into her eyes. "Exactly. You…she…will go back to saying no. I'll go back to wondering why, as you did once." His thumb rubbed her lip. "Now that I've got my head around you only knowing me for two weeks, and me knowing another Addison for three years, tell me how you feel about me."

Stumped, she revisited Jon's purple door, and again separated the true from the new, coming to the stand-off last Saturday.

"I don't know. But, since meeting you, you've been kind, respectful, and assertive." Addison smiled. "Who knows what I would feel, had you kissed me in your hallway last week."

Instead, Addison felt torn between two no-hopes, because when she returned, she'd have neither. Laszlo would be alive, but without a clue of who she was. Strangers, like she and Jon, wherever he might be...used to be? Besides, there would be two Addisons for six weeks and then only one. It wouldn't be the original fading into non-existence, but the version she had become now. And Addison Original didn't know either man.

"Where did you live before Lechlade? Because in my world, Arnold still owns the shop."

"Dinner. And then I'll tell you. But promise me something. When you go home, look me up. At least I can think one of me is happy with one of you."

With her heart in a flurry, Addison nodded, hoping that her eyes hid her uncertainty. Addison Real liked him, but she didn't know him well enough to decide if she wanted to hook up with him. Addison New did, and she loved him. Would Addison Original?

Despite her own feelings, if Addison Real could choose the man for her original self, she'd choose the safer Jon.

He interlaced his fingers with hers. "Do I have to ask this time?"

Her mind tugged in turmoil. *Yes. No. I don't know.*

It was only one kiss. What harm could it do? Much less than another rejection. As long as it didn't make things harder for him.

Still uncertain, but afraid to hurt his feelings, Addison shook her head. It was just a kiss. She could do that for him. She could also let Addison New lead while she hid away and licked her guilty wounds.

Jon didn't hesitate. Soft and unrushed lips met hers, tongue sweeping like a delicate petal as his fingers brushed her sleeve on the way to her cheek. Its touch ignited a desire-fuelling spell, feeding Addison New. The see-sawing emotions tugged between Real and New, and Laszlo and Jon.

"Will you two remember where you are? I feel like I should leave the room."

Addison blushed, suddenly realising Jennie was there, along with Travis and his expectant smile and raised eyebrow.

Jennie laughed and flicked her fingers. "Go have dinner or something."

~

Dinner was a takeaway pizza alone in Derek's dining room with the dimmer switch low. A date-setting Addison didn't mind. She didn't want to run or think about Laszlo and compare the two of them. Having Addison New lingering in her mind made it easier, and she gave Jon the respect he deserved, dining with him as if she'd never stayed at Laszlo's house. As if she had never met him.

Addison took another slice of pizza from the box on the table. "So, come on. Whatever your reasons are, they aren't the same where I come from. I won't be carrying your secrets."

Jon finished chewing his mouthful and swallowed. "Recently, I vividly relived it. I thought Laszlo was one of them."

"Who?"

Jon washed the pizza down with a glass of Coke. Between burps, he explained. "My name is Jackson Lowe. I used to work prestige private security. Minding celebrities, dignitaries and the odd politician visiting the National Space Academy, and the VIP door at Leicester FC. Occasionally, the club paid for the players to have a night out, and five years ago, on one of those nights, I witnessed a murder."

Addison mouthed an O, half-chewed pizza balled up in the corner of her mouth.

"I knew who the people were on both sides—all dangerous people. And if I'm honest, I didn't want the drama, so I walked away, unseen. But not cleanly. Forensics found my DNA on a cigarette butt at the scene. It placed me there. The police arrested me and tried to pin the crime on me, suggesting that, because of my career, I had the skills to carry it out. I had little choice but to tell the truth, despite knowing the murderer's capabilities. It put me in emergency witness protection for two years, segregated from everyone but the cops assigned to protect me. Then, after the court case, I moved to Lechlade as Jon Wells."

Stunned, Addison couldn't form a reply right away. Of all the explanations, she didn't expect that. Was he even supposed to be telling her?

"No," he replied when she asked. "But you returning with the name Jon Wells won't take you to me. Word of advice, though." He laughed. "Don't mention we've met in the turning point."

"I don't know what to say. It must have been horrible."

"Horrible isn't close. It's why I was off with you when you turned up soaking wet and bringing drama to my door. Then, when Barnes had me, I thought that drama was the reason they'd found me. I didn't expect to get out of the flat, to be honest."

"I felt the same escaping the fire."

His hand cupped hers. "I should have believed you. Sorry."

"It's a unique situation."

"Yes, but shifting identities overnight isn't easy, and you had signs like me when I first started out as Vinny Jones, running a local country shop."

"Why a country shop?"

He grinned like a proud cat. "For my mum, at first. She grew up in one on the outskirts of Leicester. Recession hit. They eventually lost the family business in 1974, eight years before I was born. She told me she never knew what to do with herself. She expected to run the shop that would be hers one day. To give to me one day. It broke her heart. You know, it's sad to admit, but I'm glad she isn't alive. Died young, agreed, but she wouldn't have coped with me leaving."

"The shop is in her memory?"

"I guess it was always in the back of my mind, even before she died. But I was young and wanted a nightclub within walking distance."

"Will you still be in Leicester?"

Nursing his sore ribs, he laughed and leaned in. "Why? Are you falling for me and worried I'll be gone?"

In an odd way, he was right. A smile grew while his eyes sucked her into their mesmerising sparkle. Another burning kiss spread over her lips, hatching a tingle at the base of her spine.

Just a kiss. One goodbye kiss.

A kiss that lingered while they finished dinner. Lingered in the lounge with Jennie, Derek and Travis. Lingered while she showered and dressed in Jennie's clothes. It was a goodbye kiss that grew roots, and separating the true from the new as she lay across the bed in Derek's spare room became impossible.

One thing was true. Addison was a murderer. Filled with guilt and shame, she shied away while the harder Addison New took the reins. She turned the guilt into justice, vengeance into fair game, and her rotten walls of shame whitewashed clean. It drew a thirst that finishing her water did not quench. She opened the guest-room door to fetch another, only to find Jon hovering on the landing.

"Oh, I was just..." they said together. He pointed to another bedroom while she held up an empty glass.

Embarrassed, he cleared his throat. "I'll fetch you one." He was no doubt keen to escape the awkward moment.

Addison stood by the window, staring out over Cheltenham, lights glowing like a blanket under the horizon's chin. It looked like a professional stock photo. She wasn't familiar with the city, but could easily spot a lit church spire in the distance.

Jon nestled behind her and rested his forehead on her shoulder.

"I don't want you to go. I finally have you in my arms and you're leaving." He buried his face in her neck and inhaled. She could feel the ache in his words, in each atom sucked in through his nostrils, and in the needy breath now rushing over her goose-pimpled skin when he groaned.

It was hard not to react. It was hard to separate her purple door feelings that were smearing into one colossal mess. She spun around, catching the inviting desire in his eye. Jon's hungry kiss melted the constraints and discipline that Addison New had put into place, defences dissolving around the ruins of a gutted heart, one that Addison Real didn't have and couldn't comprehend. As she slid onto the windowsill, craving him as if he bound her with shackles of addiction, she submitted to his assiduous lips peppering her throat.

Addison New didn't let Laszlo enter her mind.

~

Sun streamed through the open curtains at half-five. It bounced off the mirror and lit the room with an unwelcome intrusion. Addison Real turned her head to avoid the light and cling to sleep. Jon lay behind her with an arm lolled across her waist. Initially, his proximity was a comfort. She smiled, remembering the slow-burning intercourse they'd shared. Jon's ribs were too sore for anything more athletic, but then, there'd been no need. Addison New had thought it perfect, just as it was.

She'd never woken with Laszlo beside her. The thought provoked awkward feelings. Bad enough to be in bed with a second man in so many days. Thinking of the other while she was, made it worse.

Addison got up, beset with the interlaced feelings of her two sides and their two men. All sizzled in her gut in different ways for different reasons, while Addison New's memories shone brighter than her own.

The familiar head-stabbing, stomach-churning, shifting ground feeling struck her at the door. This time it distorted her vision with the zig-zag aura blur of a retinal migraine. She grabbed the wobbling wardrobe, patted the air until she felt the mattress, and eased herself back into bed. The pictures of Jon behind her eyes brought more than memories. They confirmed Addison New's dreams and fantasies. She saw her regretting the times she'd declined Jon's advances, how hard the last few had been, and how afraid she'd been of relenting. She knew the instant he kissed her, she would be all his.

If only Jon had kissed *that* Addison and not this one.

She remembered being at work, sitting on those awful yellow chairs, feeling alone and unable to confide her feelings for Jon to anyone, or share the undercover, world-discovering major political cover up that spanned twenty-five years.

"Addison!"

The blue door memories that were drilling out their spaces evaporated.

"Can you hear me?"

Yes, but I can't speak right now.
"Addison?"

"I'm okay," she eventually stuttered, focusing on an engine chugging in the street. It drove off as a door slammed and a holler boomed from downstairs. A minute later, a hurried knock bumped the bedroom door before it flew open. Vishnu staggered in, looking like he'd just climbed from his grave.

"Good to know you've had a pleasant night." He nodded at their semi-nakedness. "Get dressed. Time is of the essence."

"More than you think. Addie fell into a trance or something."

Hand bandaged and in obvious pain, Vishnu limped to the bed. While he held her wrist, he checked her eyes. "Coherent?"

"Yes," they replied together.

"What have you forgotten?"

Addison frowned. Her thoughts were like tangled spaghetti. "I don't know."

"Get dressed. Fast as you can."

At the top of the stairs, Vishnu yelled for everyone to wake up. Soon, creaks came from the bedrooms. Despite rushing, Addison was the last to appear in the kitchen and feel the extent of Vishnu's anger.

"She needs to leave. Now. She should have gone yesterday. Instead, she had another blackout. You shouldn't have left me. I called a taxi the instant I woke." Vishnu slapped a receipt on the table. "This is my expense claim."

Jennie and Derek defended their reasons for leaving him while he unpacked medical supplies. He placed a bag of clear liquid and a few items in packets on the kitchen table. Addison was too weary to care what they were and gratefully received the coffee Travis gave her as she sat on a wooden chair.

Vishnu tugged on a latex glove and came towards her. "There isn't much I can do. If infused quickly, iron sucrose might help take the stab out of the latest attack. Do you remember Mason?"

Mason was linked to a car accident, which led to many other links, one of which was Laszlo. That, plus Sting and the Jockey, took her to a dusty, scratched red door. Childhood memories of a boy growing up waited behind it.

"Yes."

"Good." Vishnu's nimble fingers stole her coffee and handed it to Travis. "Put it in a takeaway cup," he instructed while rolling up Addison's sleeve. "As soon as the cannula is in, we're leaving."

~

Vishnu's lab, frigid, stark, and filled with an eerie blue light from the computer screens, made Addison shiver. As soon as the mechanics and electronics of the booth-cruise were ready, Vishnu invited her to stand inside the cylindrical vessel. She brushed her fingers over the cold, white metal as she stepped in, another shiver rippling through her. A screen flickered on the right, illuminating a window in the open door, and a large, white, egg-shaped bulb above her head that shone like a precious stone.

He handed her several items. "Cash, key to your house, a copy of your driving licence and the memory list we got off your cloud. This, too." He pushed a memory stick into her hand. "Evidence of what you know from here. Sneak home and get some of your own clothes. Things you won't miss. Make sure you don't meet yourself. It isn't worth the drama. And I mean it. In six weeks, the time will be yours again. Well, hers."

"Why won't I inhabit my own body there? I don't understand."

"You aren't her. Your biochemistry has adjusted to the New. It won't match the original Addison's. You can't occupy her. Besides, who says we inhabit ourselves? It's a common consensus. If I went back to 1683, would there be a me to occupy?" Vishnu laid a hand on her shoulder. "You will go. For a little while, at least. Long enough to put an end to it."

"But the turning point…"

"…combined two realities and made one. Don't you see? You remember and live both. Like me. The rest of the world lives the combination without knowing it."

"So why didn't I come the same way as you?"

"Your ferritin levels kept your memories safe. As for hitchhiking? You're the first one I've met, and we've no time for you to become my guinea pig. You need to leave. Remember what I said. Don't encroach on Addison Original. Just do what you need to do to make sure she has a future to stay in."

"Okay."

"Feel alright?"

Addison sighed. "For the millionth time!"

"You're a bit tetchy. You sure you had sex last night?"

Shocked, she laughed.

Vishnu kissed her cheek. "Farewell, Addie."

He shut the door, and a millisecond flash of the egg-shaped bulb wrenched her from the ground to journey six weeks back in time.

Twenty-Four

26th February 2023, 10:15 – The Real

The delicate spray of her best *Yves Saint Laurent* perfume mingled with the fresh-linen aroma of Addison's bathroom was instantly familiar. It told her she wasn't standing in Faringdon anymore. She opened her eyes, uncertain which reality she would find.

Unsure of the time and who might be in the house, Addison crept onto the landing. The digital clock glowed 10:15 through the open bedroom door. She whistled for Sting. If he came running, it meant Mason hadn't been to collect him. Ergo, nothing had changed, and Mason was still dead.

Sting didn't come. His lead wasn't hanging by the door. The emptied dishwasher contained a rinsed plate and dirty cutlery. Mason had been.

Containing her excitement, she moved into the lounge, checking her mental list. The photo frames and pictures were correct, and the tall plant stood where it should instead of a fancy mirror.

Addison laughed, relieved to be home and glad it was late February. She flew upstairs to hunt for clothes she wouldn't miss and stubbed her toe on an old laptop in the bottom of her wardrobe. It lagged, but worked, and it would serve a purpose for now. She stuffed it into her bag and hunted out a utility bill. Hiring a car was a priority. Her next task meant a trip around the country looking for Laszlo and Jon/Jackson. And then stopping Laszlo and his friends from bringing global doom.

Downstairs, she found the faster laptop, opened it on the dining table, and began her hunt for Laszlo Sándor—starting with a Palowa credit check.

~

Slipping out after lunch without being seen was easy on Sundays. Addison Original would be with Mason or their mum, and this end of the street was always quiet. Many didn't venture out after a roast dinner. Except Mrs Tonks. But she would be at her painting club and unlikely to spot Addison's doppelgänger leaving with a packed bag.

Needing to know if she loved it as much as she thought, she stopped at the Jockey first. To see it fixed and pretty again brought joy to her heart. It might not be as handsome as it used to be, but it looked considerably better than the last time she'd seen it. She tugged the secure padlock and sighed. Keyless, she staggered around the side and smiled at the pellet hole as she nosed through the window. The inscription wasn't visible in the shadows, but the name Mason Rae would surely be there.

Addison raced to the shop to see Arnold, and her heart leapt at the jingling bell. He flashed his sixty-five-year-old dentures as he came around the counter.

"Addie. You not with your mother today?"

"I'm on my way. Just popped in for a sausage roll. Got any fresh?"

"As it's you, yes. But don't tell Mrs Tonks. She'll call it favouritism and raise merry hell." He frowned, noticing her bag. "You going away?"

"This? Oh, no, um, it's for the charity shop."

"Ah. You're a nice lady, Addie. Why aren't you snapped up?"

"Because being single is less painful and complicated." She laughed, fobbing off the truth with jest. After paying for her sausage roll, she kissed his cheek and headed around the corner to Mason's flat. She couldn't visit him, but she could peek at his front door to see if it looked as pristine as it should. It did, except for the chewed step.

Snorts from the garden enticed her. She approached the gate, risking Mason seeing her. Sting's black nose sniffed under the hedge, tail up and ears happy. Mason sat in a cheap deckchair, holding a cigarette. Though she couldn't see them, she knew his fingernails would be ingrained with engine oil. No matter how much he scrubbed, he could never get them clean. Chloe had hated it. Being more of a girly girl, she despised dirt.

Mason chugged out a row of smoke rings, in between wittering to Sting. Teases about chasing rabbits and pheasant stilled a wagging tail. Sting's nose looked for a scent as his head lifted.

Addison yearned to hug them. To finally have Mason and Sting back and not hold them was excruciating. Backing away was a struggle, but she forced herself to go. She left her heart in the alleyway and moved on to the car hire depot. After that, she would drive to Bath, stopping to buy a cheap phone on the way.

~

Everyone stayed at home on Sundays. Right? Usually. Unless they worked, or were having a dirty weekend somewhere. Laszlo was more likely doing one of those than attending the church she'd just passed. Any of them would be preferable to abduction, murder, and killing dogs. She speed-walked along his street, psyching herself up to face him, and reminded her heart of the despicable crimes he'd committed. She let herself remember his dead face to dampen the love she still suffered for him.

Relieved to see a familiar Audi parked outside the house, she smiled. Laszlo was home, so she didn't need to hang around or brace herself to do it another day. She approached and rang the doorbell, her fragile heart beating at the rhythm of an express train.

A clean-shaven Laszlo answered, his dark hair ruffled, and the same mystery in his ice-blue eyes. Icier than she'd seen before, but back then, he'd faked emotion.

"Hello."

"Hi," she greeted him with a beaming smile. "Can I come in?"

She stepped up to the threshold, but Laszlo's sturdy fingertips at her chest stopped her mid-step.

"Name?"

"Addison Rae."

"Purpose?"

"That'll take some explaining, but I promise not to shoot you this time."

He side-smiled, frowned and raised his eyebrows all at once. Addison could only imagine what he thought.

"Profession?"

"Senior reconciliator at Palowa Enterprises. For now. Until I've written my resignation letter."

"Shoot me...this time?"

She cocked her head. "Well, you did kill my dog."

"Are you sure you have the right man?" His eyes twinkled above an amused smile. A soul-trapping expression that weakened her resolve.

The hate vanished at the sight of his exquisite face. In its place, a spark re-ignited and caught the tinder of the feelings she'd had before she'd discovered his betrayal. She recalled the shower where he'd kept her on the cusp of a climax, forever it seemed. Then, with just one subtle move, she'd rippled with silent, breath-held pleasure and could only manage a small squeak as it faded.

She licked her lips. "Absolutely."

"I know that look. Women have gazed at me like that enough times. But I don't recognise you. So, why are you wearing it?"

"What look?" she asked innocently.

He bent towards her, lips close to hers. "The one that says, 'I've been here before, and I want it again.'" He straightened while Addison's blood pressure shot up.

"That is also going to take some explaining," she stuttered. "Please, can I come in?"

"No. I'm going now."

The door closed. She loitered on the steps, deciding how long she should leave it before ringing the bell again. He ignored it anyway, twice, but on the third, the door opened with a snap of the handle.

She stepped back, seeing the side of Laszlo that Jon and Sting had.

"What do you want, Miss Addison Rae of Lechlade, Gloucestershire?"

He'd looked her up.

"I want to prevent a crime that becomes something I'm willing to kill to avoid. And you, Laszlo Sándor, are the only one who can stop it."

"Why me?"

"Because you commit the crime and assassinate Robert Naise."

He laughed. "The Mayor?" He laughed again. "What is the point of that?"

"I don't know. What was the point in killing Duncan Frost when he'd already killed Izsak? What you did the second time made more sense."

She watched comprehension dawning on his stunned face. Then his fist clenched her coat and dragged her unceremoniously into the hallway. He kicked the door shut and held her against the wall.

Addison cocked her head, unshaken. "If you're going to get rough, at least pin my wrists to the shower tiles again."

"The purpose of your visit?"

"In four weeks, you will assassinate Robert Naise."

"No."

"Yes. I'm here to make sure you don't."

"If I were going to assassinate the Mayor of London in four weeks, I would be planning it now. And I'm not. You're wrong."

"You already did! Then you made a deal with politicians and changed history. Sort of rewrote history in another reality."

"Are you some kind of crackpot?" His face looked as if he thought as much.

"Are you the kind who likes restaurant-quality foods, and is so stubborn and obsessively fussy that you taught yourself to make them? Or the kind who listens to classical music to calm or incite a mood? If you lived in the house you had in The New, I'd show you a shower like nothing I've seen before, and a silver box your brother gave you for your birthday which holds the savings he challenged you to reach. Ten fifty-pound notes."

As she watched his face contort in surprise, she put her hand above his right nipple. "Here you have a freckle that is almost black." She dropped her fingers to his left thigh. "Here, a scar from falling off your bike when you were young. I wouldn't know these intimate things about you unless we'd met. Because you don't love easily. Do you?" An astonished Laszlo didn't respond. "Then again, what you had with me wasn't love. You pretended the whole time."

"And now I know you're lying. I haven't or wouldn't do that. It's one of my rules. I respect women too much."

"I'm willing to think you aren't the same man you become, but you did do that." Addison dropped her eyes. "And a lot more besides."

"I certainly don't kill dogs."

Her terrorising eyes snapped up. Laszlo flinched as she shoved a fang in his face.

"You knocked out his tooth!" she snarled with an aggressive, almost canine curl of her lip.

A darkness fell across his face. He didn't like to be accused. "Why?"

Addison's rage boiled to trigger-pulling levels. She smacked him in the chest and pushed him away. "See for yourself!" She searched her pockets for the memory stick from The New, but found only a scribbled note of her contact details. "Dammit!"

Laszlo bent and picked up a slim, white USB from the laminate floor. "Looking for this?"

She relaxed her shoulders and closed her eyes with a controlled sigh of relief. It must have fallen out when she fished out Sting's tooth.

He gestured to the lounge and opened the door. "You'd better come in then. I'm intrigued, at the very least."

The first thing she noticed was colour. Although predominantly neutral beige, splashes of soft green furnishings and a darker feature wall behind an enormous TV added personality. Flat screen. Some things never changed.

"Woah. So different from your other house."

"How?"

"Your lounge used to be white and glass."

Laszlo smiled. "Then I didn't consider it a home."

"And this is?"

"Yes."

What was so special about Bath?

The USB files loaded onto his TV and, one by one, they reviewed the evidence, with Addison explaining and adding her experiences. The dealings in The New, between Jarvis, Naise, and Coleman were damning, some too vile for comment. Addison let him explore them alone.

A defensive Laszlo stirred when he read his own past emails. "I haven't written these. I don't know these people. These two I do, obviously, but who are Henry Coleman and Ross Barnes?"

"Do your own homework. You do it so well."

She recognised the deliberating look, but didn't expect him to circle the sofa and stand in front of the lounge door.

"How did you find me?"

"My access to credit searches at work."

"Who do you work for?"

"Palowa. I told you that. Ross Barnes is my boss."

"Where did you get that?" He pointed at the footage of Anton Jarvis in a strip club playing on the TV.

"It came in Addison New's box, so I don't know. Why?"

"It's mine."

"How do you know?"

"My lens is…unique. It's definitely my recording…but I haven't recorded it."

"Yet."

He scratched his face, struggling for something to say. In the end, he chose the truth. "I can't get my head around it. Are you saying you're from the future?"

"Only by six weeks. You went back twenty-five years."

"How does going back six weeks change me going back twenty-five years?"

"Please, don't ask."

"But I am."

And so, for the next hour, she explained what she knew, but even seeing the evidence for himself didn't persuade him to believe it.

"Prove it."

"Only you not planning to assassinate Robert Naise with chlorine trifluoride will do that. I could take you to my house where you'll find another me. The two of us will be around for six weeks. I don't have a twin sister, just a younger brother. Again, thankfully. You will also find my colleague Marsha alive and well." Addison opened the recent photos. "This is her in the boot of my boss's car the other day."

Laszlo shook his head and looked away. A moment passed before he responded. "I don't like the person you say I am."

"I did. Until I found out he was fake."

"I wouldn't have been fake. Deceptive, maybe. But not fake. It would make me too sick."

Barnes's words echoed. *'As it turns out, neither did he. Laszlo likes you. He prevented us from taking you out.'*

She swallowed as visions of shooting him in the head enveloped her mind. Her shaking fingers handed him the note from her pocket.

"My number and address. You won't find me there, but you will find her. Oblivious, so best not to set off any alarm bells. You can get me on this number." She went to leave, but he didn't move from the door. "Assuming I'm free to go?"

"I'm reluctant, I admit. You know more about me than anybody."

"As much as I did before I knocked on your door. I'm not bribing or threatening you, nor hiding anything from you. If I wanted to go to the cops about Mr Frost, I would have done that first. My care, my only concern, is keeping my life as it was. Which means you must not kill Robert Naise."

"Which means someone else will. I'm not Naise's keeper."

"But I am my brother's, and I won't live peacefully in a reality without him in it. And you won't get the chance to be with Lorrie, the barmaid at Swindon Babbons hotel. The woman you said you might have married."

She elbowed him out of the way and stepped into the hall. Perhaps that surprised him because he didn't stop her from leaving. Halfway back to the hire car, her phone buzzed. She saved the new number into her address book and stared at Laszlo's message as she walked.

I'll be in touch.

Her heart thrummed. She hoped he would, and simultaneously that he wouldn't, as she pressed down on the deluge of blue door emotions and pistachio-green sheets. In denying her heart its need, she succumbed to the carried-back sadness of Addison New. This mingled clinging of loss and abandonment that had, in truth, happened much later for the real Addison, and by someone less important than her parents. But now she was breathing Addison New. Living her. Feeling every shred of her pain as she hankered for Jon Wells. Jackson Lowe.

Twenty-Five

5th March 2023, 21:30 – The Real

Simms was a classy bar in the centre of Leicester. Light floors and pale wooden tables with deep-green furnishings, chrome fixtures, and mirrors. It brimmed with impeccably dressed clientele adorned in fancy jewellery, all able to afford the drinks behind the bar. In comparison, Addison looked destitute in her tatty jeans.

She paid for her pricey Pepsi with an appalled cough.

"I'm looking for Jackson Lowe. Do you know him?"

The bartender smiled and pointed at the door to the rear exit and the back of a man's tobacco-brown head. "You and many other women in town."

She picked up her drink and wound through the revellers, questioning the logic of meeting him when she would disappear soon, unsure what to say when she reached him. She'd toyed with the idea of spending a few magical weeks with him, dropping the Lechlade shop into conversation and hoping it planted a seed. Life would go on for Addison Original—the version of her that Jackson Lowe needed to meet—so any length of time was out of the question. Meeting him at all was stupid. If Jackson met the Lechlade Addison after a three-week, manic love affair, he'd think it weird that she thought him a stranger, as Jon had when he discovered she didn't know him after three years. Jon, who knew himself best, recommended she didn't reveal the truth about how they met to Jackson.

She was reluctant to approach, and the closer she walked, the more hesitant she became about keeping her promise. What would be the point? But something in her gut spurred her on. Addison New/Real didn't have the answers, but she hoped the future would if she trusted her instincts. Somehow fate would find a way for Jackson to meet Addison Original, the lonely version untainted by Laszlo. She deserved a nice man and a happy ending.

That possibility stirred her. She wanted Jackson for her original self.

What was he looking at? She liked his ruffled, wavy hair, but she'd rather see his mischievous smile. She looked beyond him to a lover's tiff growing rough outside the toilets.

"I only touched up my makeup," the meek woman said.

"You left me alone too long at the bar. It looked like you'd bolted."

Addison cringed at the sound of the man's punishing slap as she attempted a strategic bump into Jackson. At the same moment, he sprang to intervene, and Addison's shoulder hit the doorframe.

As she stumbled forward, a fist came towards her. The lover's tiff had spilled onto spectators and innocent passers-by. She tried to duck, but it caught her brow bone.

"Oi! Watch it!" she yelled, but Addison New's ever-present instinct also reacted. Her left fist swung out and clocked him between the eyes as the other handed her glass to someone.

The man stared, surprised.

"George. Let's go," his companion said.

In reply, George elbowed the poor woman in the nose.

Surprising herself as much as George, Addison stabbed three fingers into his throat and followed it up with another punch. "Hit a woman, would you? Disgusting man."

The stunned George slid down the wall as she entered the ladies to inspect her eye. It wasn't bleeding but would bruise. She took out a wad of hand towels for the woman's nose and returned to the hallway.

"You can learn to defend yourself. The local council funds classes and, if you can't go out, there are free online videos. It isn't hard to learn. Getting the confidence to know you can is the hardest part. You deserve better than this." She turned to Jackson Lowe. "And shame on you for just standing there and waiting for it." When she took in his face, she ended her rant with a faint, "Wow."

Jackson frowned, burying his chocolate eyes further beneath his thick eyebrows. "Now, hang on."

But Addison New couldn't stop staring. Even though they were the same, he looked younger than Jon. Clean-shaven, less rugged, and less wise.

He came towards her. "Who are you, and what do you know about it?"

"I'm the innocent victim strolling by to receive a fist in the face. I'm fine, by the way. Thanks for asking." *Jerk*. He wasn't as chivalrous as Jon, either.

Addison had feared comparing him to Laszlo, never the New version of himself.

"Sorry. But you shouldn't make assumptions. It's rude. Are you okay?"

She walked away, not wanting to know this version of Jon, but Jackson took her arm and pulled her aside.

Lowering his voice, he said, "She's my ex. She chose the money and married that." He nodded to the place where George had been. "It wasn't easy to watch or intervene."

Swallowing a little pride, she blushed. "Sorry. I was wrong."

Jackson held Addison's chin and inspected her eyebrow, catching her eye and smiling as he did. "We should ice this."

We?

She grabbed his arm as he went to leave. "Don't go to the bar. I don't want a fuss. I'm fine."

"It's already swelling."

"Then I'll see to it at home."

"I bet you mine is closer…if you're that embarrassed."

"I'm fine."

"Hospital then?"

Horrified, she cried, "No!" Then fake laughed. "I'm sure that won't be necessary." A black eye noted on her medical records wouldn't be good for the original Addison who, at this present moment, was likely to be snuggled up with Sting watching TV.

Jackson led her to the rear exit. "See that tall building over there? That's my block of apartments. Nothing fancy."

Addison didn't look. She couldn't tear her gaze away from his slow-motion lips, and when they parted to say something else, the enthralled Addison New grabbed the front of his shirt and kissed him. The surroundings dissolved into Derek's spare room and the intimate vibe they had shared that night.

Jackson pulled away and smiled. "My place it is."

"I am so sorry. I've no idea what made me do that," she lied, knowing full well Addison New's feelings were as overpowering as hers were for Laszlo. "Just for an icepack, then."

"Nightcap? Okay."

She laughed, abandoning all common sense as Jackson's hand pressed the small of her back and edged her forward. She let him. What was wrong with her and why did she keep going to strangers' houses? First

Laszlo. Now Jackson. Not that Jackson was a stranger. Well, Jon wasn't.

"You don't need to worry. I've seen you fight. You're perfectly safe."

"I am. But are you?"

Jackson's quiet laugh sounded nervous. His brooding eyes explored her sparkling, playful ones before deciding she must be joking.

Smiling, she looked away, stomach swirling like a wash cycle spreading foamy suds into her thoughts. Barely able to answer the simple 'getting to know you' questions, like her name, while they walked to his apartment. Unable to think up a cover story, she gave him the Addison Original truth.

She relied on the cavern purple doors separating her memories correctly as he gestured her inside his tidy, but lived in, home. She glanced at the abstract paintings on the wall, a car magazine on the coffee table, and a photo of an older woman on the bookshelf. His mum?

As Jackson rooted through his freezer, she smiled at the paperwork and empty beer bottles cluttering the kitchen worktop and opened the door to his seventh-floor balcony.

"What brings you to Leicester?" he asked.

Stumped, she turned from the city lights and perched on the black leather sofa while she thought of an answer. Without red-door data to give, she used a shaving from a blue one. "I made a promise and I'm seeing it through the best way I know how."

Jackson came from the kitchenette holding a frozen fish wrapped in paper with its grey head poking out, mouth open, and round silver eye staring.

Addison made a face and pulled her head back. "Why are you holding a trout?"

"Best I've got for an ice pack."

"Ice cubes in a tea-towel?"

"Don't have any."

"You have nothing better than fish?"

"I have pie?"

She laughed, doubtful. "Peas? A cold bottle?"

"There's wine. But I thought we could drink that." The silver eye closed in.

Addison recoiled, thrusting her hands between the fish and her face. "I am not putting that on my eye."

"It doesn't smell yet. It's still frozen."

"I'll take the wine," she said, unable to stop her laugh.

Jackson shrugged and swapped the fish for wine, pouring it before handing the bottle to her for deswelling duties.

"Why do you have a trout wrapped in paper with its head sticking out?"

"Because I caught it."

"You fish?"

"Yeah. Why?"

"No reason." But she guessed the fishing haunt, Horseshoe Lake, had been a deciding factor in which country shop he ran. Hopefully, she wouldn't see Jon again to ask him. "Lechlade has a stunning carp fishing lake."

"Gloucestershire? Never been. Fishing is something I do to think, and it's usually nearby. At least I didn't offer you the bag of frozen maggots."

"Urgh! Now I'm glad I turned down the fish. Remind me never to eat here."

He laughed. "There used to be mice as well, but Flappy died."

She lowered the wine bottle and he used the opportunity to fill their glasses.

"Flappy was my snake."

"Ha. I didn't expect that. Why Flappy?"

"Because of his tongue." He rolled his eyes, tutting as if she should have known, and she laughed.

"How old are you? Like, five?"

"I did it to tease my mum. She hated snakes. Stick the bottle on your eye and shut up." He grinned. "How long will you be in town making assumptions, anyway?"

"Maybe a couple of weeks. Definitely until this dies down." She lowered the warm wine, wondering what use it was now.

"Where are you staying?"

Grinning, she pointed across the main road. "The hotel over there. My just-as-close place where there would have been an ice pack."

Jackson laughed, remembering the bet he'd now lost.

Having only recently recovered from a bitten lip, Addison sighed, disgruntled. Now, she would have to deal with bruised knuckles and a black eye. She swapped hands to press the bottle to her face, wincing at her protesting fingers when she tried to straighten them. "With everything else going on, I can't believe I have injuries."

"I would have protected you had I known you were there, but I ain't got eyes in the back of my head."

"I don't need your protection, thank you. If you weren't standing in the way, I'd have seen the punch coming sooner."

"I'd have let him hit me instead if that makes you feel better. How about we even the score?"

"What you gonna do, blacken my other eye?"

"I meant me." He stared at the hall door frame while flicking his tongue rapidly across his top lip. Then he bent over, rocking his hips like a playful kitten preparing to leap, and rubbed his hands together, willing himself to run and knock his face on it.

The amusing build and satisfactory run-up were praiseworthy. His enthusiasm, more so. But the abrupt halt with his hands reaching out, and the light head-bump to the frame at the end, was a real letdown.

Addison smirked, then let out a forlorn sigh. "He wore two rings, you know."

"Two rings?" Jackson quoted with a wobbling head. "All right."

More of the same puffery ensued, resulting in the same cowardly finish. Addison rolled her eyes and teased him with a yawn.

"Third time lucky?" he asked.

She couldn't stand to watch the preparations a third time, despite his sexy tongue licking his lips in readiness again.

"Let me do it," she said, the black leather sofa creaking when she rose.

"No thanks. I've seen your punches."

"I promise to be gentle." She closed in, rolling up her sleeves. "Just a little flick. That's all it needs."

"I think I'll stick with–" He dodged Addison's nippy fist. "What the...?"

Addison laughed. "So much for solidarity."

"I can't help my instincts. It's what happens when a fist–"

"Comes at you?" she finished for him, while throwing a right and then left punch. He looked surprised at her skills, but blocked them and laughed. She circled him, jokingly affronted. "You sneaky f–"

"It's ingrained training. I can't help it," he interrupted.

Addison squinted at her new opponent. "I sense this is getting tactical. Okay, bodyguard. Show me whatcha got."

Jackson raised his hands in surrender. "Noooo. I wouldn't want to hurt you."

"Arrogant much?"

"Realistic."

Eyebrows arching, she felt the rise of Addison New's stubborn pride. After sweeping for hazards, she dived into a sparring session, pushing Jackson nearer to dangers he was most likely used to seeing, like the corner of the sideboard poking into his hip as he retreated from her persistent jabs. The lampstand teetered as he rounded the armchair, laughter growing louder when Addison tripped on the rug and fell face down on the sofa.

He came to her aid as she scrambled up, afraid to let him get the upper hand. Her elbow smacked into him.

"Ow!"

"Sorry!" She looked around and saw Jackson nursing his left cheekbone. "Ha! Did I even the score?"

"By foul play! You didn't win."

"The deed is done. My elbow won. So, go fetch the trout." She couldn't stop her chuckle.

"How do you call that a win?" He walked to the freezer still holding his face. "It was an accident."

"Ah, but was it?"

"Good timing at most."

"You're not a good loser, are you?"

Jackson flopped into the chair, slapping the trout to his eye as Addison glanced away, pressing her lips together to stifle a laugh.

"Depends on the fair game, Addison Rae. Would you really pull a dirty trick?"

She considered her answer. Addison New would cheat to win if it were serious enough and saved lives. Addison Original didn't live with the same fears, and never cared about winning. Whereas Addison Real...

"An enemy in battle? Heck, yes. But not friend to friend."

"So, was it a dirty trick or an accident?" he asked with that same cheeky smile. His mischievousness hadn't changed, no matter how smooth and young he looked now. It was more than being clean shaven. He had a zeal for life in his eyes.

"All right, then," she conceded. "An accident. But I win by default."

"In that case, the victor buys the wine."

"Not tonight, she doesn't! I really need to go."

His expression clouded with disappointment. "So soon? Is the fish turning you off?"

She grabbed her jacket, laughing again. "It's not a good look."

Jackson threw the fish back into the freezer. "I'll walk you to your hotel."

"It's only across the road."

"Then it won't take long."

With their eyes flicking to avoid each other, the seven-floor lift ride seemed to take longer than her Leicester car journey. The awkward silence continued until they stood outside Addison's hotel and their eyes finally met out of politeness.

"Can I see you tomorrow?" he asked.

"Aren't you working?"

"I'm due holiday." He winked. "Anything up to two weeks."

"Plan on showing me the sights?"

"Why not? Ten?"

"There are ten sights?" she teased, then laughed at his amused expression. "I'll see you then."

A shy grin spread. Jackson bowed, circling his hand like a viscount in a period drama before walking away.

~

Addison switch on the lights as they entered her hotel room, confident now of which turned on what, and closed the blackout curtains on the carpark outside. Fawn cotton dragged on the beige carpet. She straightened them and sat in the chair while Jackson pulled the cork from a bottle of white wine.

They'd had dinner. Properly. In a restaurant, dressed-up and almost loved-up, but not intimate. Although Addison New desired it, Real wanted Jackson to experience Addison Original, and for her to experience him, for the first time, but how that would happen remained a mystery. Over the last fortnight, a friendship had sprouted between them, building on the default win and trout humour foundations. She'd learned so much about him. Perhaps even more than Addison New had known.

All Addison had to do was stay focused. Jackson was for the future, not now. She had her memories of Jon, the version that wanted her when she craved Laszlo.

The Laszlo of today sent her periodic messages. She left them unanswered, but she never ignored them. Worshipped his attention would be nearer to the truth.

Jackson deserved better. He ought to have the nonaggressive version, untainted by the Laszlo touch. The one who wouldn't putrefy beside a worn purple door, aching for another's flesh, and likely pulsing the same need in her eyes as Jackson had for her now. He craved her. It had been tough to decline at times, but she couldn't fight the ripening vibe in their gazes as he placed a wineglass on the table. Fingers entwined, he edged forward, hesitant. His searching eyes seemed to seek her approval. As his gentle lips moved with hers, she remembered Jon peeling off her damp clothes, then her dry ones, followed by that exquisite night.

His fingers combed her short hair, soft kisses drizzling along her jawline.

"We should slow down."

"Any slower and we'll be back in primary school," he whispered, mouth brushing her neck.

"But I don't have much time left and–"

"Better make the most of it then."

"–I won't see you anymore."

"I'd walk the earth to find you." He nibbled her ear.

"Bet you would. Stalker."

Jackson laughed.

"Well, I guess an Addison Rae is easier to track down than a Jon Wells." Realising her faux pas, she closed and rolled her eyes as Jackson's lips froze. He recoiled as if she were something nasty.

"How do you know that name?"

She bit her lip, surprised he knew it, too, assuming the witness protection programme had chosen it.

"This isn't the first time. I thought you'd said things before. Me being a bodyguard, for example. I put it down to the wine and forgetting I'd mentioned it. Now…I'm suspicious. How do you know me?"

Jackson's glare searched her eyes for deception now rather than permission to kiss her. The tension heightened as she worked out how to respond.

Her phone rang, loud in the knife-edge moment. The static-prickling atmosphere dissolved. Her face tightened when she pulled it from her pocket and saw Laszlo was calling. Who else would it be? While the interruption was welcome, he was not.

Her heavy sigh echoed her mood. "Why do you keep messaging me? What do you want?" Her tone forced Jackson off.

"Help me."

Laszlo's breathless whisper pierced the flimsy shield around her soul and heart. His purple door burst open with memories she shouldn't want to see.

"What's happened?"

"Come. Please. Starlight Hotel, Henley-On-Thames…"

She hunted the hotel drawers for paper, focusing more on remembering the address than the rest of what he said. "Did you say shot? And supplies like what? What can I do? Go to the hospital."

"I did what you asked," he mumbled, followed by more incoherent words. "Please. Come."

"That will take me hours. Hello? Laszlo?"

Annoyed that he had hung up, Addison went to ring back and was shocked to find his phone still connected, but silent.

"Jackson, I'm sorry, but I need to go."

"We've unfinished business, and you aren't leaving without answering me."

Out of curiosity more than suspicion, she asked, "How do you know the name Jon Wells? Tell me, and I'll tell you. It will come as a shock. You probably won't believe me." She started packing her small case.

"It's my biological father's name. I'm adopted by my stepdad. Your turn."

"I didn't know."

"Why would you?"

She dumped her suitcase on the bed and opened it. "Summarised version."

Jackson's face morphed from blank to shocked and back to blank as she explained, trying to simplify how she had woken up in a reality that she hadn't lived. She purposely planted the seed of Jon-Vinny-Jones Wells owning the local shop. "You once advised me not to tell you we'd already met. Hence why I didn't. I guess you'd know best, right? If the realities hadn't collided, then who knows who the original me would have ended up with because I didn't know you. But, in the reality I visited, she would have been with you if she could. Your safety meant more to her than her feelings. I admire that about her…er…me."

She packed the last of her clothes and remembered her toiletries. She returned zipping the bag, tossed it into her case, and checked the room for anything she might have missed.

"You're confusing me now. Are you saying there are two of you?"

"There's actually three if you count the original. Okay, in the original reality, I'm in Lechlade and you're in Leicester, and we haven't met. Then, in the other reality, you have been running my local shop in Lechlade for three years. That Addison wanted to know you, but she lived too dangerously. When those realities collided, I, from here, was suddenly there in a life similar to mine but not the same, residing in a body that had a different life to mine." A sock snagged as she closed the case. With a frustrated growl, she tucked it in, adding, "Fast-forward to it all coming out and Jon Wells learning the truth."

He raised a sceptical eyebrow. "Why was I living there under a pseudonym?"

"I don't know," she lied as they left the room. She didn't have time to explain, or the right to give away the details. If the murder had occurred in this reality, Jackson Lowe would know the people involved. "You asked me to look you up when I returned to undo the mess. I still hope I can do that. Today, in this reality, you and I are in Leicester, and she, the original me, is living in Lechlade, waiting to meet you. I'll be gone when time catches up with me, so maybe you can meet her."

While a confused Jackson tried to process her words, she checked out of the hotel and braced herself for his questions as he followed her to the car.

"Okay, I'll play along. Gone where? Do you mean I've got to do this all over again?"

The boot of the car opened at the push of a button and she threw her suitcase inside before peering at him. "Do what?"

"Get to know you. Her." He shook his head as if the idea was stupid.

"She won't have a clue who you are because she hasn't had her life turned upside down and threatened yet. She doesn't have the other Addison's heart that loves you, but...she has the same heart as me, and I... You two should keep it special between you. If you choose to go."

Regret stabbing, she started the engine and drove away, staring in the mirror as he ran after her until he blended with the cars. She hoped he believed her, for herself and Jon, but it didn't look good.

Twenty-Six

6th March 2023, 21:30 – The Real

Laszlo watched the traffic through the café window, sipping a cappuccino and ignoring the giggles and mutters about him from the girls behind the counter. Even together, they couldn't handle him. They were too green and would run screaming if he pulled one of his crude tricks. It had taken all week, but he'd scoured for every morsel of information he could find on Anton Jarvis, Robert Naise, Henry Coleman, Ross Barnes, Mario Spinzer, Lorrie James, and Addison Rae. He'd compared the USB data to private government files, looking closely at Convolve Ltd and their finances. Most of their funding had come from Palowa Enterprises until the acquisition, although Palowa's accounts didn't show a payment to Convolve. Their Finance Director? Ross Barnes.

Following his crusty, stale breadcrumbs led Laszlo to files with security beyond his skills. Opening them required a specialist, and Arizona Snowy in Fairford had been happy to assist. He could pull apart IT security like loose knitting.

"Well, I'll be damned, man. You sure do pick 'em. This organisation is developing time travel. They ain't gonna thank ya for snooping on their stuff."

"Are you sure that's what they're doing?"

"Absoroaringlutely! I watched a vase get smashed, and come back together again. And they've discovered ways to travel realities, I think. *I think*."

Confirming the scientific abilities shared by Addison Rae stilled Laszlo's heart, and his next stop that morning was her house in Lechlade, where a dog barked at his knock.

Great. He preferred cats.

Addison answered. She'd actually answered. Yet the phone number she'd given him was active in Leicester.

"Hi." he flashed a wide grin. "Have you seen a ginger cat hanging around?"

Her knee wrestled with the yellow head of a well-built Labrador trying to squeeze through the door. "Get in, Sting! No, sorry."

"Could you check your garden and shed? I'd appreciate it."

"Of course. Hope you find it." She hustled Sting inside and closed the door, too distracted to pay attention to Laszlo or his cat.

That Addison clearly didn't know him. It seemed there were two versions of her after all. He had confirmed everything else the first Addison said, even the job to assassinate Mayor Naise. An appointment for which he was now unspeakably early and killing time in this coffee shop just along from Spinzer's nightclub.

Sparing him and the giggling baristas more embarrassment, he threw a £20 note onto the table beside his empty cup and stood. He'd rather slowly walk to the club than listen to any more of their childish chatter, though he couldn't help donating a cheeky wink as he left. The echoes of delighted screams followed him through the door.

Turning left, he walked the littered street, struggling to push away the person tattooed on the insides of his eyelids as he passed takeaways and closed boutique shops. Even the sexy barmaid at the Swindon hotel couldn't surpass the face of the cheeky mare who had stood on his doorstop, fronting him out with spunk he hadn't seen in a long time. Though short-haired and bony, the opposite of his type, Addison's personality was on-point. Passionate. Assertive. Brave.

As he turned into the car park of Spinzer's club, he tried to get her hazel eyes out of his head. Eyes with specks of soul-reading green that screamed impatience as he held her at bay with his fingertips on her chest. He'd seen hate, violence, and desire in them, too.

A lanky scout whistled from the rear door and signalled down the hall. "The office is open. Mario's waiting."

The room was silent when Laszlo entered, expecting the club owner to be alone. The whistle had also alerted Spinzer's five-man team…uh, four-man-plus-one-woman team. He frowned at her pigtails.

"You'd better have a good explanation for this job."

Eyebrows rising at the utter cheek, Spinzer rose and rounded his desk. The man was short, and Laszlo understood why he had five bouncers on hand.

"What's it to you? You came highly recommended. Do you want the job or not?"

"That depends on why I'm doing it. This is the mayor! You won't get many takers." Spinzer pushed out his chin. Laszlo clearly wasn't his first call. "As you've already found out. Tell me your reasons and I'll give you my answer."

"Robert Naise is about to push for legalising residential arms in Britain. I don't want to risk my lucrative earner."

"That'll never happen. The US is even calling for a change in the law. The constitution. Civil uproar. Can you see the British government saying 'aye' while that's playing out with our American cousins?"

"But it is. And they will. It has solid backing."

"And just as solid opposition, I'd imagine."

"It is what it is, and the job still stands. Do you want it?"

"750k?"

Spinzer dipped his head.

"If you're sure of what you say—"

"I am."

"Then…yes. I want it. Half now. No argument."

Spinzer dipped his head again.

"I'll be in touch when I come up with a plan that I can achieve in three weeks."

"The plan is all ready, and here is your team.

Surprised they were prepared and expecting him to agree, Laszlo sniggered. "Is it now?" He curled his lip at *his team*. "I work alone."

"Not this time, Lassie."

"My name is Laszlo."

"I don't know you."

"Exactly. I'd be worried if you did. I work alone because I'm not a snitch."

"Neither are they, and it's a deal breaker."

Laszlo sucked in his cheek, thinking, accepting the man's ignorance of his integrity and eventually opting to compromise. "One, then. Which of you is intelligent?"

A solid, capable looking man, who Laszlo assumed to be team captain, stepped forward. "Depends on what you mean by intelligent. Lara has a weird logic, but she's a genius, if a bit strange. I have street wisdom and I can fight."

"I'll take the girl."

"You'll take Dan as well. I insist. Now, transfer details. Then we'll move on to the plan."

A plan that Laszlo declined at once. He refused to burn a house with Naise's wife present and threatened to double his fee if Spinzer remained adamant. Instead, he offered his own suggestion.

"We'll do it away from London. At his club lodge in Henley-On-Thames. And I'll do his friends for free."

"Friends?"

"Oh, the company he keeps is especially colourful."

~

The party was easy to arrange. Almost as simple as throwing high-school leaflets down a stairwell for the sheep to grab. Everyone loved a good shindig, especially when the drinks were free. The hardest part was getting legitimate access into the turreted building of the club lodge.

Ordinarily, Spinzer would be something Laszlo wiped off his shoe, but the man proved capable. They hatched a plan to engineer a birthday celebration for the now missing member Dorian Gates, digitally impersonating him and inviting along the vilest selection of lodge regulars from Laszlo's research.

The chlorine trifluoride effect would be spectacular inside those efficiently sealed doors. The huge black doors against white painted brick that 'catering manager' Dan now unlocked. Lara hopped to place the precious canisters inside the square structure. Dan's warning had been right. She was childlike.

Laszlo marched across the tiled foyer, doubtful that flames could take root with nothing but air to burn. He needn't have worried. The party planner Spinzer employed had adorned the main hall with elegant fabric tablecloths, napkins, and champagne bottles chilling in buckets, ready to pop. Flammable, thick mustard curtains and a patterned carpet would help. The blue and yellow swirls gave the impression of movement as he walked to the two rear exits.

Laszlo's priority was to ensure no one escaped.

The lock mechanisms only took seconds to weld and ten minutes to clean meticulously behind him. Most traces of DNA would be burnt, but he'd sooner take no chances. He returned to the main hall to check if Lara was behaving. Her pert backside poked from under one of the long tables as she crawled beneath it with a bag of canisters bouncing along behind. When her hand plunged inside the bag to lay another, she noticed his shoes beside her.

"It's a shame we don't have miniature ones for the ice buckets." She winked and pointed at the nine chintzy standing vases bursting with bloom…and water.

He peered closer, noticing a canister among the stems only because he looked for it. It faced the water and would shoot vase fragments and droplets of flame to rain across the hall.

Dan was right. Lara was a genius.

When the guests arrived, her excitement grew intolerable. Laszlo sent her outside before she gave them away. Her twitchy fingers and zeal to watch the place burn made him nervous.

The stars of the show, led by Mayor Naise, came last, querying the whereabouts of the no-show party host. They helped themselves to a complimentary glass of champagne and mingled, while Dan rounded up the smokers, persuading them back inside before performing a final perimeter check. Lara watched the merrymaking through the window as Laszlo unpacked his welding equipment, grateful for a milder wind. He then started on the front door. Spinzer reckoned the guests wouldn't have time to escape. He said sealing the doors wasn't necessary. But Laszlo didn't know how ferocious chlorine trifluoride could be, and he didn't intend to risk it.

With the door lock welded, he packed his equipment and drew out the canister remote as he rounded the corner. Lara continued to stare through the window, waiting as patiently as her excitement would allow, while Dan returned from his perimeter check.

Her brown eyes widened at the remote in Laszlo's hands. Like a begging kitten, she looked up, fluttering her eyelashes. Laszlo rolled his eyes and handed it to her. Gleeful screeches thanked him as she held it up like a winning trophy. While it was in the air, she pressed the button.

Explosions vibrated beneath their feet, the window flickered with flames, and fire engulfed the room in milliseconds. Lara wouldn't come away, despite Laszlo's insistence.

Dan shouted.

Distracted, Laszlo's reactions were slower than usual. An echoing gun crack became horrendous pain as a bullet ripped into the back of his left shoulder and knocked him to the ground. The window exploded, bursting glass and drowning out Laszlo's yell as air-sucking flames lit the dreary moonlit evening. Lara soared into the air like a starfish and landed on the neat lawn. When Laszlo coughed, a searing pain sliced his chest. Through the rippling heat haze, he watched a figure approaching. Cold metal pressed to the back of his head.

Waiting for the inevitable, Laszlo raised eyes drawn to slits, thinking about Addison. Thinking it might be too late to consider a career change. Thinking it was too late to change anything.

Another shot fired. Dan lowered his weapon, and the shooter fell, his vinegar feet coming to rest beside Laszlo's nose. The pungent aroma persuaded him to stand, his heart racing with adrenaline. The pain zoomed out. It became a dot on the horizon of a long, straight road as an unexplainable strength gripped him.

Dan ran to Lara. Laszlo snatched up the abandoned canister remote, cleaned it in case their gloves had transferred forensics, and then shoved it in the shooter's hand, pressing his oil-stained thumb to the button.

Dan returned, shaking his head. "Twenty-five years old. She's a goner. You alright? I'll take this one." He bent and grabbed the shooter's smelly shoe.

Laszlo circled his large hand around Dan's wrist. "Don't drag him. Carry him. Make it look like he got up and walked. His fingerprints are all over this." Laszlo tossed the remote onto the grass and released a heavy sigh. Lara would be his burden to take to the car.

Distant sirens wailed. Dan hoisted the shooter onto his shoulder with a deep grunt and strolled off. Despite his injured shoulder, Laszlo took Lara's arm and, crying in pain, pulled her off the grass into the shadow of the parked cars. He reached the pavement, breathless and sweaty.

The sirens grew louder. The sound provoked a burst of adrenaline, which dispelled his sudden dizzy spell.

Dan laid Lara on the back seat while Laszlo stumbled into the car and removed his belt to make a sling. As they drove away, a crowd gathered. Potential witnesses. Loose ends.

Dan looked him over. "You should get yourself some help. I'll take care of the bodies."

Laszlo saw only one option. "Take me to my hotel."

"You need a hospital."

Weary of Dan's demands, he rolled his head to the side to glare at him. "You tell me how I explain a bullet in my shoulder?"

Dan continued to drive.

"My hotel, please."

~

Every breath felt like a twisting knife. Even reaching the bathroom in his hotel room had been an ordeal. Laszlo broke into another sweat. He caught sight of his grey-green face in the mirror. No wonder the couple waiting for the lift declined to share it when he looked like this.

He dampened his face, the urge not to procrastinate if he hoped to survive growing stronger. The wound kept bleeding, despite strapping his arm and shoulder as best he could. The bullet was still lodged. He couldn't reach it to remove it or stitch himself. Although he knew how, he'd never needed to put the skill into practice.

He only wanted one person. The only one he trusted. Weirdly. Laszlo trusted no man. But Addison wasn't a man.

Decided, finally, he rushed to the bed. Too fast. The room spun into a kaleidoscope. Instead of reaching for his phone, he collapsed onto the carpet and gave in to the excruciating pain. He yelled in frustration and struggled to stay alert as he pulled on the bedcovers until his phone dropped.

"Why do you keep messaging me? What do you want?" Addison's abrupt tone startled him.

"Help me."

His genuine desperation must have thawed her because her voice softened.

"What's happened?"

"Come. Please. Starlight Hotel, Henley-On-Thames. Bring vodka and my medical supplies. I've been shot."

Paper rustled in the background. She wasn't taking him seriously.

"Did you say shot? And supplies like what? What can I do? Go to the hospital."

"I did what you asked. I can't go to the hospital. And now I'm dying. Please. Come."

"That will take me hours…hello? Laszlo?"

Twenty-Seven

22nd March 2023, 22:30 – The Real

Addison pulled into a gravel car park. Stones crunched beneath the tyres as she parked beside the entrance. *Starlight* blinked above it in neon pink. Vegas, baby. Classy. It didn't suit the boutique hotel's Tudor design at all.

Pulling a small case filled with medical supplies instead of her clothes, she crossed the dark wooden floor and approached the service desk.

"I'm here to see Mr Sándor."

Nostrils flaring, the unimpressed receptionist looked her over. "Name?"

"Laszlo Sándor."

"Your name."

"Addison Rae," she snapped. Not that her name should be any of this woman's business.

"Top floor. Room twenty-six." The snooty, over-made-up receptionist handed her a card and continued working as if she weren't there.

Addison looked around for the lift, feeling the woman's eyes on her back as she left. Did she fancy her chances with the assassin Laszlo, only to have her hopes dashed when she discovered he'd left an access card for another woman?

The lift doors opened on the third floor. She followed the hall to his room and slid the card into the slot with a preparatory breath. She dipped the handle and paused, running through her 'keep it together mantra' before seeing his face. Because then, he had every chance of making her do whatever he wanted.

But Laszlo couldn't make her do anything while lying still and topless on the floor with a phone loose in his hand. Blood had soaked through the wet, balled-up rag on his shoulder and seeped into the carpet. The metallic smell whooshed through her nostrils and filled her mouth with saliva. She swallowed, hoping it took the nausea with it.

Dread hit her as the cavern walls closed in. The Perfect Man door wrapped itself around her face, suffocating her lungs with pain more agonising than Addison New could ever imagine. The thought of him dead, again, was too shattering.

Abandoning her suitcase, she raced over, yelling his name, and then knelt beside him, checking his warm neck for a pulse. It tapped her fingertips like a steady drum. She exhaled, grateful he wasn't dead, and she didn't have to call the cops. Not yet anyway. How would she explain? Not just this, but also the two of her, present in the world at the same time.

She leaned to his ear, calling his name, and praying for a response. The monumental relief rushed with a silent "whoop" when he finally roused with a weary groan, although he didn't get up.

"Addis...?"

"I'm here." She lay down, peering into his washy eyes, diluted and wraith-like. "You need the hospital."

In between rapid breaths, he whispered, "No. Can't. You."

"Can you stand? I'll help you to the bed."

"Bath...room."

He closed his eyes, wincing with the draw of a determined breath as Addison helped him to his feet. It was more of a hoisting. Leaning on her for support, he shuffled unsteadily to the bathroom and splashed cold water over his face.

"Did you bring the stuff?"

"I hope so. The pharmacist gave me an odd look." She headed towards her case. "So, what am I doing?" she asked, knowing what he expected, but she couldn't do it. She would vomit.

"The vodka. Pharmacist?"

"For supplies, like you asked."

Laszlo looked blank. Didn't he remember?

"First, go to my car. Under the backseat, driver's side, is a compartment with a case inside. Bring it. But before you go, I'll need the vodka."

While he guzzled it, Addison raced down the stairs, psyching herself up to face his sticky blood when even the rusty smell made her want to heave. She asked herself why she would be keen to assist an assassin as the receptionist's hawkish eyes followed her out of the door. Then she realised precisely why she would help him. She had no choice. She liked him.

Loved him.

And neither version of them deserved it.

Not the seventy-year-old in a forty-five-year-old body with the knowledge and wisdom of a pensioner, nor the man here today, who had yet to explain how he got shot.

An unfamiliar caution crept in as she searched for the car and then the case. The sort Addison New would know so well. Downcast, she returned to room twenty-six.

The case brimmed with supplies, including utensils Addison would usually use for eyebrows and clothes. Ignoring the needles and tweezers, she took the saline as instructed and dabbed the wound but, even after several tubes, the black-crusted blood wouldn't fully wash away.

She doubted she was doing it right and sighed, frustrated. "It isn't working."

"Use the shower. I have antibiotics in the case."

She set it to a gentle flow and rested the nozzle on his shoulder, letting the warm water run over the wound. Eventually, the crust loosened. Addison couldn't watch the flakes swirl down the plughole in streams of washy pink or look at the bullet hole glistening with brass. She closed her eyes, fighting the squeamish urge to cry out like a child.

Laszlo tapped her hand. "Now, sterilise it." He passed her the vodka bottle, rolling his chin at what it would mean, and gripped the sink in anticipation.

Despite everything, she took no pleasure in his pained growls and muttered curses as she drizzled vodka into the wound, or the hiss through his teeth as she pressed the gauze. But when he offered her a set of tweezers, she backed off.

"I can't."

"You have to."

She spun round, ready to claim she didn't have to do anything, but mellowed when she saw his alabaster face. "Don't you have people for this?"

"Yes."

"Then why me? Why do I have to?"

"Because they're too far away."

"Further than Leicester?"

"I can't drive there."

"I can."

Frustrated and shivering, he sighed. "I don't want him to know."

"Why? Isn't he paid to keep your secrets?"

He stared at the floor without answering.

"I won't do it. It will make me vomit. I can't even watch this stuff on the TV."

"Please."

"No. I'll drive you."

"He isn't stupid. He'll connect this with how it happened."

"Which is?"

"I did what you asked. I also researched and uncovered more about Convolve's dealings than you did. Four-fifths of the problem is done. To finish it, you need to finish here." Between his teeth, he added, "So, please. Take the tweezers, press them around the bullet, and pull it out."

Gloved hands shaking, Addison gripped the tweezers, staring at the nine millimetres of brass, unable to proceed. She needed something to distract her.

"Four-fifths?"

"The foursome is finished."

Mulling that statement over led her to Naise, Jarvis, Coleman, and Barnes.

"Naise is dead? Again? I didn't ask you to do that. I asked you *not* to do that. You've ruined everything! The exact thing will happen again."

The squeamishness vanished. In its place came the rapid burn of Addison New's temper, then a desensitisation to the job as she gripped the tweezers around the bullet and yanked it out, not caring if it hurt or that he yelled.

"You don't know what you've done!" She threw the bullet and tweezers into the sink. "I knew better than to trust you."

Laszlo grabbed her wrist as she walked away, anger sparking in his eyes. "It's you that doesn't know. Do you live in a fantasy world? Am I the only person Mario Spinzer can hire? If not me, someone else would have taken the job and nothing would have changed. This way, his friends aren't around to initiate another turning. The last fifth is taking out Convolve. Then we're sure it can't happen again."

"You killed three more people."

"They were not people. Not with their deeds. You don't want to know. Trust me, their victims would be satisfied. Some of them are children."

"You're right. I don't want to know. Okay. The bullet is out. You can heal up and drive home. So, I'll be off. I think that's best."

It was for the best. Half of her detested him. The other half had embedded him so far under her skin that she couldn't think rationally in his presence.

Left arm loose at his side, he leaned forward, holding his head in his other hand. She'd never seen him so vulnerable, not even in front of his brother. Suddenly, the blue-door Laszlo feelings sweated through her skin, and the hatred dampened.

"Please don't go. There are lots of reasons but, right now, the priority is I can't sew it up myself." He looked up, lifting watery eyes. "I need you."

Laszlo, who was always in control, always had a plan, and never worked with others, was now asking for help.

Addison walked out of the bathroom but couldn't leave. She sat on the bed to gather her thoughts. To swallow her pride at being forced to do something she didn't want to do and find the courage to do it.

When she returned, he had taped a cannula to his arm.

"I thought you left." He fumbled through the case for a bottle and syringe.

"I just needed a minute." She pointed at the cannula. "I don't know how you can do that yourself."

He finished the injection and pulled a sewing needle from the case. While threading it, he smiled half-heartedly and replied, "Lots of training to learn how to diagnose and treat myself. This is the first time I've had to put it into practice—and I can't. So much for planning, training, and rules. Especially if I get complacent and don't stick to them."

"Why? Have you broken them?"

"By the looks of the future, I have, yeah."

"I said you conned me." She fought an itch to punch him.

The needle pierced. Firm flesh tugged as a gagging Addison pulled it through and the skin came together. She didn't relish the other three stitches and only peeked when she inserted the needle. His hisses and winces appeased her discomfort as she counted down and pulled the last one. After tying off and applying a dressing, she removed her gloves, set on leaving.

Laszlo followed her out of the bathroom. "Please don't go."

"Why?" she snarled. "I'm no one to you. Just finish the job. Soon, or I will have to find a way of giving myself a heads-up on who to call if Palowa ever turns yellow. Because of you. She won't know what it means, but she'll remember the name I leave her. And you? You won't even know about it this time because you killed the man who hired you." Addison mumbled "Idiot," under her breath.

"You've got some front. You rock up on my doorstep accusing me of murders and dog killings, demand I save the world, and then call me an idiot?"

"I didn't accuse. It's true. And you are!"

"What did you do? Nothing! You handed it to me."

"Killing Robert Naise started it all. Who should I have given it to, other than you? What other links do I have? There isn't a resistance here, unlike in the turning point."

"Then let me do it my way with the knowledge I have about these people. What would you have done?"

"I would not have killed Naise! If I had to, I'd get rid of Mario Spinzer."

"He isn't the problem. Parliament was about to be bombarded with passing a residential gun law."

Pfft. He had an answer for everything.

"It would never pass."

Laszlo nodded. "Eventually it would. Because in the room with the 'four-fifths' were people exceptionally skilled in political coercion. I know of them. Men with which Naise had clout. So, yes, eventually, it would pass. You might disapprove of what I did, but it was the logical move."

The man just didn't get it. She rolled her eyes. "I'm more concerned about the outcome."

"Then help me take down Convolve—their reputation, funding, and findings—so the outcome is certain to keep us in the real world."

Her hand tightened around the door handle as she considered it. Without the science or the company, no one could use the turning point.

"Are there any government links to Convolve? From memory, I remember they were a privately funded company. Who else might know is what I'm asking?"

"No links to the government. Two influential people have invested, but they're in it for profit, so neither would have copies of the data."

Addison stared at the carpet, edging towards leaving. She expected half of her to want to go. However, the part belonging to Addison New presented an eagerness far beyond her coping skills. It buried her doubts. But any mission creating excitement in the New version of her would probably not bloom with joy.

"I'm sorry I...*he* killed your dog. I must have been pretty desperate."

She released the handle and turned, sarcasm dripping. "I'm sorry I shot you in the head. I guess I was pretty desperate, too."

"Touché."

"Why do you hate dogs so much?"

"I don't, really. They don't like me."

"Funny. They say animals sense things." Addison caught the hurt in his eyes.

"Just go. I'll get the train to Bath and deal with Convolve myself. Somehow. Because if you won't help, and I can't ask anyone, who else is there but me? I can't even drive. So just go if that's what you want."

He disappeared into the bathroom and closed the door.

Addison didn't leave. She sat in the chair under the window, experiencing a perfect balance of hate and love. A line finer than a strand of baby hair. She pondered how different this Laszlo seemed. He wasn't trying to win her over, and he showed an aggressive side that he'd kept hidden in the New. Even the hostility attracted her.

She heard the tap run, and after he washed, he packed the supplies and closed the case with two deep, plastic clicks. He came back in carrying it, still wearing only black shorts. Addison's eyes slid down his sturdy body. She rolled her chin, knowing he'd seen it and, no doubt, with that look he'd spoken of. Both the timing and her feelings were inappropriate and conflicting. She hated that she loved him.

She matched his stare. "I'll take you to Bath, and I'll help you take down Convolve. Then we're done."

Twenty-Eight

11th April 2023, 19:45 – The Real

Planning the takedown became their focus over the following weeks. It distracted Addison from hating the man who, in a different world, had beguiled her with fake words and killed her dog. With Laszlo in such proximity, she had to put Sting's tooth away, reminding herself that she'd seen him happy with Mason and he wasn't dead here in The Real. She let the truth wash over her and decided, for the sake of working together to achieve a successful mission, she would try to forgive.

At least be tolerant until they completed the job.

Witnessing him secure the few items they needed helped and listening to him discuss explosives with an American called Snowy was as mesmerising as watching him cook—the Vulnerable Victims officer of the New vs the assassin of the Real. Today, Laszlo didn't need to hide his true nature from her. A nature that hooked the mixture of Addisons she had become. A duality needed to enact what Laszlo had in mind as they approached the pub frequented by an off-duty Convolve security guard.

Laszlo undid a button on her shirt. She smacked his hand away, but he was too swift to stop.

"Why can't we just steal the access card?"

"You know why. It has to be this way. You keep him busy while we borrow, scan, and return it. I've done the legwork. Now it's time for you to…do another kind of legwork." He sniggered.

"I'm not a cheap tart! So, watch it," she said, fighting a smile, "or I'll punch you in the shoulder."

An American drawl crackled over her comms. "Now, now, children. Business first. Catfight later."

The punters' laughter and chatter hid the squeaky door hinges as she entered, with Laszlo not far behind. He disappeared into the crowd. His eye would be on her, no doubt. She slipped past the wooden tables and closed in on the day-guard scrolling on his phone at the bar. In this soft lighting, she could swipe the card sticking out of his jacket pocket right now. He wouldn't notice, but the obsessively fussy Laszlo would only complain that she hadn't followed his instructions.

She exhaled loudly. Part sigh, part huff, aimed at Laszlo and his leg plans.

"Bad day?" the guard asked, his brown eyes full of genuine concern before they frisked her.

"My boyfriend's an arse." She winced. Mentioning a boyfriend wasn't the best way to start. "Stood me up for the last time."

"Work commitments?"

"Control issues. He likes things his own way."

From the corner of her eye, she saw the loitering Laszlo shake his head with a small smile.

The guard held out his hand. "Malik."

"Chloe," she lied as the bartender approached.

She studied the optics, unsure what to choose. Time wouldn't permit a long gin, but would allow for a quick kick. She smacked £20 on the bar. "Double Cointreau."

"Let me get you that," the guard offered, wetting his lips. As he held his phone out to pay, Laszlo swept past his stool—so light-footed that Addison didn't see he had the access card until he shoved the last of the neck strap into his pocket while heading to the door.

Act one, complete. For act two, Addison would have to really distract Malik until Laszlo returned.

She knocked back the Cointreau and held her breath, barely tasting the zesty freshness but feeling its sweet burn.

Her face contorted as she lowered her empty glass. "Thank you," she replied. "Bastard ain't getting me down."

"Good for you. Another?"

No, but if she must, she would buy it herself. She held up the twenty crying inside for Laszlo and Snowy to free her from this awkward nightmare.

Malik's eyes undressed her, dissecting so intently that she felt naked of her skin and her clothes. Was it any wonder he drank alone after work most days with no woman to go home to? She'd known him for ten minutes and already couldn't wait to leave.

The lecher drooled as if he were in with a chance. "Your eyes are mesmeric. You have specks in them that remind me of canary yellow diamonds."

That wasn't as cheesy as she expected. "Yellow diamonds?"

He leaned in, exploring her face while Laszlo returned the card to Malik's pocket just as nimbly as before. "Diamonds that have absorbed nitrogen. The impurities modify the light."

Her eyes widened. He was having her on. Diamonds didn't come in colours. "For real?"

"It's true. Other colours are rarer, but they do exist. Including brown, green, and yellow. Sparkly, just like your eyes."

The cheese layered now. Addison lifted the Cointreau to her lips and Malik backed off. With a quick flick of her wrist, she drank it and braced herself for the rush while collecting her change from the bar.

"Right. Well, it was nice talking to you. Reckon I'll be off now."

"So soon?" he replied, disappointed. He felt inside his pocket, eyes narrowing with suspicion. It vanished when, she assumed, he found his card.

Wow. For a letch, he was vigilant.

"Long day. Thanks for the drink." She walked away, ignoring his mumbled complaints, and weaved through the punters towards the door.

As she slammed it open, Laszlo came up behind her, whispering, "Canary yellow diamonds? Nice–"

"Oh, don't you start!"

"–play. Bet he says that to all the ladies."

Despite her ongoing attempt at forgiveness, she couldn't help sniping as he ran ahead. "Takes one to know one, I guess." After all, he had conned her in similar ways.

Someone grabbed the back of her jacket and thrust her face into the wall at the side of the bar. They pressed themselves against her, hot breath at her neck and a hardness pressing into her coccyx as an ambulance siren drowned out her scream.

"You're such a tease." Malik's words sent a chill down her spine. "You can't leave yet. I've only imagined your clothes on the floor. Now I want to see them there."

Using his frame to cage her, he twisted her arm behind her back, scratching her cheek on the brick. Bucking her hips to put space between them, only appeared to excite him. Held with a mighty strength, she released a futile, muffled scream. Addison New's shouts to kick him didn't reach her foot, and when his fingers slid inside her underwear, she froze.

The force that yanked him away and sent him flying made her lose her balance. She landed on her backside as Malik hit the ground with a yell. A brutish Laszlo loomed over him, clenching his fist. His colourful words drowned out Malik's fearful cry as he dragged him up and punched him back to the floor. He raised his fist to smack him again, but turned to her instead, pulling her up and guiding her to the car. She climbed into the backseat, hardly believing what had happened, and how close it had come to being much worse. An icy shiver like a rod fusing with her spine kept her upright for the silent two-hour journey to Bath. Shock abated with every mile, allowing the conflict of her feelings to surface. More anger than shame. Another close encounter had soiled the celebration she should be having, and her muted disgust for the deceitful dog killer now fought with the noble act of him saving her from Malik's grubby fingers. She hated the turmoil it brought to her heart.

"How you doing?" he asked, eventually breaking the silence beyond indicator clicks as they turned off at the Bath motorway junction.

She caught his concerned cerulean eyes in the rearview mirror. The angst of love and hate churned in her stomach, along with Malik haunting her thoughts. "I'm all right."

He stretched the muscles in his neck and winced, obviously uncomfortable.

"How's your shoulder?"

Laszlo pressed on the accelerator, confirming his pain, and another spell of silence ensued. She thought about the time she had left and pondered if she minded leaving so much. Part of her loved a man she wanted to hate. She would never truly forgive his sins. They'd scupper any chance of a relationship they might have. Perhaps it was better this way. She didn't want a life without her brother and Sting. Addison Original could start afresh. Unknowingly. Maybe with Jackson Lowe. Hopefully, she'd find happiness with him.

Meantime, would Addison Real simply disappear, or would she fade like the pictures did in *Back To The*

Future? Would her cells disperse into the air and vanish with little sparks?

As they pulled onto Laszlo's drive, she decided it didn't matter how. It was going to happen. Addison New lived her reality as it should have been. Addison Original lived her reality here. Addison Real was homeless and about to expire.

At the moment, she'd welcome it over stiff hips as she struggled to get out of the car.

"I feel like an old woman."

He threaded his good arm under hers, pulled her to him, and supported her to the door. Her resistance cracked, and her stomach leapt when his natural musky smell, drizzled with adrenaline, swirled in her nostrils.

"I'm angry and I need to cook. De-stress." He peered at his blood-spattered knuckles. "I'd better get cleaned up first."

Laszlo rushed upstairs. Addison shuffled into the kitchen, splashed water on her face, and poured a glass of chardonnay from the bottle open in the fridge. Feet curled beneath her on the sofa, she supped, soaked in her thoughts and riding the waves of Addison New's restlessness while wrestling with the memory of Malik's breath on her neck and his fingers at her groin. Then Laszlo's intervention, and his concerned eyes staring from the rearview mirror. She didn't know what to make of that—or how to feel when he strolled into the lounge smelling divine and looking as if he might burst out of his tight black t-shirt.

"Alena, activate the failsafe."

"Failsafe activated. Entryways secure. No approaching guests."

"Best be safe." He lifted his eyebrows, face still tense. "The music is about to get despicably loud."

"Are you going to make pasta on the worktop in the middle of the night again?"

"Do you know how weird that sounds?"

She smiled. "Yes. Just as weird as me telling you about a possible wife you haven't met yet."

Ignoring her, he collected her empty glass and entered the kitchen, pensive. He made two fancy vodkas with green syrup at the bottom before pulling vegetables from the fridge.

Addison sat on the stool indifferent to what he was making, yet enthralled as he chopped mushrooms and onion, listening to Vivaldi Winter blaring from the lounge. The melody moved her. Her heart rushed, calmed, then rushed again, the electrodes in her brain sparking as it swept her in. Tears falling, she understood why Laszlo relied on Winter to centre him. It did the trick. He lowered the volume, downed the rest of his vodka, and shook his head with a grimace as he continued working.

"Have I said this is exactly like your other kitchen?"

"Is it?" He didn't hide the gloom of his mood. "Funny that. I guess tastes never change."

He didn't look up, and having seen this mood before, she queried it. "Despite what happened to me, the mission was successful, so what's wrong?"

"I'm furious. He's lucky you were there."

"No, this is something else."

"I didn't like him hurting you." He sighed, pausing before he opened up. "When I got shot, I thought that was it. The last thing I expected was to make it to the hotel. I came-to now and then, wondering if you'd come and what I'd do if you didn't, but I couldn't get off the floor. I tried. Didn't have the energy, and it hurt too much. It bled more than I thought."

Visions of a soaked rag with blood dripping onto the hotel carpet smothered the reminder of Malik. In that moment, the fear of losing Laszlo felt like an overwhelming virus. Her anger looked small in comparison. Even the thought of going to her grave did not match him going to his. Not again.

He raised his voice over the sizzling chicken and vegetables. "I honestly thought I would die in that hotel. Too late to ponder a change of career then."

"And do what?"

Genuine excitement flashed in his eyes. "Cook. I can run the restaurant. You can do the accounts."

"I won't be here, Laszlo."

His joy dimmed.

"You should find Lorrie. Didn't you go to the hotel?"

"I went. But..." His voice trailed off into the steam.

"What?"

He turned his back on her and focused on the roux. "I looked at her and saw you." Her lips peeled open, and she frowned. Didn't he once say he'd have married Lorrie from the Swindon hotel? "No one was more surprised about that than me," he added.

"Why?"

He removed the pan from the hob. "Because she's more my type than you are. What is it about you, Addison Rae?"

She moved off the stool and onto the worktop, ignoring the pain in her back from her fall. "Maybe it's because you don't have the upper hand for once, Mr Obsessively Fussy." She cocked her head, a small smile forming. "I'm the mystery now."

He leaned closer, tongue at the corner of his mouth and an affection in his eyes that she had only ever seen once—while lying on his pistachio-green sheets. "You are. It's delicious."

Addison pulled away. "What's the point? I won't be here, and I'm the one who knows you. She doesn't. The moment the world turns will be the instant I go."

"I'd already gathered that, which is why I want you now, however inappropriate it might be to say, under the circumstances."

Despite herself, she grinned. "I'm actually rather hungry."

"I can see in your eyes how hungry you are." He returned to the pan with a smug smile. "If this is your last night, then why not spend it with me?"

Jackson's mischievous face surfaced, along with a fresh rush of Addison New's feelings. She denied them, hoping the original Addison would embrace them—if the chance arose. One version of her had no reason to say no.

"Why with you?" she asked.

"You've been under my skin since the day you rocked up on my doorstep with enough fire in your eyes to melt a nuclear power station. Sass and bravery. Despite knowing who I am and what I'm capable of, you came armed with Duncan Frost's name. That could have caused you all kinds of trouble."

"I had a mission to fulfil and nothing to lose."

"That all?" he asked, correctly deducing the mission wasn't the only reason.

She didn't reply. Instead, she weighed up the least painful way off the worktop and turned sideways to slide to the floor. He eased his thigh between her legs and put his arm around her waist, drawing her to him. She slipped down his body to her feet, holding his wicked gaze and wishing she wouldn't hate herself if she kissed him.

"I should go for a shower."

Desire faded into disappointment, and he closed his eyes. "You've less than ten minutes."

"I'll be quick." She ran up the stairs to the bathroom and to his ordinary shower. The running was less painful than giving in to the moment. She turned the temperature down to cool off the smouldering lust inside her. Perhaps her passion would warm her muscles while she cleansed her mind under the freezing water.

Her lust didn't wash away. She secretly hoped he would walk in and snatch her wrists again. Though not the same shower, it was Laszlo's. She let the memory ride, legs as jelly-like now as they were then, when he tantalised her.

The wide-open blue door with strings uncut by Vishnu, and still labelled My Perfect Man, enticed her as much.

She switched off the pointless water and dried herself. What use was it if all she could think about was Laszlo? She dressed in casual joggers and joined him in the kitchen.

His fingers brushed her hand as he gave her a fresh vodka. "You're freezing."

"It was a cold shower." She sat in front of a chicken and mushroom pasta and laughed. "I can't believe I'm eating this impromptu again." She poked it with her fork. "No prawns?"

He mouthed prawns, confused, probably trying to remember her mentioning them.

"The first dish you made me was this with prawns." She noticed a tidier kitchen this time. "Did you finally succumb to dried pasta?"

"Ha, not a chance. I had some made up in the fridge."

Though they ate in silence, his eyes said plenty as he stared. She caught him a few times, watching her draw loose spaghetti into her mouth and lick her lips. He didn't seem to care. He made his intentions known. She battled with desires that she shouldn't have. Despite his heroics, she continued to wrestle with her feelings. She hated to love him.

"I'm sorry I hurt you. He...hurt you. Because I think you're pretty great. It's hard to accept you saying he used you. I could never imagine myself doing that. Sex isn't a transaction to me. It's too personal. So, if I think you're great, then he would have felt the same."

"You know he's you. Right?"

"I disassociate myself from him because I haven't done what he has. I haven't...even kissed you."

He came closer. Visions of the multiple times Laszlo had kissed her battered her fragile defence walls and, little by little, they fell.

"I don't hate you. I never really hated him."

His cautious laugh showed he doubted it. "You shot him in the face."

"I was angry."

"The fact that you could shoot anyone is actually damn sexy." He wet his lips, close enough to touch hers. Was he holding back for her to retreat if she chose?

She licked her lips automatically, need racing through her body as much as his by the way he kissed her. Tender lips massaged hers. Tongue sweeping. Fingers trailed her spine, brushed her neck, and sought the places where she quivered. She'd already succumbed to wanting him while in the shower, so when he pulled her to his hips and lifted her, she felt relieved, anticipating the pleasure he would bring—several times as they messed up his pistachio-green bedsheets. Trapped inside her mind, Addison relived that enviable week with a desire she knew only he could satisfy. Since being with him, no one else could compare. No one else's fingers would arouse the same craving. No body could mould so perfectly with hers, and no stimulation would be as attractive as his touch.

Addison Real would be forever Laszlo's.

~

The sex conjured an awkward mood as they recapped the Convolve details in the car in the early hours of the morning. Addison wasn't keen on Plan B. Lately, heights and ropes were chilling reminders of near-death experiences and Laszlo on the helicopter, waiting to take her memories. Instead of confessing her fears, she used them to keep herself in check. Successfully, until they approached the Convolve perimeter fence on foot.

"I've never abseiled before."

"You tell me that now?" he barked as he cut into the mesh. "Follow my lead." He stole across the tarmac to the back door. As expected, the access card let them in without alerting the guard making his rounds from the west side. It also took them through the corridors lit with night lights and to the server room on the fifth floor within the ten-minute timeframe, allowing the virus ample time to upload and bed into the system before the guard returned.

The virus would hide their entry alert and keep the on-screen corridors empty while they planted the explosives Snowy had pilfered. It would also attack any device linked to the server. If an outside laptop should connect, it would corrupt.

With the server room armed, they rushed to the west wall on the fourth floor and activated another bomb for remote detonation. Laszlo's idea to destroy Convolve's structure walls made sense. Collapsing the legs would bring the upper floors down faster and safer. They moved down a level, towards a structure wall on the east side of the building. The granite-like resin floor shone and its random flakes glistened in the low lights. Her trainers kept squeaking on it. After Laszlo's fifth disgruntled glance, her irritation spiked. "Prefer I take them off and whack them around your head?" She huffed. "What's the point of destroying Convolve if the scientists can rebuild it somewhere else?"

"If they have the tech, equipment and money. You're not worried about it coming back to us, are you? Because you needn't."

"No. Addison Original probably hasn't left Lechlade. Good luck to the officials trying to pin it on her."

"They won't find anything to pin. Trust me. I know what I'm doing."

"Destroying the place is all good, but what if they have data backed-up off-site?" she asked.

"They don't. I checked. There isn't a payment for one."

"What about at Palowa?"

Laszlo raised his eyebrows as he armed an explosive. "If that's the case, let's hope no one other than Ross Barnes knows about it." He glanced at his watch. "Twenty-six minutes. We're ahead of schedule."

"Let's not dally and waste it then." Addison smiled and headed for the door.

"Dally?"

"A yellow-brick-road skip and dance. You took me on one once."

"Didn't," he whispered. "*I* didn't. Can't speak for the other me." Plainly insulted, he rushed ahead as they descended to the first floor, south side.

Sudden guilt enveloped her. Of all the occasional digs she'd thrown at him, this was the first to have a comeback, or at least to show an impact. She followed him into a large room filled with workstations, divided into blocks of four, the odd light glowing. She handed him the last bomb.

Shadows moving in the corridor caught her eye. She tiptoed to the door and looked through the blinds.

Malik was running his grubby fingers through his hair, a black eye brewing, and wearing an expression just as dark.

"It's Malik."

The bomb activated with a quiet beep.

Twenty-Nine

12th April 2023, 02:37

Laszlo curled his lip as he recalled the disgusting man abusing Addison. He zipped the bag as silently as he could and hid behind a grey workstation. "I obviously didn't hit him hard enough."

Addison crouched beside him. Her fast breaths and fearful expression touched his heart. He held her hand, encouraging her to look at him, and mouthed numbers to calm her.

The door crashed into the wall. She jumped but didn't make a sound as she stared into his eyes. The tiny specks of yellow in them glowed like sunlight through pin-pricked curtains. His ears focused on Malik's movements after he had passed the workstation.

Laszlo accessed the camera on his phone and pointed the lens over the desk partition. The villain sat with his back to them at a computer four blocks away, muttering *'little bitch'* as he hammered on the keyboard. Laszlo contemplated Malik's last breath. A quick snap of his neck. A few seconds, and she would never need to worry about him again. Malik wouldn't see it coming and Laszlo didn't mind serving another dreg of society to the devil for free.

He nodded at the door with his finger on his lips and, head down, crept towards the last block of workstations. The remaining three metres were out in the open, risking exposure. Unclipping his knife, he calculated the distance between them and Malik and the force needed for the kill.

She stilled his hand, shaking her head.

"Precaution," he whispered, and after checking on a preoccupied Malik, he flicked his eyes at the swing door. "Go."

She stayed low. Clever girl. Her trainers didn't squeak on the tiles as she slipped through the door. Laszlo followed, eyes on Malik, watching faces flash up on the screen. His ears caught a growl of *'I'm gonna find you, Chloe,'* as the swing door shut. If the bomb didn't get him, Laszlo would.

They raced towards the stairs.

"What's he doing back here?" Annoyance flared on her cheeks. "We can't detonate the bombs now."

He rolled his shoulder and stretched his neck, unable to stop his involuntary wince. Though the stitches had healed, his shoulder wasn't at full strength.

"Looking for you—or rather, the original you who will be clueless. Still want to wait?"

"Yes. No lives taken, we agreed."

"Even at the risk of your own?"

Her wary eyes flicked away.

"We agreed to innocent lives like the security guard, not attempted rapists who make us late." He guided her up the stairs.

"Where are we going? The door is that way."

"We only have thirty seconds left until the innocent guard starts his rounds at that door. I hoped to avoid Plan B, but now we can't."

It left six minutes to abseil the east wall and escape through the perimeter fence before the guard skirted the corner.

At the roof door, he pressed the access card and opened it, letting it shut as they raced across the concrete. He took two climbing ropes from Addison's bag and, while he secured them to the metal fence around the maintenance electricity supply, she put on a harness. Straps checked, he pulled the ropes tight through the belay clamps and tugged hard on Addison's. She stumbled, throat rippling as she swallowed. Despite his simple crash course, fear still shook her body. Cupping her face, he stared into her wide eyes.

"Fear is a liar. It will try to deceive, break, and own you, and its voice is smooth and believable. It's fake, and you need to master it. Channel it into determination, and it becomes success, most of the time."

"I don't like heights since the Horseshoe Lake incident."

He frowned, looking for a connection between water and heights. He didn't have time to ask, or navigate this unfamiliar tugging in his heart that kissing her seemed to appease. It might have been nerves, but she returned his kiss.

"It'll be fine. Do what I do." He kept his hand on the belay as he stepped over the roof edge, feeding the rope through and explaining every move as she followed him. "Lower your hips and pretend you're walking backwards... Good, that's it."

She gained confidence and sped up, gradually catching up with him. "It's not as bad as I thought." When he pushed off with his feet and dropped a floor in seconds, she laughed. "Show off."

At the fourth floor, he slowed, waiting for her to reach him, and chided himself for admiring her curvy backside. The memory of his tongue trailing the constellation of freckles above her breast a few hours ago lingered without conflict. As did the feel of her soft skin against his, and her sensual touch.

Her rope jerked, then jerked again. She fell, screaming, hurtling towards him faster than she should. Her and the rope tumbled past unlit windows, then him. Instinct reacted. He reached out and caught her with his injured arm, yanking her into a swing.

A searing knife ripped through his shoulder. He yelled. His arm jolted in protest, but he didn't let go.

With pain in his eyes, shock in hers, and breaths hissing through gritted teeth, they stared, sweat forming on his brow. He couldn't lift her, and he couldn't hold her.

Dangling four floors above the ground and calmer than expected, she whispered, "Let go."

"What? No!"

"I'm going anyway. It doesn't matter. Let me go."

"No," he growled. "Can you grab my legs?"

Agony raked through him as she reached for his foot and pulled herself closer, but only to the bottom of his jeans.

Laszlo opened his belay clip and descended, faster than before, but much slower than falling. One floor down, he felt her hands slipping.

Slipped hands.

She was falling again.

Surprisingly, she didn't scream. Nor did her eyes leave his as he chased her. They both landed at the same time.

He unclipped his rope and ran over. "Shit, Addie!"

Her eyes rolled, and blood pooled on the tarmac under her head. He unhooked her belay and felt for broken bones. His fingers skimmed over a frayed rope. It must have been rubbing against something sharp.

"Where do you hurt?"

"Nowhere," came her frail whisper.

"I'm so sorry. The rope–"

"Hey! You there!" The guard ran from the south corner, torchlight bobbing.

Finding no breakages, and knowing he couldn't leave her there, Laszlo picked her up, not giving his shoulder a chance to complain as he ran.

"I'm getting too old for this shit," he cried, arriving at the opening in the perimeter fence.

"I know I'm tired of it," she slurred.

He went through backwards, holding her close, letting nothing but him touch her. Then he placed her gently under the trees. When he glanced up and saw the guard still chasing, he took out the remote detonator. It left them with no alternative. They needed an urgent distraction, Malik inside or not.

"We need to take cover now."

She frowned, blinking, and unfocused, but the fierceness in her eyes seemed to speak for her.

"If the guard catches us, I will have to kill him. So, will it be his life or Malik's?" He pressed the button.

The phenomenal noise rattled all other senses. He'd experienced thousands of explosions, but enduring their effects never became easier. It felt as if the ground thumped him. Pummelled him. Pressure, followed by heat, swept up his back as he shielded her, arms now screaming in protest as he resisted the force trying to pin him down. The rumbling stopped. Ash, dust, and fine debris swirled like a sandstorm, covering them, while chunkier pieces lay behind the dented mesh fence. The guard staggered to his feet, scratching his head with an awed expression, while the culprits faded in his concerns.

Laszlo brushed grit off her face, paler now since he'd placed her under the trees. She trembled, teeth chattering. He collected her in his arms and ran to the car, her chilled skin forcing him to confront the truth. She was dying.

He climbed into the backseat less clumsily than he expected, covered her body with a blanket, and her face with gentle kisses. She responded with a murmur. It bubbled in her throat and she squinted to look at him.

Her fingertips tickled his hairline. "You have zigzag colours on your head."

"It's the head injury–"

"It's the turning point," she replied between wheezy breaths. "Everything is tilting and I'm dizzy. I'm leaving."

Denying the truth, he slid out the medical case stored under the seat. The plastic catches clunked when they opened. He unwrapped a piece of gauze.

"Stop. I'm going anyway. It was only a matter of hours."

A new strain of grief possessed him. This wasn't a dying brother, child, or father figure. His chin wobbled, stubbornly refusing to admit the truth. She couldn't go, not now he had realised his feelings. With a heart throbbing harder than his shoulder, he snuggled beside her. His lips met hers with such affection that it felt like heaven. It equalled more than all other kisses combined.

He drew back, eyes wet with tenderness and mouth reluctant to share his thoughts. But this might be the only time he could.

"I think I love you," he stuttered, and kissed her again.

Then the blanket flattened, and he was alone.

~

The nightmares were mere additions to the drudgery of his sleepless nights. Mabel, Izsak, and Duncan Frost were already regular visitors. Addison's fearful expression as she fell to the ground was the cherry on his cake. The freshest. Rawest. Nevertheless, it quietened the critical voices in his head. Even his demons feared the anguish in his heart.

He placed the notecase and Pocahontas painting into the lockbox he kept at the bottom of his wardrobe. Addison's ring he'd found in the bathroom hung on the chain around his neck. Now he removed it and added it to the box. All his losses in one place. Tears spilled, and no scathing voices teased him. Two months of silence, as if he had paid his penance. Living with her death was punishment enough, and he was tired of surviving on only his memories. He wanted more, needed it. He needed her.

Thirty

22nd July 09:30 – Three months later

Heavy padded feet thumped off the bed and hurtled down the stairs at the sound of Addison's whistle. A fluffy yellow ball of lusciousness met her at the front door, yipping with excitement, and furiously wagging his tail at the dangled lead.

"Breakfast." She was desperate for the English 'grill-up' she'd fancied since she woke.

Sting replied with a deep woof, as if he knew a sausage would appear in his bowl later. His gratitude for it would come in the manner of stinky farts all afternoon, but Addison didn't mind. Plus, the removal lorry parked next door had pricked her curiosity enough to get off her backside to go to the shop.

She opened the front door, avoiding the urge to stare at the lorry beside the neighbour's lawn as she locked up. From this angle, she saw nothing but a few stacked boxes, though she could hear the shoving and banging well enough. A bout of swearing followed, and the scraping of more boxes. As she neared the end of her drive, she peeked in. A well-built man with floppy black hair and a tan looked along the rack for something. He wore black trousers, shoes polished to a high sheen, and a white shirt, open at the neck with the sleeves rolled up. He looked too well dressed to be the removal staff, even if he did have the body for it.

The man scratched his chin and turned to the side, revealing a stubbly cheek and precision-trimmed moustache beneath a sculpted nose. He looked around her age, possibly older, but absolutely gorgeous. Rooted to the spot, she didn't consider that he might turn any second and see her drooling with her tongue poking out.

A delighted yelp sounded, and he smiled, baring his immaculate teeth. He lifted a box down to his chest, then rolled his neck and shoulders, catching her gaze in a side-eyed glance.

Tucking chin-length hair behind her ears, she rushed off, muttering to Sting about his lack of wingman skills. Why couldn't he have been sniffing everything like normal instead of sitting patiently for her to move? At least it would have looked as if she was waiting for him.

"Good morning." Gravelly voice. Unaccented. He'd obviously moved around.

Her tongue hit the corner of her mouth as she turned to see his face and cheeky smile full on.

"Hi." She sounded like a moron. Gathering her thoughts, she added, "I didn't want to intrude. And I'm a bit shocked. I didn't know we were getting new neighbours."

The man looked at the view between the houses. Something about him felt familiar. "I fell in love with the place." He drew magnificent cool-blue eyes back to hers and her stomach rolled. "It's beautiful here."

Addison cleared her throat. "It is. A nice neighbourhood. Very friendly."

"I can see that," he replied, still smiling. He put the box down, stretched his shoulders, and walked over holding out his hand. "Laszlo Sándor."

"Addison Rae. It's nice to meet you."

It's really nice to meet you. It's really, really nice to meet you.

"You, too."

"This is Sting."

He offered the back of his hand for the dog to sniff. When Sting wagged his tail, pleased at the attention,

Laszlo stroked his head with a "Nice to meet you too," and a wide smile.

"I'm popping to the shop. Can I get you supplies while I'm there? Milk and bread?"

"Oh. I hadn't even thought of that. If it isn't too much trouble?"

"No trouble. It's my pleasure."

Any excuse for a reason to come back, she thought, with a spreading grin.

She turned right towards the end of the cul-de-sac rather than left to exit the street.

"Isn't that the wrong direction?"

"Having a dog encourages you to uncover all the shortcuts." She smiled. And probably more besides.

She could feel his eyes tickling the back of her neck as she walked away. Determined to fight the impulse to check if he was watching, she kept her eyes ahead and lengthened Sting's lead, convincing herself that she didn't need to catch another glimpse of him. Demanded herself, more like.

At the corner, she turned her head, disobeying her own command, but it was worth it. As he walked backwards across his garden, the box in his hands, he nodded. Then her view became a boundary hedge, leaves and twigs up close as Sting ran the length of his lead, pulling the besotted slowcoach down the alleyway. She tugged the strap, drawing it and Sting back. She couldn't stop smiling. *That* was now living next door to her.

Then, the horror set in. A vision of delectability had moved in only a garden away. He might see her every day. The thought wouldn't be so awful if she looked immaculate, at least presentable for work or a rare night out. Not lounging in her pyjamas at midday, answering the door to delivery drivers. She was grateful to be dressed this Saturday morning. Granted, only in a tracksuit and trainers, and her hair was a mess, but it was better than tatty pyjamas. She would have to keep the curtains drawn, she decided, especially while her hair grew out.

No one needed to see that. Least of all the sexy Laszlo.

Walking along the lane into town, she pondered his name. Foreign. Eastern European, perhaps. His natural, sun-kissed skin indicated a warmer climate than Britain, though she couldn't know for sure.

The town was abuzz with visitors. The café tables were full, inside and out. Chloe sat at one until she spotted Addison waiting to cross the road.

"Addie!" she yelled for all of Lechlade to hear.

Addison waved as Chloe ran towards them with her blonde ponytail swinging and her long arms flailing. Addison couldn't help her laugh. "What do you look like?"

Chloe flashed eager blue eyes. "I'm excited. So what? How did it go yesterday?"

"I bottled it."

"I knew you would."

"Is it so bad to want him to ask me?"

"How is Mr FD going to invite you to my wedding?"

Addison smiled. "You know what I mean. Plus, he's my boss and might not be interested."

"Coward. You won't find out if you don't ask."

"Gimme a break. I'm already growing my hair at your insistence."

"Begging, you mean. ...I know! I'll tweet the picture of your legs in that Charleston dance outfit. He'll be interested then." She added a purr.

Addison laughed. Adam Grant had probably hated her since their first encounter. She'd shooed the cheeky chancer out of her seat the day after Ross Barnes went missing, not knowing he was her new boss. Finding out about Barnes' murder came as a double shock. That he was part of a secret society surprised her more. She didn't realise he had the kudos to become a member of one.

Of course, that was only a rumour. Allegedly, the government said, with so many influential people inside the Henley-On-Thames building, it had been impossible to know who the target or targets were. Light of a mark, the authorities couldn't find a motive, and without forensics and witnesses, the suspect pool was too vast. The case remained unsolved to this day.

When a gap appeared in the traffic, Addison rushed off, Sting pattering alongside her. Chloe tagged along behind, still wittering about Addison's social skills as she tied Sting to the post.

"I reckon you're better off out of the game, anyway, because people are strange. Seriously, Addie. I had someone call 111 last week saying they'd swallowed their septum and didn't know what to do!"

"How does one swallow their septum?"

Lost for words, Chloe shook her head as they entered the shop.

Addison approached the fridges, aghast at the milk selection. Blue, green, red, and yellow tops. Filtered, lactose-free, or calcium and vitamin-enhanced. Too enthralled with her new neighbour's sexy face at the time, she'd forgotten to ask for his preferences. She chose semi-skimmed. Most had that, right?

When she reached the bread aisle, she faced a similar dilemma between the variations of white and brown as she spotted Arnold showing a new member of staff the ropes. A brawny man with tobacco-brown hair lifted crates of tinned food without breaking a sweat and started filling the shelves. His sweet, but rugged, face turned and clocked her watching. Mesmerising brown eyes searched hers, almost intrusively. Intimately. As if he knew her.

Somewhere inside she felt as if she knew him.

She couldn't help her reaction. "Wow. Lechlade is getting buff."

The man laughed. "It just got buffer."

Addison blushed and looked back at the bread, grabbing two loaves at random.

Cringing, Chloe jabbed her ribs. "Lechlade is getting buff? Addie, you're embarrassing."

"It slipped out! Besides, you haven't seen my new neighbour!"

"Ooh. Is he nicer than the finance director?"

Addison smirked. "A few months ago, there were zero men. Now, there's an abundance of buff!"

"Ah! Ladies." Arnold rushed up and linked his arms with hers and Chloe's. "Come meet the new chap." He pulled them to the end of the aisle. "Jackson Lowe, meet Addison Rae and Chloe Brompton. Chloe's getting married next month."

"Nice to meet you both." Jackson shook their hands, Chloe's last. "Congratulations."

"Thanks. You're welcome over at The Crown after. Everyone's invited. If you're still here, that is."

"Are you that much of a rogue boss?" he asked Arnold.

Addison laughed. "What Chloe means is you don't look the type to be skivvying for too long."

"Which brings me to the reason I introduced you. Addie, I've known you for thirty-three years. Like many in the community, I've watched you grow all your life, but an offer came our way that we just couldn't resist, and Marge and I are ready to settle by the coast to see out our last days."

"You're retiring?" she asked, surprised but warm about their choice.

"We are. And Jackson here will be the new owner."

Reality stalled. Laszlo living next door, Jackson running her local shop, and Adam in control at the office.

Did she really have to look immaculate twenty-four seven?

"It's all happening rather fast, but we're grateful. Now that we've decided, we're excited to go."

Jackson smirked at their stunned delight. "I arrived to find I'm buying a larger shop than expected. Hence, the training from the bottom up while the sale completes."

"And I'm going to enjoy the help and handover while we pack up." Arnold laughed as he walked away.

She watched Jackson stack tinned baked beans with beefy hands, fussing so the label faced the front. "You didn't view the shop before you put in an offer?"

"Not from Leicester. But I wanted Lechlade. It has a well-maintained fishing lake, and it's a pretty place. Stunning views and oldie-worldie buildings. My mum would have loved it here. This—" he waved his hands, "is for her."

"Aw," gushed Chloe, "that's really sweet. Addie's single, by the way. And looking."

Addison's mouth popped open with an embarrassed smile. "Excuse us." She dragged Chloe away, not caring if the basket jabbed her in the side. "You're killing me. Get out of the shop!" She pushed her shoulder towards the door.

"Hey. We're supposed to have babies together. Get a move on."

"I'm just going to pay and go home."

"Yeah. Go watch *Bridget Jones*," laughed Chloe.

Smirking, Addison replied, "Shut up!"

"And after that, watch *Fifty Shades*."

Addison shook her head. "I will never watch that. Seriously. Get out of the shop!"

Chloe laughed. "See you tomorrow night?"

"Yes."

Cheeks scarlet and heart thumping, Addison queued to pay, grateful she was next in line and able to flee quickly from the humiliation. The hope was short-lived. She glanced down the aisle nearest the exit and caught Jackson's eye. He stopped straightening the milk cartons and nodded goodbye with a mischievous grin worming its way into her heart.

Addison pulled the door open. "See you later."

"Hope so."

She untied Sting and left in a rush. Sting looked back at the fields, likely wondering why they were walking along the road. Faces floated in her mind. The pert-bummed, blond Adam as he passed to use the photocopier. Jackson's strong, cheeky face as he said goodbye. The steamy, blue-eyed Laszlo with his thick black hair and stubble around cushy lips… Then the alluring clean-shaven version standing at her front door a few months ago suddenly catapulted into her mind.

She'd seen him before.

Pausing at the corner, slightly apprehensive, she watched him talking to Mrs Tonks, still holding the same box as when she had left. Whatever he said made her laugh. If anyone could smell a rat, Mrs Tonks could, but her harsh face looked delighted.

This confidence spurred Addison on and, for once, she walked at a pace that Sting enjoyed.

"Have you been yakking this whole time?"

He turned around, surprised, then looked back at the alleyway. "Uh, yes. Mrs Tonks is grilling me about my life."

"It's been an interesting one. Did you know he solves people's problems? I could do with hiring him." Mrs Tonks' eyes flashed as she hooted a laugh.

"What are you, a counsellor?"

Laszlo laughed. "Far from it. More, uh, freelance for whatever came my way. Company issues. Private investigation requests. Security detail. All involving problem-solving. However, I'm retired now and plan to open a restaurant."

Mrs Tonks laughed. "Yeah, I should hire him."

Addison didn't laugh. Instead, she studied him. His piercing eyes fell on her, eyebrows tightening. Her breath froze.

Sting cold-nosed her hand, impatient for his extra breakfast. Brought back to earth with a wet nose-bump, Addison took a noisy breath. "Did you knock on my door once?"

"Yes," Laszlo gave her a guilty smile.

Hmm. Sneaky.

"Checking out the neighbourhood, were you?"

"Yes."

"There wasn't a lost cat?"

"No."

"Didn't come and see me!" blurted Mrs Tonks. "I'd remember."

Addison raised an eyebrow. "Really? Just my door, was it?"

Laszlo smiled again, reddening a little. "Well, as it happened, the neighbourhood was lookin' pretty fine."

She blushed. Again. It was bordering on ridiculous.

"On that note, I'll leave you to it, Addie, love." Mrs Tonks nudged her arm and walked off, muttering to Taffy about a cuppa.

"Milk and bread. I forgot to ask what you usually have. Sorry, I just grabbed whatever one." Which turned out to be the worst shop-brand sliced white, and probably the unhealthiest bread on the planet.

"It's fine. I appreciate it. Thank you. Enjoy your breakfast."

"There's plenty if you'd like some. I'll cook it all because Mason's a pig and will finish what I don't eat."

Laszlo crouched in front of Sting. "That's not a nice way to talk about you, is it?"

Sting woofed and licked his face, then nudged the bag with an impatient snort.

"That's Sting. Mason is my brother. The offer's there," she said as the fur-ball pulled her to the door. She waved and closed it behind her, then ran upstairs to have a gander at him from her bedroom window.

Her heart leapt to find him still watching her door, holding his precious box. He took a step back and turned towards his new house. As he did, he gazed up, and straight at her, a hint of relief lining his face.

Mortified, she backed away and rushed to the kitchen, overthinking his expression as she prepared breakfast. He'd caught her staring for the third time, making her feelings clearly, albeit inadvertently, known. Why was he so relieved to find that she liked him?

Greasy fat sausages, soft bacon, eggs, mushroom, pepper and onion cooked in butter, filled her plate. Pools of yellow and oil formed. Folk called it a heart attack city, but she didn't care. Famished, she was about to sit and demolish it when the doorbell rang. It wouldn't be Mason. He wasn't due for another hour at least, and he'd simply walk in.

She plucked up a sausage and bit it as she answered the door. Lazlo stood outside with an empty cup.

"Good timing. Did you change your mind about breakfast? Because I've just dished up."

"I have all the trappings for a coffee but the actual coffee. I can't find it." He sighed and held out a cup. "I wondered if I could borrow some of yours."

"Sure. Come in." Addison tucked her hair behind her ear, still getting used to it growing, and searched her cupboard for the spare jar she'd bought yesterday. When she handed it to him, she caught him staring at the congealed fat around the leftover food. "Sure I can't tempt you?"

"Uh… No," he replied, unimpressed. "Thank you. I'll just borrow the coffee if it's all the same."

The smile he fought gave him away.

"What's wrong with it?" she asked, biting off another piece of sausage.

He shook his head. "Nothing. Perhaps one day, you'll allow me to make you breakfast."

Addison stopped chewing.

"I didn't mean…" He lifted his hands and laughed, embarrassed. "That didn't come out quite how I meant it. The restaurant, of course."

She raised her eyebrows, teasing him further as she considered his hint at taking her out on a date.

"I'm going to go now." At the front door, he added, "Truthfully, though? You eat like you need looking after."

"Says the restauranteur. I do just fine, thank you."

She watched him go with a beaming smile, if only for his cheek. Sting cocked his head at the strange vibe.

Three faces hung. Laszlo on her right, Jackson on her left, and Adam up ahead. Each one appealing, a settle-down-with possibility.

Addison couldn't date them all, and she approached a crossroads of decision. There were no men three months ago. Now she had Laszlo and Jackson. And on Monday, she would go to work and see her new finance director, who was equally inviting.

Did she go left, right, or straight on?

Coming Soon…

Penned on my Wall – 2025

By popular request, a selection of poems and prompts written for #vss365, #NAlove, and more, on TwitterX will be available late spring.

Servant Killer - 2026

When tragedy falls, not once but twice, Lieutenant Laszlo Sándor's grip on his temper crumbles. Revenge for his brother's murderer contains it, a short-term salve feeding the idea that births a servant killer.

About The Author

"The part I most want to zip and padlock inside a #suitcase and hurl off the Bella Coola Road into a sea of Jack pine trees is the about the author section. I hate it. #vss365"

Emma Bloor is an accounts administrator living in Wiltshire with her husband and grumpy teenager. Besides writing her own novels, she ghost-writes and has a piece of flash fiction published in the 2021 compilation book *Triumph from Tragedy*. She is also a regular contributor to writing prompts on Twitter/X and Bluesky @emmabloorbooks.

Author's note

Writing gives me such joy and I am grateful to have rekindled my passion for storytelling in 2020. What began as a mental health exercise developed into a seven-book dystopian thriller series, fictionalising Biblical end-times prophecies akin to *Left Behind* by Tim LaHaye and Jerry B. Jenkins. After many requests from my friends for printed copies, I self-published.

Who knew how far the writing would take me?

Since then, the wonderful VSS community and writing groups on social media have enhanced and improved my craft. One day, I will find the time to refresh the prose of a truly thrilling series.

Acknowledgements

I have so many people to thank for supporting me this far, and I wish I could put each one at the top of the list. My first port of call goes to my 'reader betas', Linda and Kirsty, who have begged for first draft chapters, read hot off the press, and debated *(argued!)* which scenes in Turned shocked them the most.

The many 'writer beta readers', Ann, Jess, Lisa, Cameron, Marie, Mel, Helen, and Laura. Without these invaluable people, Turned wouldn't be the book it is today.

To Thorne from Penguin Random House, whose comments lifted me to believe the premise is absorbing and would capture readers' imaginations. If not for the small speculative element, she would have added Turned to her book portfolio. This wonderful lady's confidence in my writing encouraged me to keep creating.

To my husband, Harvey, who hates reading, has no interest in fiction, and believes any word will do, for always being available—even when he rolls his eyes, heart sinking at the thought of what I might ask him!

To Sabrina and The Carp Society for allowing me to visit the private Horseshoe Lake in Lechlade and allowing its name in my published works.

Finally, to my amazing editor, Marie Keates, to whom I have much to be thankful. I am incredibly grateful for her insight and ability to simplify my neuro-divergent sentences.

Without you all, I would never have had the confidence to come this far.

Thank you.

www.ingramcontent.com/pod-product-compliance
Lightning Source LLC
Chambersburg PA
CBHW030226100526
44585CB00012BA/233